ISBN 978-1-332-13703-9
PIBN 10289683

1 MONTH OF
FREE
READING

at
www.ForgottenBooks.com

By purchasing this book you are eligible for one month membership to ForgottenBooks.com, giving you unlimited access to our entire collection of over 700,000 titles via our web site and mobile apps.

To claim your free month visit:
www.forgottenbooks.com/free289683

THE

HISTORICAL COLLECTIONS

OF

A CITIZEN OF LONDON

IN THE FIFTEENTH CENTURY.

CONTAINING:

I. JOHN PAGE'S POEM ON THE SIEGE OF ROUEN.
II. LYDGATE'S VERSES ON THE KINGS OF ENGLAND.
III. WILLIAM GREGORY'S CHRONICLE OF LONDON.

EDITED BY

JAMES GAIRDNER.

PRINTED FOR THE CAMDEN SOCIETY.

M.DCCC.LXXVI.

WESTMINSTER :
PRINTED BY NICHOLS AND SONS,
25, PARLIAMENT STREET.

[NEW SERIES XVII.]

INTRODUCTION.

AMONG the MSS. now in the Egerton Collection in the British Museum is a small folio volume, numbered 1995 in that collection, which was purchased in 1865 at the sale of the books of the late Earl of Charlemont. The contents are varied, consisting of poems, statistics, scraps of various kinds, a rhyming chronicle and a prose chronicle; but, with the exception of a very few idle scribblings of more modern date in the margins and fly-leaves, the handwriting throughout is of the fifteenth century, and the whole appears to be the work of one scribe only. The volume consists altogether of 223 leaves of paper; but the prose chronicle at the end is imperfect, and one or two leaves have probably been lost.

Originally the MS. seems to have formed two volumes, which are now bound together in one. The sheets in each separate quire of paper are distinguished by signatures at the bottom, " a 1," " a 2," &c., and a new set of signatures begin at folio 110 with Lydgate's verses on the Kings of England. Not a single leaf appears to be missing to make up a quire except at the very end.

The matters contained in the book are as follows:—

1. An English version of the poem called " The Seven Sages of Rome," beginning—

> Herkenyth lordynges, curteys and hende,
> Howe thys gentylle geste shall ende.
> Sum tyme there was an Emperoure
> That ladde hys lyfe with moche honowre.
> Hys name was Dioclician.

This extends over **104** pages, beginning at fol. **3**.

2. A short poem on the words: " Memento, homo, quod cinis es et in cinerem reverteris." It is a rather expanded version of the well-known lines, " Earth upon Earth," fol. 55.

3. Notes of the " properties " of a young gentleman, the conditions of a good greyhound, a vocabulary of the terms of venery, &c., fols. 55*b*—58.

4. A poem on courtesy, beginning—

> Litylle chyldrynne here may ye lere
> Moche curtesy that ys wretyn here.

5. A few scraps, among which are rules how to interpret the weather at Christmas, &c., as presaging future events, fols. 60—62.

6. A classification of beasts of venery and of the chace &c.; also of the different kinds of hawks; fols. 63, 64.

7. " A nobylle tretys of medysyns for mannys body," fols. 65—77.

8. " Sapiencia phisicorum," a poem on the preservation of health, fols. 77*b*—78.

9. " For bloode latynge," another poem, fols. 79, 80.

10. The assize of bread and ale, as in Statutes of the Realm, i. 199, fols. 80*b*, 81.

11. The names of the churches in the City of London, fols. 82—86.

12. A poem on " The Siege of Rouen," fols. 87—109.

13. Lydgate's verses on the Kings of England, fols. 110—112.

14. A Chronicle of London, fols. 113—222.

It is clear from this table of contents that the MS. is a commonplace book, into which the writer has transcribed a number of things that interested him. But with regard to the Chronicle at the end the appearance of the MS. seems to favour the supposition that the latter part at least is an original composition, not transcribed from any other MS.; so that if we could only determine

the author we should probably be justified in assuming that the
whole book was in his handwriting ; for the heaviness of the
hand, the irregularity of the spelling, and the gross transcriber's
errors that abound in some parts, indicate a writer who was not
well trained in regular clerical labour. Yet in this latter part of
the work, from the middle, or at least from the close, of Henry the
Sixth's reign onwards, though clerical and grammatical errors are
abundant enough, there is no evidence of that special kind of
blundering which marks the work of a copyist, and which is very
frequent in the earlier pages—nonsense made by the omission of lines
or the misreading of words, confusion of the original punctuation,
and misapprehension of the author's meaning. In this part the
errors are rather like those of a hasty careless writer, who composed
with pen in hand, omitting sometimes a word or part of a word in
his haste, but leaving the sense of what he meant to write sufficiently
obvious.

The different treatises and scraps contained in the book seem
to have been entered in the order in which they stand, the handwriting exhibiting just such a gradual change from the beginning
to the end of the volume as naturally takes place in the character
of any man's writing in the course of several years; and it is
probable that the first treatise, " The Seven Sages of Rome," was
transcribed when the penman was rather a young man. It is
certainly far more carefully written than the latter contents of the
volume.

But who was this penman and chronicler? In a modern note
written on a fly-leaf at the end of the book it is said that the
author of the Chronicle was one Gregory Skinner (meaning William
Gregory of the Skinners' Company) who was Mayor of London in
1451, the thirtieth year of Henry VI. And when we turn to the
Chronicle itself the fact seems to be pretty well borne out by what

the author himself says in the record of that year. For the words he uses are as follows:

And that year came a legate from the Pope of Rome with great pardon, for that pardon was the greatest pardon that ever come to England from the Conquest unto this time of my year being mayor of London.

When it is considered that " Gregory Skinner, Mayor of London —Anno xxx " stands at the end of this paragraph, the inference appears to be sufficiently obvious that he was the author of the Chronicle, and, therefore, that the whole contents of the volume are in his handwriting. This opinion, indeed, seemed to me to rest upon so sure a basis that I had no hesitation in calling the narrative " Gregory's Chronicle," with which title I have printed it in this volume. But at the last moment, while seeking for materials for Gregory's life, I was fortunate, or unfortunate, enough to discover evidence the most conclusive that he died a year or two before our Chronicle comes to an end; for his will, which I have printed at the end of this Introduction, was proved on the 23rd January, 1466 (or, according to the modern computation, 1467), while the Chronicle is continued in the same hand to the ninth year of Edward IV. (1469). It is quite clear, therefore, that, if William Gregory wrote the part relating to his own mayoralty, he could not have been the author of the whole Chronicle or the writer of the MS.

I must own that the effect of this discovery was at first to make me doubt whether the name of " Gregory's Chronicle " was not altogether a misnomer; for it was not, after all, quite clear that even the passage in which his authorship seems to be asserted was really his composition. It was open to dispute that the expression, " this time of my year being mayor," did not necessarily mean the time of which the passage in question treated, but the time at which

it was written. And it was even conceivable that the real writer
and the year of his mayoralty were originally disclosed at the end
‾of the work, which is now lost. But on the whole it seemed to me
more probable that this was really Gregory's Chronicle, transcribed
and continued by another hand; and on careful examination of the
text I found various evidences that tended to confirm me in this
opinion.

In the first place—though the fact might suggest an opposite inference—it was a little remarkable that in this thirtieth year not
only the name of Gregory himself as mayor but also those of the two
sheriffs are entered in a manner quite unusual in this narrative. Only
the surnames without the Christian name of any one of the civic
officers at first stood at the head of this mayor's year, although in the
ease of Gregory himself the omission has been supplied in a later hand.
Not a single other instance occurs in the whole Chronicle in which
the Christian names of all three civic officers have been omitted;
for, though there are cases in which the sheriffs are mentioned only
by their surnames, it is never so with the mayor.

Now it is true the omission of a man's own Christian name does
not look much like a sign of authorship, for it is a thing that could
hardly have been occasioned by modesty, and if owing to ignorance
the argument, of course, tells conclusively the other way. But
there is a third cause, slovenliness, to which it may more reasonably be attributed; and the fact that in this instance surnames only
were jotted down both of the mayor and his two sheriffs agrees
very well with the supposition that the labours of office had inter-
fered with the work of continuing the Chronicle, and that the
writer had left it off just at that point, with a very brief memo-
randum of what was done in the year of his own mayoralty.
Gregory's Chronicle may then have been transcribed by another
hand, which continued the work to the year 1469 or later.

And this hypothesis seems rather to be confirmed by another fact, viz., that whereas the record of the years immediately preceding is remarkably full and accurate, especially for the twenty-eighth year, the year of Cade's rebellion, it is quite otherwise just after the thirtieth year is passed. The record of the five or six years immediately following, though it was a time of great political excitement and witnessed the beginning of the Wars of the Roses, is singularly jejune, especially as regards great public events, and the chronology is vitiated by the entire omission of one year from the annals. So remarkable a change in the character of the narrative—from fulness to emptiness and from accuracy to in-accuracy—is perhaps the best reason for supposing that the Chronicle as far as the thirtieth year was really the work of Gregory. For it seems as if just after that year the work must have been laid aside, and that it was taken up—presumably by a different' hand—several years later.

Moreover, in the part which we suppose to be Gregory's, viz. from the nineteenth to the thirtieth year of Henry VI., a minute examination reveals some errors which may have been very well due to the transcriber. In the twenty-third year it is stated that the King made forty-six Knights of the Bath on Thursday the 26th day of May. This is wrong according to the calendar of the year, and the error is evidently due to a misreading of the numeral " xxvij." as " xxvj." Again, the twenty-sixth year of the reign is altogether omitted—not even the names of the mayor and sheriffs for that year are given. Yet the chronology is not vitiated by this omission as in the case of a similar blunder in the later part. It is an omission pure and simple, and the general account of the events is such as could only have been written by a well-informed contemporary. There is however a piece of erro-neous information in the twenty-seventh year, which I think may be best accounted for by supposing a sentence or two to have been omitted by a careless transcriber. It is as follows:—

That same year was a treaty of truce taken with the Scots by Master Adam Moleyns for four years, that time he being ambassador into Scotland, and after Privy Seal, and then y-made bishop of Chichester, and within short time after put to death.

The 27th year of Henry VI. extended from the 1st September 1448 to the 31st August 1449. Adam de Moleyns, Bishop of Chichester, was put to death in January 1450, so that the above paragraph might very well have been written not many months after the conclusion of the truce referred to. But unfortunately the truce was not made for anything like a period of four years; it was in fact only for six weeks, from the 10th August to the 20th September 1449.* Adam de Moleyns does not seem to have been ambassador in Scotland, for the negociations took place at Winchester; and most certainly it was not "after that" that he was made Privy Seal and Bishop of Winchester, for he had enjoyed the latter dignity since the year 1445, and the former from the year 1444. I do not see any perfect explanation of this maze of errors; but, if (as is quite possible) Adam de Moleyns was ambassador to Scotland on a former occasion, we may suppose that a line or two may have been omitted by the transcriber just before the words "for four years." If the errors be not due to some such cause as this, the passage must be an ignorant interpolation of later date written from a confused recollection of the facts. There are no other inaccuracies comparable to these in the part we attribute to Gregory.

With these remarks we must leave the Chronicle for the present,

---

* Rymer, xi. 232.

as there is other matter in the volume which ought first to claim our attention.

Of the fourteen separate articles contained in the MS., almost every one except the Chronicle is to be met with elsewhere, and, the three last alone being of a historical character, they only are printed in this volume.   Of the others there is little need to say anything except as to No. 11, which is a list of the parish churches and monasteries in the City of London.   A similar list is printed in Fabyan's Chronicle (pp. 295-8, Ellis's edition), and another in Arnold's Chronicle, (pp. 75-77).   But these lists do not correspond, the churches being named in each in a different order, and even with different totals as to number.   Thus the whole number of parish churches in London (within the city) is according to Fabyan 113, according to Arnold 118, and according to our MS. 115.   But the total number of churches and monasteries in and about London, including the suburbs and also Southwark and Westminster, is given in our MS. as 153.   Besides the mere names and number of the churches, however, special descriptions are given of the character of one or two of the monastic foundations, which are so curious that we transcribe them here:

Pappy Chyrche in the Walle be twyne Algate and Bevysse Markes. And hyt ys a grete fraternyte of prestys and of othyr seqular men.   And there ben founde of almys certayne prestys, bothe blynde and lame, that be empotent; and they have day masse and xiiij d. a weke, barber and launder, and one to dresse and provyde for hyr mete and drynke.

Bartholomewe ys Spetylle.   Hyt ys a place of grete comforte to pore men as for hyr loggyng, and yn specyalle unto yong wymmen that have mysse done that ben whythe chylde.   There they ben delyveryde, and unto the tyme of puryfycacyon they have mete and drynke of the placys coste, and fulle honestely gydyd and kepte.   And in ys moche as the place mayo they kepe byr conselle and hyr worschyppe.   God

graunte that they doo so hyr owne worschippe that have a-fendyde.
Amen.

A chyrche of Owre Lady that ys namyde Bedlem.* And yn that
–place ben founde many men that ben fallyn owte of hyr wytte. And
fulle honestely they ben kepte in that place ; and sum ben restoryde
unto hyr wytte and helthe a-gayne. And sum ben a-bydyng there yn
for evyr, for they ben falle soo moche owte of hem selfe that hyt ys
uncurerabylle unto man. And unto that place ys grauntyde moche
pardon, more thenne they of the place knowe.

Seynt Marye Spetylle. A poore pryery, and a parysche chyrche in
the same. And that pryory kepythe ospytalyte for pore men. And
sum susters yn the same place to kepe the heddys for pore men that
come to that place.

In Southwark :

Mary Overaye. Hyt ys a pryory of Mary Magdalene; in the same
——ᵇ Chanyns.

Thomas Spetylle.ᶜ And that same place ys and (*sic*) ospytalyte for pore
men and wymmen. And that nobyl marchaunt, Rycharde Whytyngdon,
made a newe chamby[r] with viij heddys for yong weme[n] that badde
done a-mysse in truste of a good mendement. And he commaundyd
that alle the thyngys that ben don in that chambyr shulde be kepte
secrete with owte forthe, yn payne of lesynge of byr levynge; for he
wolde not shame no yonge women in noo wyse, for byt myght be cause
of hyr lettyng of hyr maryage, &c.

The Abbay of Barmondesay, Mary Magdalene ther by. That Abbay
ys of Blacke Monkys, and there ys grete offeryng unto the Crosse that
ys namyd Syn Savyoure.

Some of the facts contained in these extracts seem to be quite
unknown; and they go far to correct certain popular misappre-

* It was then near Bishopsgate.
  ᵇ There was a blank here in the MS. which has been improperly filled up by the
rubricator with a mark ¶, indicating a new paragraph.
  ᶜ St. Thomas's Hospital.

CAMD. SOC.

hensions touching the useless unpractical character of monastic institutions before the Reformation swept them all away. The charities of the middle ages were perhaps not more redundant or more misapplied than those of our own day, and many of them were eminently beneficial. There were hospitals for the sick and infirm, lying-in hospitals, asylums for the aged, the impotent, and the insane. Bedlam existed then, and was devoted to the same purposes as at present. And, whatever may have been the system of treatment adopted for the patients, it appears that some were cured; and the charity of the age extended a large indulgence to all who were so afflicted.

The poem on the Siege of Rouen has already been printed from other MSS., but not in a complete form. It was first brought to light by the Rev. J. J. Conybeare, who in the twenty-first volume of *The Archæologia* printed it from an imperfect copy in the Bodleian MS. No. 124. The conclusion of the poem, which was wanting in this MS., was afterwards supplied by Sir Frederic Madden from two MSS. in the Harleian Collection (Nos. 2256 and 753), and was printed by him in the twenty-second volume of the same publication. But never till now has the poem been published as a whole, so as to be easily read through or consulted in one volume. Moreover the text contained in the Egerton MS., from which we now print it, differs a good deal here and there in phraseology from that of the other MSS.; and though, perhaps, on the whole, a trifle less polished, being, it appears, taken from a first draft of the poem, it is on this very account all the more interesting, as the relation of an eye-witness written while the impression on his mind was still recent and vivid. At the end, too, the author gives his name, which is suppressed in other copies of the poem, with an excuse for the ruggedness of his rhymes, which apparently he afterwards improved, as he says he intended to do:

> With owtyn fabylle or fage,
> Thys procesce made John Page
> Alle in raffe and not in ryme,
> By cause of space he badde no tyme.
> But whenne thys werre ys at an ende,
> And he have lyffe and space he wyll hit amende.

It thus appears that the poem was written during the continuance of the war, very shortly after the events which it relates. As an account of the siege of Rouen by Henry the Fifth it certainly stands unrivalled. No other contemporary writer states the facts with so much clearness, precision, minuteness, and graphic power. Yet the language is simple and unpretentious, the author only seeking to impart his own knowledge of the facts in the plainest possible form:

> Lystenythe unto me a lytylle space,
> And I shalle telle you howe hyt was.
> And the better telle I may,
> For at that sege with the Kyng I lay,
> And thereto I toke a vyse
> Lyke as my wytt wolde suffyce.

That his information was not only minute, but on the whole exceedingly accurate, we have little reason to doubt. Yet it abounds in details which are met with nowhere else; for although, as remarked by Sir Frederic Madden, the chronicler Hall appears to have been acquainted with this poem, even he made but slender use of it, and scarcely any modern historian has hitherto made use of it at all. Hereafter we may presume it will not be so neglected.

The siege and capture of Rouen were the crowning events of Henry the Fifth's second invasion of France. His first expedition against that country was signalised by the splendid victory of Agincourt; but no territorial advantage accrued from it. The English only saved themselves from being cut to pieces or crushed by overwhelming numbers. In his second invasion the case was different. Town after town in Normandy opened its gates or was taken by assault in the summer of 1417; and in the course of the following year almost the whole duchy was in the hands of the English. Rouen, the capital, however, still held out; for here the enemy had gathered all their strength, and were prepared to make the most obstinate resistance.

The following is a brief outline of the narrative contained in the poem. After the capture of Pont de l'Arche, which opened to the invaders a passage over the Seine (for hitherto their conquests had been all on the western side of that river), the King despatched his uncle, the Duke of Exeter, to Rouen to summon the city to surrender, which it scornfully refused to do (p. 2). The Duke then returned to the King at Pont de l'Arche, and those in command of the city preparing for an attack destroyed the suburbs * (p. 3). The fortifications of the city are then described, with the further preparations for defence (pp. 4–6). The king came before it on Friday before Lammas day, the 29th July, 1418 (p. 6). The positions taken up by his lords and captains are related (pp. 6–10). The Earl of Warwick after taking Domfront was sent to Caudebec, which surrendered conditionally, agreeing to do as Rouen did, and allowing the English meanwhile free passage up the Seine (p. 10). Warwick then joins the besiegers, as also does the King's brother

---

* M. Puiseux points out that this " cursed deed," as the poet calls it (involving as it did the destruction of a number of churches), was dictated by considerations of prudence, the importance of which had been recently illustrated in the case of Caen. The reluctance of the inhabitants to destroy the abbeys of St. Etienne and Ste. Trinité had been the chief cause of the loss of that city.—Siège et Prise de Rouen, 56.

Humphrey Duke of Gloucester, coming from the siege of Cherbourg (p. 11). It is then reported that the French King and the Burgundians are coming to relieve the city, and Henry prepares for them (pp. 12, 13). The captains within are named and described (pp. 13, 14). The King orders a ditch to be made round the town (p. 15). Renewed tidings of the coming of the Burgundians cause the citizens to ring the bells with delight, but it turns out to be a false rumour (p. 16). The King, however, endeavours to profit by it, and adopts a stratagem to induce the citizens to come out and attack him (p. 17).

The writer goes on to tell of the failure of provisions within the city, the extraordinary prices given for horseflesh, dogs, cats, rats, and mice, besides more ordinary food, such as eggs and apples (p. 18); and he draws a fearful picture of the sufferings of the inhabitants:

> They dyde faster every day
> Thenn men myght them in erthe lay.
> There as was pryde in ray before
> Thenn was hyt put in sorowe fulle soore.
> Thereas was mete, drynke, and songe,
> Then was sorowe and hunger stronge.
> Yf the chylde schulde be dede,
> The modyr wolde not gyf hyt bredde,
> Ne nought wolde parte hyt a scheve
> Thoughe sche wyste to save hys lyve ;
> Ne the chylde the modyr gyffe ;
> Every on caste hym for to leve
> As longe as they myght laste.
> Love and kyndenys bothe were paste.
> Alle kyndenys love was besyde,
> That the chylde schulde fro the modyr hyde,
> To ete mete that shulde hyt not see,
> And ete hyt alle in prevytè.
> But hungyr passyd kyude and love, &c. (p 19)

In the end it was found necessary to drive the poorer inhabitants outside the city, where they remained in the ditches dependent for food on the charity of the besiegers, and some died of cold (p. 20). On Christmas day the King as an act of charity sent heralds to the city, offering food to all who were in want of it, either within the city or without, and safe-conduct to come and receive it. Those within affected to despise the offer, and would scarcely allow two priests and three men to come and relieve those outside (p. 21). But on New Year's eve, as "hunger breaketh the stone wall," the citizens proposed to treat (P. 22); for which purpose they conferred with Sir Gilbert Umfraville (pp. 23–25). Umfraville carried their message on New Year's day morning to the King, who consented that twelve of the citizens should wait on him next day (pp. 26, 27); and on the next day accordingly twelve delegates from the city waited on Henry at St. Hilary's Gate (p. 28). Their interview with the King is then described (pp. 29–32), and the King's lofty and unmoved demeanour is particularly reported (p. 30). Next day tents are pitched for a conference (P. 33), and the author is led to contrast the splendour of heralds and pursuivants with the misery of the poor people who had been put out of the city and had scarcely clothes on their backs to protect them from the weather, which was at that time very rainy. Still more dreadful was the case of others:

> There men myght se grete pyttè,
> A chylde of ij yere or iij.
> Go aboute to begge hyt brede.
> Fadyr and modyr bothe were dede.
> Undyr sum the watyr stode ;
> Yet lay they cryyng aftyr foode.
> And sum storvyn unto the dothe,
> And sum stoppyde of ther brethe,
> Sum crokyd in the kneys,

And sum alle so lene as any treys;
And wemmen holdyn in hyr armys
Dede chyldryn in hyr barmys,
And the chyldryn sokyng in ther pappe
With yn a dede woman lappe. (p. 35.)

The conference was unsatisfactory, as the demands of the English greatly exceeded what was offered on behalf of the city; and at the end of a fortnight negociations were about to be broken off (p. 36). The city delegates, however, prayed that the truce might be continued for one night; and the clamour of the citizens compelled them again to treat (pp. 36-39). In four days more they came to terms, and it was agreed that the city should be surrendered in eight days if no rescue came in the interval (p. 40). On Thursday the 19th January the keys of the city were delivered up (p. 41), and the poem concludes with an account of the King's entry into the city and the process of taking possession (pp. 42-45).

Of the three other MSS. of this poem above referred to not one supplies a complete and satisfactory text. In the Bodleian MS. the latter part is wanting; while, on the other hand, in the two Harleian MSS. it is the latter part alone that has been preserved to us in its original form. Both these MSS. are copies of the well-known English chronicle called *The Brute*, which used to be attributed to Caxton, because printed by him in 1480, with a continuation to the accession of Edward IV. Neither the printed copy nor almost any other MS. of the Chronicle contains this poem, but in these two Harleian MSS., and also in a MS. mentioned by Sir F. Madden as being then in the library of T. W. Coke, Esq. at Holkham, the poem is incorporated in the narrative, the earlier part of it being translated into prose, sometimes with very little verbal alteration, while the latter part is preserved in its original form as metre.

As the text of the Bodleian and the two Harleian MSS. has already been printed, I have not thought it necessary to note the varieties of reading, except where the variations are material or where the reading of another MS. seemed preferable to that of the Egerton. In the footnotes I refer to the Bodleian MS. as B., the Egerton as E., the Harleian MS. 2256 as H., and the Harleian MS. 753 as H 2.

The Verses on the Kings of England which follow occur in several MSS. They are commonly, I doubt not justly, attributed to Lydgate. A copy in Ashmole MS. 59 is in the handwriting of Shirley, the transcriber of Chaucer, and must have been written as I am informed about 1456. The poem, however, was added to by other hands after it was composed. A further stanza relating to Edward IV. (which I have printed in a footnote at p. 54) is con-tained in MS. Harl. 2251, a volume full of Lydgate's poetry. The poem was printed in 1530 by Wynkyn de Worde with additions continuing it to the reign of Henry VIII., but this tract is exceedingly rare. A copy occurs in the Public Library at Cambridge, bound up along with Stephen Hawes's " Joyful Meditation on the Coronation of Henry VIII."

As to the Chronicle, we have already seen that it was in all probability partly written by William Gregory, who was Mayor of London in 1451-52, the 30th year of Henry VI; but that his authorship does not extend to the conclusion of the work, and probably does not go beyond the year of his mayoralty. It seems hardly necessary to add that the earlier part of the work is not more his composition than the last part; for all who have the least

familiarity with mediæval chronicles know quite well how one
writer transcribed the works of others, only adding to them at the
end some original information of the facts of his own day. But
William Gregory, though not the only author of this Chronicle, is
the only one whose name is known to us; and the very little that
is known even about him may here be briefly stated.

He was the son of Roger Gregory of Mildenhall in Suffolk, and
though I find nothing else about his family it appears that he was
entitled to bear arms, which are described as: "Party per pale, argent
and azure, two lions rampant guardant endorsed, counterchanged."
Of the date of his birth there is no precise evidence; but as he was
a widower, who had been three times married and had at least
eleven grandchildren when he made his will in 1465, fourteen
months before his death, it could hardly have been later than about
the year 1410. Indeed we may with great probability carry it still
further back and suppose him to have been born before the close of
the fourteenth century. He was, as we have already mentioned, a
member of the Skinners' Company; but at what date he became so
we have no means of knowing, as the records of that Company do
not extend so far back. He served the office of sheriff in 1436 and
was elected mayor in 1451. At the time he made his will he was
living in the parish of St. Mary Aldermary, where he directs that
he should be buried; but if Stowe be correct he was actually
buried in the church of St. Anne Aldersgate. In that church,
too, according to Stowe, he founded a chantry, and there are MSS.
at the Guildhall which say that he endowed this chantry with
19*l.* 17*s.* 4*d.* per annum out of all his lands. No monument of
him, however, existed in the church even in Stowe's day,[a] and
among the many benefactions in his will the name of St. Anne's
church Aldersgate is not even once mentioned. To the church of

---

[a] Stowe's Survey, iii. 102.

St. Mary Aldermary there is a bequest of 16*l*. 13*s*. 4*d*. in aid of the " church work," that the parishioners might pray for his soul; and there is another to Master Duffeld, " one of the chauntry priests of Aldermary church aforesaid," for the like purpose.

At the time he made his will he had two married daughters, of whom one named Margaret was the wife of John Croke, and had a family of five sons and two daughters. The second, Cecily, was the wife of Robert Mildenhall, and had two daughters. The will also mentions a William Gregory, who is perhaps a son of the testator, but is not so designated, who has a wife Mary and a son and daughter.

For other points of interest we must refer the reader to the will itself, which is very curious in many ways. The very large bequests for the good of the testator's soul, the charitable legacies to the poor in hospital and elsewhere, the sums left for the relief of prisoners and for the repair " of the foulest ways about London," may create some little surprise that greater provision is not made for the testator's own relations. But they were probably in good circumstances and did not need his generosity; for he makes his son-in-law John Croke his executor, which certainly implies that there was no coolness between them, and the way in which he provides for servants and dependents forbids us to suppose that he was insensible to any natural claim upon him.

The Chronicle is one of those city chronicles of which we have several examples, the best known being that of Robert Fabyan. Events, sometimes only of civic importance, and sometimes such as affected the whole kingdom, are in these compositions recorded in the form of annals, the names of the mayor and sheriffs of London in each year being prefixed to the record of that year. The Chronicle of London, printed by Sir Harris Nicolas in 1827, bears a considerable resemblance to that of Gregory. Both begin

at the same date, the first year of Richard I., and are evidently
derived from a common source down to the time of Richard II.
There are, however, considerable variations, our Chronicle being
less full in some places and more in others; but the Chronicle
printed by Nicolas is itself derived from two different MSS., which
exhibit some variations among themselves; and in the account of
the last years of Richard II. one of these (the Cottonian MS. Julius
—B i. which I have referred to in footnotes as J.) corresponds much
more closely with our Chronicle than the other (Harleian, No. 565,
which I have referred to as H.) Another city chronicle which
corresponds still more closely with ours is contained in the Cottonian
MS. Vitellius A. xvi., which I have cited in footnotes occasionally
as V. It is evidently derived from a common source until the
19th year of Henry VI., after which the text is a good deal like
that of Fabyan.

The variations between these different MSS. are occasionally
instructive. We can see in some cases how facts were exaggerated,
not only in the telling but even in the transcription, as time went
on. Thus in the fifth year of Edward III. our Chronicle mentions
the defeat of 40,000 Scots by a handful of 2,000 Englishmen; but
in the Chronicle of London printed by Nicolas from MSS. H. and
-J. the number of the Scots is given at 12,000 only.

In the present Chronicle, as also in J. and V., a number of
capitulations for the surrender of places in France during the wars
of Henry V. and at the beginning of Henry VI.'s reign have been
inserted in the narrative. In these the transcriber's errors are so
numerous and so gross in our MS., that it would have been utterly
impossible in very many places even to conjecture the true reading
of the text if there had been no better transcript. But as the
original treaties are enrolled in the Norman Rolls, and have for the
most part been printed by Rymer from that source, I have been able

to give the right readings in the text, pointing out the extraordinary blunders of the MS. in footnotes. As examples of unintelligent and inaccurate copying they would certainly be very hard to match.

It is in all probability from the nineteenth year of Henry VI. that William Gregory's part in the Chronicle begins. At that date, as we have already said, the similar chronicle in the Vitellius MS. begins to differ from ours, and to follow a source to which Fabyan is largely indebted. It is probable, I think, that the whole of the preceding part in which the Vitellius MS. and ours correspond, was derived from an older chronicle, which terminated in the eighteenth year, and that from the nineteenth year to the thirtieth William Gregory took up the pen and made a continuation. We cannot say much for it as an example of literary art or style in composition; nor is there much that he records that is even of great importance from its novelty until we reach the twenty-eighth year. But his account of Cade's rebellion in that year is certainly of no small value.

Our author agrees with Fabyan in saying that the leader in this rising was originally chosen by the people; but, being so chosen, he adds that this captain "compassed all the gentles to arise with him." The people in some part of Kent had found a leader for themselves; and he proved to be a man of such remarkable energy and tact that he soon got all the country gentlemen of Kent to go along with him. They formed a regular encampment on Black-heath, or, in the words of our authority, "made a field dyked and staked well about, as it had been in the land of war." This showed real military capacity, "save only they kept [no?] order amongst them (for as good was Jack Robyn as John at the Noke, for all were as high as pig's feet) unto the time that they should commun and speak with such states and messengers that were sent unto them: then they put all their power unto the man that named him

captain of all their host." This remark seems to make the movement a degree more intelligible. The man chosen as leader
whatever may have been then known about him—possessed little
or no influence with the squires and yeomen, who only wished to
combine with their fellow countrymen in setting forth their
grievances to the King. But when the time for joint action came
his power and skill as a military leader was so manifest that all
readily submitted to him. Yet even this submission might only
have been momentary, for the multitude seems to have had no
intention of taking the offensive. When the King, after sending to
know the cause of the rising, was answered by the captain that it
was "to destroy traitors being about him, with other divers points,"
another message was immediately sent by the King and his lords,
and proclamation was everywhere made, that loyal men should
immediately quit the field. "And upon the night after," says our
chronicler, "they were all voided and a-go."

The insurrection, seemingly, was almost at an end. The King
rode armed through London at the head of his lords, who mustered
their followers at Clerkenwell to the number of 10,000 men. Un-
happily a small body, detached from this force, went in pursuit of
the captain under Sir Humphrey and William Stafford. They
were defeated at Sevenoaks, and their leaders slain. The King and
his lords were seized with a panic. They separated and withdrew
into the country, leaving London open to the insurgents, who
entered the city on the 3rd July. Here, according to our chronicler,
and also two days before at Blackheath, although they professed to
be under the same captain as before, they really had a new one who
went by the same name. This is quite a novel piece of information,
and whether true or not is exceedingly curious as bearing upon the
history of the movement. Evidently, the original leader was not
well-known, and the facts were not well-known. Apparently it

was conceived by some that the first captain had been killed at Sevenoaks, and that the fact had been concealed, another man being artfully put in his place. If so, then, a further question arises whether the name Mortimer assumed by Cade was not the real name of the first leader in the movement. It is quite clear that Cade's assumption of that name passed unchallenged till after the rebellion was over, for under the name of Mortimer he actually received a pardon, which was invalidated when it was found he had no right to it.[a] The only circumstance which renders improbable this substitution of one captain for another is the total absence of corroborative testimony to the fact. But this, it must be owned, throws serious doubt upon it.[b]

There is little else deserving of special comment in the portion of the chronicle which we believe to have been written by Gregory. But as being, to all appearance, a strictly contemporary record of the times, it will undoubtedly merit the careful attention of future historians in other matters besides those we have pointed out. Immediately after the year of Gregory's mayoralty appear those evidences to which we have already alluded of a later hand having continued the record of events some years after the events were passed. The mayor and sheriffs for the thirty-second year of Henry VI. are omitted, and the later years of the reign are each made a year too early.[c] The first battle of St. Albans, the battle of Bloreheath, and the encampment of the Yorkists at Ludlow in

[a] I have already pointed this out in another publication (Paston Letters, vol. i. Introduction, p. lv.), quoting as my authority a MS. in the Lambeth Library, which I hope shortly to edit for the Camden Society.

[b] The story of Jack Cade, however, is attended with difficulties from any point of view, and it is remarkable that when Cade's body was brought to London it was taken to the White Hart at Southwark, where he had lodged before his entry into the City, and identified by the woman who kept the house (p. 194). We hear nothing of its being identified by anyone who had seen the leader before the battle of Sevenoaks.

[c] See page 198, note [a].

1459, are all, owing to this cause, misdated. Moreover, a matter of no less consequence than the first illness of Henry VI. at Clarendon in 1453 is only mentioned retrospectively after the battle of St. Albans in 1455. It is clear that during the remainder of Henry VI.'s reign, or at least till the last year of it, the continuator does not chronicle the facts so immediately after their occurrence as Gregory did before he was mayor.

The great events of the period, too, are but slightly mentioned for the most part, and a good deal of space is devoted to occurrences of no great political interest. In the thirty-third (which ought to be the thirty-fourth) year the principal subject of the narrative is an extraordinary and very barbarous case of single combat between two men, one of whom had accused the other falsely, the conditions of the fight—degrading as they were—being apparently prescribed by some old law or custom applicable to such cases.

In the thirty-fifth (thirty-sixth) year an incident is recorded showing the high importance attached to the pulpit in those days. During Lent, the Court being then at Coventry, an order was made that no preacher, however highly qualified, should preach before the King without first showing his sermon to an official, whom the author does not name, but indicates by the letters A. B. C. Political allusions in sermons seem to have been much more common than agreeable to royalty, and A. B. C. instructed each preacher what passages he should leave out on pain of going as he came, without meat, drink, or reward. But a certain Master William Ive, bachelor of Divinity, came up from Wykeham's College at Winchester to preach before the King, and, after showing his sermon to the official, not only disobeyed the instruction to omit certain passages, but declared from the pulpit before the King that it was A. B. C. who had made the sermons previously preached before him, and not the preachers themselves; for they, be said, had allowed their purpose to be turned upside down, and " had made lovedays as Judas made with a kiss with Christ." Ive's reward for this boldness was simply a thankless ride of 160 miles—to Court and back again.[a]

The account of the battle of Bloreheath,[b] besides being out of place, is a little confused, so that it would be hard to understand from the writer's slipshod grammar, if we had no other authority to go by, that it was a Yorkist victory at all. Nor is the story quite consistent with that contained in other sources, for it is said the battle lasted from one till five in the afternoon, whereas according to Hall it began early in the morning. The disparity in numbers between the two parties was, moreover, extreme; for Salisbury had but 500 men against 5,000 on the Queen's side, "a great wonder," says our author, "that ever they (Salisbury's force) might stand the great multitude not fearing, the King being within ten miles and the Queen within five miles at the Castle of Eccleshall" It is not safe of course to rely on the strict accuracy of these numbers, which differ considerably from those in other authorities, —but it is hard to say what authority is more trustworthy. According to the Act of Attainder against the Yorkists (which, however, in all probability magnified their numbers to mitigate the disgrace of a Lancastrian defeat) the Earl had 5,000 men with him. This estimate is even exceeded in the English Chronicle edited by Mr. Davies for the Camden Society in 1856, where it is said that he had 7,000 well arrayed men. On the other hand Lord Audeley's force is stated by Hall to have amounted to 10,000, and the number of the slain to 2,400. Under any circumstances it seems clear that Salisbury fought obstinately against great odds, and though victorious just saved himself from being surrounded. Indeed, our author

[a] Page 203. The Continuator was probably a personal friend of this William Ive, whom he mentions again shortly afterwards with praise for the part he took in a controversy with the Friars. As Ive belonged to Wykeham's College at Winchester, and other matters of local interest are mentioned in this part of the Chronicle, I am —inclined to think the Continuator must have been a Hampshire man.

[b] Page 204.

says that he would have been taken if after the day was over an —Austin friar had not kept firing guns all night to cover his retreat.

Again we have a totally new piece of information on page 207, as to the intoxication and want of discipline that prevailed among the King's forces after the Yorkists had dispersed at Ludlow.

At pp. 208-210 likewise is a hitherto unknown account of Queen Margaret's adventures after the battle of Northampton; how she was robbed by a servant of her own in whom she had placed confidence,— how she at last reached Harlech Castle in Wales with no more than four attendants,—how, after being relieved and comforted there, she removed privily for fear of capture and joined the Earl of Pembroke,—and how she was in continual danger of being betrayed by counterfeit tokens sent to her as if they had come from the King her husband. But the messengers who brought those tokens, being of the King's or the Prince's household, and sometimes of her own, gave her warning not to trust to any but a special token agreed to privately between herself and the King just before the battle of Northampton. Margaret accordingly stood on her guard, and, sending messages to the Duke of Somerset and others, arranged to meet with her supporters at Hull, which was planned with so great secrecy that 15,000 men were assembled before the Yorkists had taken the alarm. When the news came to London the Duke of York himself set out to meet them. The result was the battle of Wakefield. All this has been hitherto quite unknown.

Our author also mentions a battle or skirmish that took place at Dunstable [*] the day before the second battle of St. Albans, regarding which other authorities are silent, except that there is a slight allusion to it in William Worcester, who says that Edward Poynings (he probably means Robert) and 200 foot were slain there. But, according to the Chronicle before us, the action seems

[*] Page 212.

to have been of an insignificant character. A few raw levies raised in the King's name to oppose Queen Margaret and her northern army were commanded by a butcher of Dunstable, and were, as might be expected, easily discomfited; on which, as our chronicler was informed, the butcher hung himself, either for shame at the loss of his men or for the loss of his goods. The incident, however, is curious as an illustration of what other writers tell us about the general fear of outrage and plunder that prevailed in the south on the approach of Margaret and her northern forces.[a]

Of the second battle of St. Albans itself we have also some new particulars. The King's army, or in other words the Yorkists, who at this time had the King in their keeping, had already pitched their camp and fortified it, awaiting the Queen's coming, when, hearing that she was still nine miles off, they unfortunately gave up their position and occupied a new one. They were well prepared with artillery and apparatus—engines that would discharge both pellets of lead and arrows an ell long, with six feathers, " with a great mighty head of iron on the other end," or cast wildfire among the enemy. They had also nets, and pavyses or large shields with apertures to shoot through, and other curious contrivances interesting to the military antiquary. But before guns and engines could be got into working order the Queen's army had come to close quarters and they were busy fighting. They thus laboured under disadvantages from the very beginning; although Whethamstede intimates that they would have won the battle had their endurance equalled their valour at the outset.[b]

There is comparatively little new information about the battle of Towton and the beginning of Edward IV.'s reign. But in the third year there is a very striking account of the easy confidence

---

[a] Hall's Chronicle. Whethamstede. Rolls of Parliament, v. 476.
[b] Pages 212—214. Whethamstede, i. 391. (Rolls ed.)

with which Edward received the Duke of Somerset into favour after he had surrendered and sworn allegiance to him at Durham. " The King," we are told, " made full much of him ; insomuch that he lodged with the King in his own bed many nights, and sometimes rode a-hunting behind the King, the King having about him not passing six horse at the most, and yet three were the Duke's men of Somerset. The King loved him well, but the Duke thought treason under fair cheer and words, as it appeared. And for a great love the King made a great justs at Westminster, that he should see some manner sport of chivalry after his great labour and heaviness. And with great instance the King made him to take harness upon him, and rode in the place, but he would never cope with no man, and no man might not cope with him, till the King prayed him to be merry and sent him a token, and then he ran full justly and merrily, and his helm was a sorry hat of straw. And then every man marked him well."[a]

The King afterwards going into the north, " to understand the disposition of the people," took the Duke of Somerset with him and 200 of his men, " well horsed and harnessed," as a royal body guard. It was like putting a lamb into the guard of wolves, our author thinks, " but Almighty God was the shepherd." The people of Northampton were indignant at the favour shown to a traitor, and would have slain him, but that the King sent him away secretly to a castle of his own for surety, and sent his men to Newcastle to keep the town, their wages fully paid.[b] Somerset repaid his benefactor next year by coming secretly out of Wales and endeavouring to betray Newcastle into the hands of Henry VI. The King, however, appointed Lord Scrope of Bolton to keep the town, and the Duke did not succeed. He was taken and beheaded, as is well known, after the battle of Hexham; but it has not been

[a] Page 219.   [b] Page 221.

known till now how deep was the perfidy thus deservedly punished.—
The Scots who had been the chief occasion of trouble (especially as
France had made a truce with England some months previously [a])
had made overtures for peace about Easter 1464, and Commissioners
had been appointed on the part of both kingdoms, who were to
meet at York. Warwick's brother, Lord Montague, as Warden of
the Marches, was commissioned to conduct the Scotch Commissioners
from the Borders. But while riding northwards for this purpose
the Duke of Somerset lay in wait for him near Newcastle, accompanied by the equally treacherous Sir Ralph Percy [b] and Sir Humphrey Nevill. Montague, however, who had fortunately received
timely warning, took another way to Newcastle, and proceeded
to Norham, when Somerset again endeavoured to intercept him
accompanied by Lord Hungerford and all the principal Lancastrians.
They were however thoroughly defeated at Hedgley Moor, and
Montague accomplished his mission. The Scottish and English
Commissioners met and a fifteen years' peace was concluded. " An
the Scots be true," adds our Chronicler, showing by the remark

[a] Proclamation was made on the 27th Oct. 1463, of a truce with France till
1st Oct. 1464. (Close Rolls).

[b] Sir Ralph Percy swore allegiance to Edward at the same time as Somerset, and
they agreed to deliver up Bamborough and Dunstanborough Castles on condition
that Percy should have the keeping of them. He abused his trust, and let the
French gain possession of Bamborough (pp. 219, 220.) Sir Ralph Grey, also, who
was made Constable of Alnwick, under the gallant Sir John Ashley, betrayed his
Captain to the enemy (p. 220), a deed for which he was afterwards condemned to
death and beheaded, his spurs being first struck off by the hand of the Master Cook.
(MS. in Heralds' College, quoted in Notes to Warkworth's Chronicle, p. 39). Yet
through all this treachery there seems to have been, with some at least, a strange
perverted notion of honour. Percy was slain at Hedgley Moor, where he refused to
fly as others did, exclaiming as it is said, " I have saved the bird in my bosom."
By this he meant that he had preserved his loyalty to Henry VI., forgetting that he
had actually sworn allegiance to Edward IV. The place where he fell is called
Percy's Cross to this day, and is marked by an octagonal pillar. (Holinshed, iii.
666. Pennant's Tour in Scotland, iii. 288.)

that he writes while the treaty was still a subject of conversation—
" An the Scots be true it must needs continue so long; but it is
hard for to trust unto them, for they be ever found full of guile and
deceit." *

Then follows a notice of the battle of Hexham, and a list of the
Lancastrians who were beheaded by Montague's orders after the
battle, both at Hexham and at Newcastle, Middleham, and York.
Immediately afterwards occurred the capture of Sir William Tailboys in a coalpit near Newcastle ᵇ with 3,000 marks in money which
he was endeavouring to convey to Henry VI.ᶜ This also is quite
a new piece of information. Tailboys, from all that we know of
his former life, seems to have been a very unscrupulous partizan of
the Duke of Suffolk in the times before Jack Cade's rebellion. On
one occasion he had attempted to murder Lord Cromwell, one of
the King's councillors, even at the door of the Star Chamber, and
Suffolk was accused of protecting him unfairly against certain writs
of appeal brought by various widows for the death of their hus-
bands.ᵈ

The romantic marriage of Edward IV. is next related; but here
our author adds little, to what we already know except as to the
circumstances of its avowal. He is ill-informed indeed as to the
exact time when it was first made known, which he says was on
All Hallows' day (1 November), whereas William Worcester says
it was on Michaelmas day (29 September); and there is evidence
to show that William Worcester is right.ᵉ There can be no doubt,
however, that the circumstances of the disclosure were as stated in
our Chronicle. The marriage, in fact, could no longer be con-

* Pages 223-4.
ᵇ The Year Book in Easter, 4 Edw. IV. says that Tailboys (there called the Earl
of Kyme) was taken in Riddesdale.
ᶜ Page 226.   ᵈ Rolls of Parliament, v. 181, 200.
ᵉ See Lord Wenlock's letter on the subject, dated Reading, 3rd Oct. 1464, in
Wavrin (Dupont's ed.), ii. 326-7.

cealed, for the council was assembled with the King at Reading, where " the lords moved him in God's name to be wedded and to live under the law of God and Church, and they would send into some strange land to inquire a Queen of good birth according to his dignity. And then our sovereign might no longer hide his marriage." In fact, as we know very well from other sources, Edward's marriage with Bona of Savoy had been mooted for some time before, and the Earl, although he did not actually go, had been expected in France, where he was to have been sent to negociate it.[a]

Edward's marriage took place secretly at Grafton in Northamptonshire on the 1st May, 1464. He had left London not long before, and it may be presumed with a retinue capable of doing him some service in war; for it had been his intention soon after Easter to go and besiege Bamborough, which was again in Henry VI.'s possession along with Dunstanborough and Alnwick by the treachery of Sir Ralph Percy and Sir Ralph Grey.[b] He reached Stony Stratford on the 30th April, and meanwhile, on the 25th, in the furthest corner of Northumberland, Montague had overthrown his enemies for him at Hedgley Moor. The work had still to be completed by the battle of Hexham on the 14th May; but Edward had probably heard that the Lancastrians had received a decisive overthrow by the time that he stole off from Stony Stratford early in the morning of May day. got married, and returned. Surely never before or since did a King get married under similar circumstances!

Meanwhile Warwick and his brother Montague, all unconscious of what Edward was about (else their zeal in his service would have cooled, as it did some time afterwards), were busy completing the

[a] See two valuable notes in Kirk's " Charles the Bold," i. 415, and ii. 15.)
[b] See a paper printed in Wavrin, iii. 183.

overthrow of the Lancastrians. After the battle of Hexham they
besieged successfully the three Northern castles. Alnwick first
surrendered and then Dunstanborough.[a] But Bamborough held
out till July, and was only won by assault with artillery.[b] It was
kept by the traitor Sir Ralph Grey, who doubtless knew that he had
no mercy to expect. He was taken and brought prisoner to the
King at Pomfret, from which place he was conveyed to Doncaster,
" and there his head was smit off and sent to London, and it was
set upon London Bridge."[c]

It was just after this that, to meet his heavy expenses, Edward
enhanced the value of the old coinage and issued new coins of
inferior gold containing more alloy. New groats of silver were
also issued and ordered to pass current at fourpence; but they, too,
were of inferior metal to the old groats. The result was what
must inevitably have taken place according to the ill-understood
laws of political economy. People did not like to receive the new
coinage. The new angels and nobles of gold were difficult to pass,
and a man might go through a whole street or parish before he
could get them changed. Silver too rose in price to three shillings
an ounce or more. Moreover at the beginning of the change
" men grudged passing sore, for they could not reckon that gold so
quickly as they did the old gold."[d]

---

[a] Alnwick surrendered at once on the 23rd June as soon as Warwick came before
it. Dunstanborough probably surrendered also the same day, as Warwick "kept
the feast of St. John the Baptist " (24th June) there. See MS. in Heralds' College,
quoted in Notes to Warkworth's Chronicle, p. 37.

[b] Fabyan.

[c] Page 227. Grey's degradation from knighthood, mentioned in a previous
note, took place, according to the Year Book, "devant mults del people le Roy
s. ses gilt spores hewes de ses pees, et son espee et tout son armour sur luy debruse
et pris de luy en le champe, et puis il decoll." This punishment was inflicted on
him about (enter) St. Benet's day (11th July) on account of "son perjury et
doubleness que il avoit fait al Roy Henry le Size jadis Roy, &c., et auxy al Roy
Edward le Quart que ore est."   [d] Page 227.

Then came the coronation of Edward's Queen; on which occasion among a number of other gentlemen five aldermen of London were made knights, whose names are given. "It is a great worship unto all the city" remarks our chronicler.[a]

What is said of the capture of Henry VI. in Lancashire is interesting, and helps, perhaps, to supply a missing link in the story of the unhappy King's adventures. Many historians have written as if he had been taken soon after the battle of Hexham; but it is now well known that the date of his capture was about a year later, and it has been supposed that he lay concealed in the North of England. If, however, our author was well informed he had again found a refuge in Scotland, for it was in coming out of Scotland that he was discovered at Furness Fells in Lancashire.[b]

The security given to Edward's throne by the capture of Henry VI. was reflected in the honour paid him by foreign princes. In the seventh year of his reign he received embassies from France, Spain, Scotland, Burgundy, Brittany, the King of Naples, and the court of Ferrara; while there also came from the Pope a legate, and from the Emperor the patriarch of Antioch. The papal legate is not mentioned either in Baronius or in Fabyan's Chronicle, and who he was we are not told, though his coming must have excited no small interest at the time. It seems that he was a good scholar " the best Latin man that came into England many years;" that

---

[a] Page 228.

[b] Warkworth says he was taken " bysyde a howse of religione in Lancashire . . . . . in a wode called Cletherwode beside Bungerly Hyppyngstones." This last-named locality is explained by the late Mr. Nichols to have been a ford with stepping-stones across the River Ribble. Henry, however, eluded his captors (at least so I understand Warkworth to imply) and was afterwards retaken, being surprised at dinner at Waddington Hall, in Yorkshire, not many miles off. All this is quite consistent with his having been first recognised in Furness Fells, from which district he might have been pursued to the neighbourhood of Clitheroe. If it be true that he took refuge at Bracewell and Bolton as well as at Waddington (see Mr. Nichols's note to Warkworth, pp. 42-3) it was probably after his flight from Clitheroe.

he was lodged " at a great place of a Lombard's " at St. Bartholo-
mew's the Less, where he kept a good household, his men being
very orderly; but that he declined to accept the hospitality of any
of the English nobility, except that on one occasion after great
entreaty he became the guest of the Archbishop of York at the
More in Hertfordshire. The cause of his coming no man could
learn with any certainty. It may have been due simply to the
Pope's anxiety to understand the state of parties in England.[a]

In the eighth year, our author writes, " were many men appeached
of treason both of the city and of other towns. Of the city, Thomas
Coke, knight and alderman, and John Plummer, knight and alderman, but the King gave them both pardon. And a man of the
Lord Wenlock's, John Hawkins was his name, was hanged at
Tyburn and beheaded for treason." The circumstances here so
slightly alluded to are more perfectly known from other sources,
but have never yet been fully recounted. Lancastrian plots were
certainly thickening against King Edward, who though easily
lulled into false security became fitfully cruel and tyrannical when
impressed with a sense of danger. More than one messenger was
intercepted with letters to or from Queen Margaret,[b] and many
whose loyalty had been hitherto unsuspected were implicated in
charges of treason. Among these was Lord Wenlock's servant,
Hawkins, who accused not only Sir Thomas Coke but also his own
master; and as we know that Lord Wenlock afterwards joined the
Earl of Warwick against Edward there was probably more founda
tion for the latter accusation than the former. As to Sir Thomas
Coke, Hawkins had but asked him for a loan of 1,000 marks, which
he refused to give, finding that the money was intended for the use
of Margaret of Anjou. He was, however, arrested on the accusation of Hawkins; but at the request of the Lady Margaret, the King's

* Pages 235-6.   b W. Wyre., 511, 514.

sister, he was admitted to bail. After that Princess's departure beyond sea he was again arrested and sent to the Tower, his goods were seized by Lord Rivers, Treasurer of England, and his wife placed in the custody of the Mayor of London. After lying some time in the Tower he was tried at Guildhall and acquitted, his offence being found to be mere misprision in the concealment of an application made to him by Edward's enemies.[a] Nevertheless he was transferred to the Bread Street Counter and afterwards to the King's Bench Prison, in Southwark, from which he was only released on payment of a fine to the King of 8,000*l.* But even so he was not quite out of his trouble, for a new demand was made upon him by virtue of an old abuse, called *Aurum Reginæ*, that for every 1,000*l.* he had paid the King he should give the Queen 1,000 marks besides. With this, too, he was obliged to comply, and he suffered no further inconvenience; but he found on going back to his country house in Essex that both house and park had been plundered of everything valuable by the servants of Lord Rivers and the under treasurer Sir John Fogge, for which it was in vain to expect any compensation.[b]

The cruelty and injustice of these proceedings require no comment. But when it is considered that they were directed against an innocent man, whom the law officers of the Crown had used every effort to convict, even by means the most unjustifiable,—when it is considered also that Chief Justice Markham for having directed Coke's acquittal was actually deprived of his office,[c] we have a picture of tyranny and injustice rarely equalled in the history of this country. It is difficult even to imagine the poor excuse that the court seriously suspected that there had been a miscarriage of justice, for Sir Thomas was exonerated from the charge

[a] W. Wyrc., 515.
[b] Fabyan. Orridge's Illustrations of Jack Cade's Rebellion, pp. 12, 13.
[c] Foss.

by his accuser himself in a manner that should have left no doubt of his innocence. The case was alluded to a few years afterwards by Fortescue in his treatise on the Laws of England, addressed to the son of Henry VI. in the following manner :

Do you not remember, my Prince, a criminal, who, when upon the rack, impeached of treason a certain noble knight, a man of worth and loyalty, and declared that they were both concerned together in the same conspiracy; and being taken down from the rack he still persisted in the accusation, lest he should again be put to the question ? Nevertheless, being so much hurt and reduced by the severity of the punishment that he was brought almost to the point of death, after he had the *viaticum* and sacraments administered to him, he then confessed, and took a very solemn oath upon it by the body of Christ, and as he was now, as he imagined, just going to expire, he affirmed that the said worthy knight was innocent and clear of everything he had laid to his charge. He added that the tortures he was put to were so intolerable, that, rather than suffer them over again, he would accuse the same person of the same crimes,—nay, his own father,—though when he said this he was in the bitterness of death, when all hopes of recovery were over. Neither did he at last escape that ignominious death, for he was hanged; and at the time and place of his execution he acquitted the said knight of the crimes wherewith he had, not long before, charged him.[a]

---

[a] Fortescue de Laudibus Legum Angliæ, ed. Amos, p. 71. Although Fortescue does not mention the name either of the knight or of the criminal there can hardly be much doubt that this was the case referred to. In fact, as an acute critic pointed out in the last century (see Biog. Brit., art. "Fortescue," p. 1992, footnote), a case so alluded to must have been notorious, and the circumstances as related in Fabyan's Chronicle exactly correspond with the way in which Fortescue speaks of them. The notoriety of the case is further shown by the reference made to it in the speech of the Duke of Buckingham before the accession of Richard III. : "What need I to speak of Sir Thomas Cooke, alderman and mayor of this noble city ? Who is of you, either of negligence that wotteth not, or so forgetful that he remembreth not, or so hardhearted that he pitieth not, that worshipful man's loss,—what speak I of loss?—his wonderful spoil and undeserved destruction,—only because it happened him to favour them, whom the prince favoured not?" (Hall's Chronicle, p. 369.) Mr. Orridge has quoted this passage from Holinshed in his notices of Malpas and Cooke in connection with Cade's Rebellion.

It is scarcely necessary to point out every touch of new light in matters which are already well known, such as the Princess Margaret's marriage to Charles of Burgundy, and the hiding of Jasper Earl of Pembroke in Wales. But the misconduct of some gentlemen in the Princess's suite in Flanders, and a disturbance which they created at Southwark after their return, from the ill will they bore to the Flemings, are facts which have been hitherto unknown. The luxury of the court of Charles the Bold seems to have destroyed the discipline of the English, while at the same the Burgundian court found it necessary to put some limit to its expensive hospitality. After a certain day the English were told that every man should live at the expense of his own master. Prices rose and accommodation was scanty, from the great concourse of people. The Chronicler himself seems to have been among those who went over with the Princess, for he writes as if from personal experience: " Meat and drink was dear enough, as though it had been in the land of war, for a shoulder of mutton was sold for 12*d.*; and as for bedding, Lyard my horse had more ease than had some good yeomen; for my horse stood in the house and the yeomen sometimes lay without in the street, for less than 4*d.* a man should not have a bed a night. Lo, how soon they could play the niggards!" *

A pretty considerable amount of feeling seems to be embodied in that last remark.

The narrative comes to a close (or perhaps is abruptly terminated by the loss of a leaf or two) in the middle of the ninth year of Edward IV., so that there is nothing more of political interest to claim the reader's attention. But it is right to say a few words on some subjects of minor interest which we thought it right to pass by at the time in order to avoid interruption. Every one interested

* Page 238.

in civic history will be grateful to our chronicler for the account of the blunder committed at the serjeants' feast in 1464, where the Earl of Worcester was given precedence over the Mayor of London, and of the way in which the mayor vindicated his own dignity and the honour of the city by at once retiring with " the substance of his brethern the aldermen " to his own place, where he had a banquet " set and served all so soon as any man could devise, both of cygnet and of other delicates enow, that all the house marvelled how well all thing was done in so short a time." The officers of the feast, deeply ashamed of the mishap, tried to make amends in a fashion not uncommon in those days, by sending to the mayor a present of " meat, bread, wine, and many divers subtleties," intended to form a banquet in itself. But when the messengers arrived they found quite as sumptuous a banquet actually laid upon the table, and the person who was to have made the presentation felt ashamed of the task imposed upon him. He, however, acquitted himself gracefully, and was dismissed with a reward. So " the worship of the city," as our chronicler proudly remarks, " was kept and not lost for him. And I trust that never it shall, by the grace of God." *

To the religious history of the times we have some interesting contributions. The first is an incident referred to by Foxe the Martyrologist, in his " Acts and Monuments," who seems to have derived his information from this Chronicle. In 1465 the chronic rivalry between the religious orders and the priesthood broke out into violent disputations and schism. A Carmelite friar of London, by name Sir Harry Parker, son of a skinner in Fleet Street, preached at Paul's Cross on the old, well-worn theme of an endowed clergy. It was an old well-worn theme even then, though it has lasted so long that it does not seem to be exhausted even in our own days; but Parker, whatever may be said of his taste and judgment, con-

* Pages 222-3.

trived to invest it with some novelty of treatment. He attacked a beneficed clergy as a great abuse, and declared it was wrong for priests to have any temporal livelihood at all, implying that ministers of religion ought to live, like friars, entirely on the alms of the people. In confirmation of this view, he maintained that not one of the Twelve Apostles nor Christ himself had any private property whatever, but all things in common; and he further went -so far as to say that our Lord was a beggar, and had nothing but what was given him in alms.

Such a reflection delivered from the most famous of London pulpits shocked and staggered people not a little. But on the following Sunday Dr. William Ive, the Master of Whittington's College, replied to the friar, " and proved that Christ was poor and kept no great treasure, but as for begging he utterly denied it, and by Holy Scripture proved it so that men understood the friar erred sore against Holy Church." The friars, on the other hand, were eager to defend the doctrine, and set up Dr. Thomas Halden to answer Dr. Ive. He again was replied to on the following Sunday by Dr. Storey, parson of All Hallows the More, who three years later was made Bishop of Carlisle. Storey seems to have been moderate in his tone, as one who was anxious to pacify the controversy; but the friars set up bills on every church door impugning what he said, and their provincial, Dr. John Milverton, attacked the beneficed clergy more bitterly than his subordinates had done before. The dispute caused also divisions among the laity, some of whom were offended at the friars and withdrew their alms from them, while others refused the customary offerings to their curates, saying that they had no right to anything except mere alms.

The question was discussed in many places. Dr. Ive lectured upon it at the Cathedral School of St. Paul's, of which he was master, as well as of Whittington College. Among the friars themsclves, a great disputation was held between Dr. Halden and a grey friar at the White Friars in Fleet Street. But the grey friar went so far that he was cited by Dr. Alcock, Commissary to the Dean of St. Martin's-le-Grand, to appear before the Archbishop of Canterbury at Lambeth. The friar refused to obey the citation. as his order were exempt from episcopal jurisdiction except in cases of heresy. But the commissary cited him for heresy, and the whole order in vain endeavoured to assert their privileges. Dr. Halden and the provincial were cited but refused to appear, and were excommunicated for contumacy, and the young friar, Harry Parker, who began the controversy, was then committed to prison, but revoked what he had said and abjured the heresy. Yet even his recantation did not prevent others from doing as he had done; for a black friar soon after preached nearly the same doctrine over again, and was compelled to recant in the same manner. Meanwhile the excommunicated provincial had gone to Rome, and some expected still that he would come back in triumph; for he had got a friar at Rome to write a treatise on the Begging of Christ, copies of which were multiplied and sold in many places. But when the matter was brought under the Pope's cognisance, the whole process being sent to him from England, he altogether confirmed what was done, found the provincial guilty in nine more points of heresy, and locked him fast in the Castle of St. Angelo.[a]

In the seventh year we have an account of the burning of a relapsed heretic named William Barlow, who with his wife had before abjured his errors. It is singular that this man's case has quite escaped the notice of Foxe, although, as we have already remarked, the Martyrologist seems to have been indebted to our Chronicle for information on another subject. Barlow denied Transubstantiation and the authority of priests to hear confession. For his reply to Master Hugh Damelet, parson of St. Peter's, Corn-

[a] Pages 228-232.

hill, who attempted to reconvert him at the stake, we must be content to refer the reader to the Chronicle itself.[a]

About the same time we are told that many of the London churches were robbed of the boxes containing the Sacrament; but this was not, as was at first supposed, the doing of a company of heretics. It was simply a set of men who had turned thieves from extreme poverty, and who mistook copper boxes for silver gilt. They made a full confession before execution and died penitent. But the most remarkable point is the statement attributed to one of them, a locksmith, who made the instruments with which they picked the locks, that being at church on several occasions after his crime to hear mass he had been quite unable to see the host at its elevation; but after his confession in Newgate he saw it quite plainly. If this was the genuine statement of the culprit himself, it is a very remarkable instance of the effect of a burdened conscience on the imagination and the senses.[b]

Finally, we have a curious ordinance, partly directed against one form of Sunday labour, but chiefly against the absurd fashion of -wearing shoes with long pikes at the toes, a piece of vanity which the highest authority in the Church thought it necessary to visit with ecclesiastical censure. The Pope issued a bull that no cord-wainer should make any pikes more than two inches long or sell shoes on Sunday, or even fit a shoe upon a man's foot on Sunday, on pain of excommunication. Neither was the cordwainer to attend fairs on a Sunday under the same penalty; for not only were fairs held on that day, but the cordwainer's services, it must be supposed, were required at the fairs to adjust the dandy's *chaussure*, just as much as, in a later age, the barber's aid was necessary to dress his wig. The papal bull was approved by the King's council and confirmed by Act of Parliament; and proclamation was consequently

* Pages 233-4.   b Pages 234-5.

made at Paul's Cross that it should be put in execution. Yet, with all this weight of authority against a silly fashion, the dandy world had its own ideas upon the subject, and some men ventured to say they would wear long pikes in spite of the Pope, for the Pope's curse would not kill a fly. The cordwainers, too, had a vested interest in the extravagance, though some of their own body had been instrumental in getting the Pope's interference. They obtained privy seals and protections from the King to exempt them from the operation of the law, which soon became a dead letter; and those who had applied to the Pope to restrain their practices were subjected to much trouble and persecution.[*]

In editing this volume it has been my general aim to preserve the text as nearly as possible as it stands in the MS., with merely such amendments in the matter of punctuation and division into paragraphs as might serve to make it more easily intelligible. The spelling of the original scribe has been strictly adhered to, except that the contractions have been extended, and where the letter *i* has been used for *j*, *v* for *u*, or *vice versâ*, the modern usage has been followed. Also to prevent the reader being perplexed by the frequent instances of a word which is now invariably treated as one word being divided into its two component parts, as " be syde" for " beside," or the positive separation by the scribe of one word into two, as in " Arche Byschop," a hyphen has been generally substituted for the blank space between the syllables in the original MS.

The only other liberty which has been taken with the text is where unintelligible readings have been corrected by comparison with other MSS.; and in these cases the fact has been always stated in the footnotes.

[*] Page 238.

WILLIAM GREGORY'S WILL.

[From Register Godyn, f. 16.]

In the name of God, Amen. The vjth day of the moneth of Novembre, in the yere of our Lord God m^l iiij^c lxv, and in the vth yere of the reigne of Kyng Edward the iiijth, I, William Gregory, Citezein and Skynner of the Citee of London, and late Maire and Aldreman of the same, beyng hoole of mynde and in my goode memorye, thanke be it to God, make and ordeyne this my present testament or last will in this maner: In the first, I biquethe and commende my soule to All myghty God my Creature and Savyour, and to the blissed Virgyn Mary his modir, and to alle Saintez, and my body to be buried where it please God to dispose it. And I will and ordeigne that, first and principally afore all thinges, alle the dettes which of right I owe to eny persone or persones be paied. After payment of which dettes I biqueth to the high Awter of the chireh of Saint Mary Aldermary of London, where as I am parisshen, for my dymes and offringes forgoten or withdrawen, and for my buriyng there to be had, xl s. Also I wille that immediatly after my deces there be celebrate for my soule and for the soules of Johane, Julian, and Jobane, late my wifes, and for all Cristen soules, ij m^l masses. And I biqueth to be disposed for the same ij m^l masses viij li. xiij s. iiij d. Also I will that myn executours the day of myn decesse dele among pouere people after their goode discrecions xl s. Also I wille that the preestes and parissh clerkes that shulbe of the saide chireh of Aldermary the day of my decesse, doo and syng every day byfore noon, from that day unto that day a moneth than nexte suyng, a masse of Requiem by note, and every day after noon Placebo and Dirige by note for my soul, and the soules of my said wifes, and all Cristen soules. And I biqueth to everych of the saide preestes and parissh clerkes that shalbe present dailly at the saide masse, Placebo, and dirige, by all the said moneth, viij s. iiij d. Also I wille that myn executouris undrewriten by v yeres next suyng after my decesse fynde an honest precst to syng for my soule, and for the soules of my said wyfes, and all Cristen soules in the chireh aforsaide. And that the same preest ley every Wednesday and Friday for my soule and the soules afor- saide, Placebo, dirige, commendacion, and the sawlter of our Lady Saint Mary. And I biqueth and wole that the same preest have yerely for his salary xj marc sterlinges. Also I wol þat myn excecutours ayenst the moneth day after my decesse ordeyne xij yerdes of blak clothe, price the yerde iij s. iiij d., to cover therwith my bere. And after my terment fullfilled I woll that the same xij yerdes of clothe be gyfen and departed among iiij pore men or wommen moost needefull to pray for my soule. Also I wille that myn executours, the day of my moneth mynde, dele, and gif to pouere men and women cs. Also I biqueth to the chireh werk of þe said chireh of our Lady Aldermary, xvj li. xiij s. iiij d. to thentent that the parisshens there pray for my soule and the soules aforsaide. Also I biqueth towarde the amendyng and reparacion of the fowlest weyes aboute London, after the discrecions of myn executours, x li. Also I biqueth to the wiyfe of John Elys, dwelling in Saint Antonynes parissh, xxxiij s. iiij d. Also I biqueth to Johan Johnson, a pouere woman, dwelling by the same John Elys wife, vj s. viij d. Also I biqueth to gyf among pouer folk liyng sike in the hospitall called Saint Mary Spitell without Bishoppesgate, xx s. And to the pouere people liyng sike in Saint Bartholomewe Spitell, xx s. And to the pouere seke people of the hospitall of Saint Mary of Bethelem, xl s. Also I biquethe to þe pouere people of Elsyng Spitell, to pray for my soule, xiij s. iiij d. Also to Richard Warners cosyn, heyng suster in the same Elsyng Spitell, vj s. viij d. Also I biqueth to the pouere people liyng in the hospitall of Saint Thomas the Martir in Southwerk, xx s. Also I biqueth vj li. sterlinges equally to be devided and departed among the prisons of Ludgate, Newgate, and the ij Counteres in London, that is to wite, to euerych of the same iiij prisons, xxx s. Also I biqueth to acquite prisoners out of Ludgate and Newgate moost needefull, x li. after the discrecion of myn executours. Also I biqueth to parte and gif amonge pouere folk moost needefull, liggyng bedred in London and the subarbes therof, xl s. Also I biqueth to the fraternite of Corpus Christi of Skynners of London to be put in their comen box to the sustentacion of pouere people of the same fraternitee to pray for my

soule and the soules aforsaid, x li.   Also I biqueth to the fraternite of
our Lady of the Skynners of London to be put in the comen box therof
toward the sustentacion of the pouere people of the same fraternite, c s.
Also I biqueth to the preest of the said fraternite of Corpus Christi to
pray for my soule and the soules aforsaid, vj s. viij d.   Also I biqueth to
the fraternite of Saint John Baptist of Taillours of London, xx s.   Also I
biqueth to the hous of freres minours in London, to. pray specialy for my
soule and the soules aforsaid, lxvj s. viij d.   Also I biqueth to the frere
Kiry, frere mynour, to pray for my soule, xx s.   Also to maister Godard
thelder, a nother frere minour, xx s.   And to maister Godard the yonger,
his brothir, a nother frere minour, xiij s. iiij d. to pray specialy for my
soule and the soules aforsaide.   Also I biqueth to the hous of frere
prechours in London to pray specialy for my soule and the soules aforsaide,
xl s.   Also I biqueth to the bous of frere Augustines in London to pray
for my soule and the soules aforesaid, xl s.   Also to þe bous of Frere
Carmes in Flete Strete in the subarbes of London, to pray for my soule
and the soules aforsaide, xxvj s. viij d.   Also to the bous of Crouched
Freres in London to pray specialy for my soule and the soules aforsaid,
xiij s. iiij d.   Also I biqueth to every prisoner convict in the prison
of thabbot and Covent of Westmynster, to pray for my soule and the
saules aforsaid, xx d.   Also I wille that oon tyme after my decesse
myne executours after their discrecions shull kepe an obite in the parissh
chirch of Mildenhale for my soule and for the soules afore rehersed.
And I will that they spend aboute that obite among preestes, clerkes,
wex ringyng of belles, brede, chese, and ale, and in distributing to pouor
people moost nedy, xl s.   Also I biqueth to Maister Thomas Sygo, my
cosyn, to pray for my soule, xiij s. iiij d.   Also I biqueth to the fraternite
of Jesu founded in the Crowdes undir the Cathedrall chirch of Saint
Paule of London, to pray for my soule and the soules abovesaid, vj s. viij d.
Also I biqueth to the Priour and Couent of þe Chartirhous next London
to pray for my soule and þe soules aforsaide, xxvj s. viij d.   Also I
biqueth to the priour and covent of the Chartirhouse of Shene, to pray for
my soule and the soules aforsaid, xx s.   Also I biqueth to the hous
of nonnes at Syon, xl s. and to my goddoughter, the doughter of
Rauf Skynner, nonne in the same hous, xx s. to pray for my soule
and the soules aforsaide.   Also I biqueth to Margarete Toon, my god-

doughter, servaunt in the same hous at Syon, xiij s. iiij d. Also I biqueth to the Prioresse and Covent of Clerkenwell, xiij s. iiij d. Item to the Prioresse and Covent of the Meneresse beside London, xls. And to þe Prioresse and Covent of Halywell beside London, xxxiij s. iiij d. to pray for my soule and the soules afore rehersed. Also I biqueth to the doughter late of Henry Thurstone, xiij s. iiij d. Also to Allelya taillour, vj s. viij d. Also I biqueth lxvj s. viij d. to be departed among poner housholders, bothe men and women, dwelling in the warde of Cordewanerstrete of London, after the discrecion of myne executours. Also I will that myn executouris of my goodes aftre their discrecions pay for pouere people dwelling in the same ward, þe next xv^th that shalbe assessed ther after my deces, xls. Also I biqueth to Thomas Curson, bedell of the same warde, vj s. viij d., and to his wif vj s. viij d., and to his son vj s. viij d., to pray for my soule. Also I wille that myn executours of my goodes after their discrecions pay for pouer people dwelling in the parish of Saint Johnnes in Walbrok, the next xv^th þat shalbe assessed ther after my decesse, xiij s. iiij d. Also I biqueth to everiche of the prisons of Kyngesbenche, the Marchalsie, and the Flete, xiij s. iiij d. Also I biqueth xx marc sterlinges to by frise to make gownes and eotes, and lynnen cloth to make shertes and smokkes, and for o paire of shone for pouer men and women hauyng moost neede, after the discrecion of myn executours. Also I biqueth ls. for to by c quarters coles to be gyven to pouere men and women in the parissh of Aldermary forsaid, and in other parisshes where moost nede is after the discrecion of myn executours. Also I biquethe to Margarete Croke, my doughter, x li. wherof I will that she haue to hir owne use c s. to pray for my soule. And the othir c s. residue of the same x li to be gyven to pouere men and women after hir discrecion to pray for my soule. Also I biqueth to everych of the children unmaried of the same Margarete, þat is to say, v sonnes and ij doughters, euerych of hem v marc. And if so be that any of hem decesse, as God defende, than I will that þe parte of him, hir, or theim so de[ce]ssing shall remayne to that othir of theim than beyng on lyve egally to be departed by myn executours. And if it fortune all the same v sonnes and ij doughters to decesso befor the day of my buriyng, than I wille that the xxxv marc by me to theym biquethed be disposid by the discrecions of myn executours in masses to be songen, finding of clerkes to scole, amending of foule weyes and feble briggys, in mariages of pouere maydens of goode name and fame, and in other warkes of charitee for my soule and the soules afore rehersed. Also I biqueth to Kateryn, daughter of Thomas Ryche, my goddoughter, xx s. Also I biqueth to Cecile Mildenhale, my doughter, lxvj s. viij d. Also to either of the ij doughters of þe same Cecile, xl s. And if either of the same ij doughters dye, than I will that the othir doughter have the parte of hir so decessing ; and if bothe ij doughters dye before that I decesse than I will þat þe iiij pounde to the same ij doughters by me afore biquethed be disposed in goode uses and waies of charitee after the discrecions of myn executours. Also I biqueth to Robert Mildenhale, husband of the said Cecile, xıȷ s. ıȷ d. Also I biqueth to my cosyn and godson, William Essex, the sone of William Essex, to pray for my soule, lx s. Also I biqueth to Maister Duffeld, one of the Chauntery Preestes of Aldermary chireh aforsaide, to pray for my soule, xiij s. iiij d. Also to either of William Fissher and his wife, vj s. viij d. Also to the wife of John Snype, Skynner, xiij s. iiij d. Also I biqueth to Walter, late my servaunt, his wife, and to their son and doughter my godchildren, xl s. Item I biqueth to Richard Tritrap, late my servaunt, xxvj s. viij d. Item I biqueth to Thomas Lansell, late my servaunt, xx s. Also to Slapton, late my servaunt, xl s. Also I biqueth to William Martyn, nowe my servaunt, iiij li. and a borde clothe, vj napkyns, and a towaill. Also to Baron, nowe my servaunt, lx s. and vj napkyns, and a towaill. Also to Alice Wylcok, my seruaunt, iiij li. and vj napkyns, and a towaill. Also to William Stanley, my godson, lx s. Also to William Lussher, myn apprentice, xx s. Also to John, the childe in my kechyn, xxxiij s. iiij d. Also I biqueth to Mary, the wife of William Gregory, xx s., and to the son and doughter of the same William and Mary, xx s. Also to Johanne, dwelling at frere Augustines,- to pray for my soule, xiij s. iiij d. Also to William More, Skynner, xiij s. iiij d. Also to the wife of þe same William vj s. viij d. Also to John Aunger vj s. viij d.; and to Jobane his wife, vj s. viij d. And to the preest of the fraternitee of the Trinitee in the chireh of our Lady of the Bowe founded, to pray specialy for my soule, vj s. viijd. Also I biqueth to John Cok, Skynner, xx s. and to his wife xx s. Also to John Laurence vj s. viij d.; and to his wife vj s. vilj d. Also I biqueth to

Anne Wheler vj s. viij d. And to Julian Arthure xxvj s. viij d. Also I biqueth to Baron the elder vs., and to his wife vs., to pray for my soule. Also I biqueth to the Recluse at Alhalowes in London Wall vj s. viij d. Also to the Ankeresse without Bisshopesgate vj s. viij d.; also to the Ankeresse without Temple Barre vj s. viij d.; and to the Ankeresse at Westmynstre vj s. viij d., to thentent that they and everyche of them pray specialy for my soule and all the soules above saide. Also I biqueth to Margarete Caryngton, my god doughter, vj s. viij d., to pray for my soule. Also I biqueth to the reparacion of London Brigge cs. sterlinges. The residue of all my goodes, joialx, and dettes above not byquethed, after my dettes paied, my enterrement doon, and this my last will in maner and forme above saide in all thinges fulfilled, I gif to myn executours undre writen, to thentent that they dispose it for my soule and the soules of my said wifes, and of my fadir and modir, and all Cristen soules, in masses to be songen, and in making, repairing, and a-mending of pore chirches and of feble waies and brigges, in finding of scolers to scole, in mariages of pouere maydens and wydowes of good name and fame, in acquiting and redemyng of prisoners oute of the prisons in London, in distributing to pouere people moost nedy, and in such other werkys and usees of pitee and charitee as they by theyre goode conscience and discrecions shull thinke mooste expedient to the pleasure of God and the helthe of my soule. And of this my testament I make myn —executouris John Croke, gentilman, my son in lawe, and John Snype, Citezein and Skynner of London. And I ordeyne Maister Thomas Eborall, clerke, overseer of the same my testament, to oversee that my willes and ordenaunces in this my testament conteyned in all thinges be trieuly accomplissed and fulfilled in maner and forme as is aforsaid. And I pray, require, and desire the said Maister Thomas Eborall, and I will that he be consaillyng, aiding, and assisting my saide executours in distributing, gifing, disposing, and doing the saide almesdedes and werkes of pitee and charitee as he wolde I counsailled and did for hym if he stode in case like. Also I biqueth and gif to the saide John Croke, so þat he take upon hym the charge of execucion of this my testament, xli. sterlinges for his labour in that behalf to be had. And I biqueth to the saide John Snype, so that he with þe saide John Croke take upon hym the charge of execucion of this my present testament for his labour

to be had in that partie xli. sterlinges. And I biqueth to the said
Maister Thomas Eborall for his diligence and attendaunce in the
premissez iiijli. sterlinges. In witnesse wherof to this my present
testament I have sette my seale. Yoven at London the day and yere
aforsaid.

In Dei nomine Amen. Ego, Willelmus Gregory, civis et pelliparius
ac nuper Aldermannus Civitatis London, compos mentis et sane memorie
mee existens, volensque certis de causis menti mee post scripcionem
testamenti mei cui presens codicellus annectitur, et post sigillacionem
ejusdem testamenti noviter concurrentibus, quedam necessaria eidem
testamento prius per me facto addere et augmentare, facio et ordino
presentem codicellum in hunc modum:—Inprimis, cum ego prefatus
Willelmus per dictum testamentum meum inter alia dederim et legaverim
fraternitati Corporis Cristi artis pellipariorum dicte Civitatis ad susten-
tacionem pauperum ejusdem fraternitatis decem libras sterlingorum, ego idem
Willelmus donacionem et legacionem illas per presentem codicellum casso,
revoco et penitus adnullo, nolens illas ullo modo executioni demandari
in parte aut in toto. Sed ob sinceram affecetionem dileccionem quas ad
candem fraternitatem Corporis Christi gero et habeo, ac ad intencionem
quod fratres et sorores ejusdem fraternitatis animam meam in suis
oracionibus Deo specialius habeant recommendatam, ad perpetuam rei
memoriam do et lego supradicte fraternitati Corporis Christi sex ollas
meas optimas argenti deauratas. Item ego, prefatus Willelmus, legata
mea de sexaginta solidis, sex napkyns et uno towaill Willelmo Martyn
nuper apprenticio meo, necnon de sexaginta solidis sex napkyns et uno
towayll Alicie Wylcok, servienti mee, in dicto testamento meo facta, casso
et adnullo per presentes, volens jam, concedens, et legans, quod idem
Willelmus Martyn habeat de bonis meis x mareas sterlingorum ac sex
napkyns et unum towayll, ac quod dicta Alicia habeat eciam de bonis
meis centum solidos et sex napkyns cum uno towaill. Volo itaque, lego et
ordino per presentes quod omnia et singula alia legata et ordinaciones
in dicto testamento meo contenta et in presenti codicello minime revocata
fideliter perimpleantur, exequantur et perficiantur juxta formam, tenorem
et effectum ejusdem testamenti mei; Salvo semper et excepto quod
cum ego, prefatus Willelmus Gregory, per dictum testamentum meum

fecerim et constituerem Johannem Snype, Civem et Pelliparium London, in
eodem testamento nominatum, unum executorum meorum, idem Johannes
jam mortuus est; qua de causa facio, ordino et constituo Margaretam Croke,
filiam meam, uxorem Johannis Croke, alterius executorum in dicto testamento meo nominatorum coexecutricem cum eodem Johanne, viro suo, tam
ejusdem testamenti quam presentis codicelli, ad perficiendum et exequendum
omnia et singula in dictis testamento et codicello specificata juxta formam
et effectum eorundem. Item, licet ego, prefatus Willelmus Gregory,
ordinavi per dictum testamentum meum quod unus capellanus idoneus per
executores meos eligendus celibret pro anima mea et alijs animabus in
eodem testamento expressatis per quinque annos in ecclesia beate Marie
Aldermary London tantum; Volo tamen, lego, et per presentes jam
finaliter ordino quod capellanus per dictos executores meos elegendus
celebret pro anima men et alijs animabus predictis ubicumque eisdem
executoribus meis melius videbitur Deo placere et saluti anime mee pro-
ficere. In cujus rei testimonium sigillum meum huic codicello apposui.
Hijs testibus, Magistro Johanne Palmer clerico, Johanne Cok, Waltero
Smert, pellipario, Thoma Hardyng scriptore, et alijs. Datum London
secundo die Januarii, anno Domini millesimo ccccᵐ sexagesimo sexto.

Probatum fuit suprascriptum testamentum una cum codicello xxiij die
Januarij Anno Domini M.cccc lxvjᵗᵒ ac approbatum et insinuatum, &c.
Et commissa fuit administracio omnium et singulorum bonorum ac
debitorum dicti defuncti, &c., citra primam Dominicam quadragesime
proximo future &c., ac de plano compoto, &c. jurato, &c. reservata pro-
testate, &c.

HISTORICAL COLLECTIONS

OF

A CITIZEN OF LONDON

IN THE FIFTEENTH CENTURY.

THE SIEGE OF ROUEN.

GOD, that dyde a pon a tre
And bought us with Hys blode soo fre,
To Hys blys tham brynge
That lystenythe unto my talkynge.
Oftyn tymys we talke of travayle,
Of saute, sege, and of grete batayle,
Bothe in romans and in ryme,
What bathe ben done be fore thys tyme.
But y wylle telle you nowe present,
Unto my tale yf ye wylle tent,
Howe the V. Harry oure lege,
With hys ryalte he sette a sege
By fore Rone, that ryche cytte,
And endyd hyt at hys owne volunte.[a]
A more solempne sege was nevyr sette
Syn Jerusalem and Troy was gotte.
So moche folke was nevyr sene.
One kynge with soo many undyr hevyne.[b]
Lystenythe unto me a lytylle space,
And I shalle telle you howe hyt was.
And the better telle I may
For at that sege with the kyng I lay,

---

[a] *Fore that he lovyde as hys own volante.* B.
[b] *Nother syche another sege sette, as I wene.* B.

And there to I toke a vyse,
Lyke as my wyt wolde suffyce.
   Whenne Pountlarge^a with sege was wonne,
And ovyr Sayne then enter was be gunne,
The Duke of Exceter^b that [lord so]^c hende,
To Rone, yn sothe, oure kynge hym sende.
Herrowdys with hym unto that cytte,
To loke yf that they yoldyn wolde be,
And alle soo for to se that grounde
That was a boute the cytte rounde;
Howe our kyng myght lay þer at a sege,
If they wolde not obey to oure lege.
When þe Duke of Exceter with grete renowne
Was come by fore the ryalle towne,
He splayyd hys baners on a bent,
And herrowdys unto þe cytte were sent,
To mcke hem to oure kyngys methe,
Chargyd them uppon payne of dethe,
Not withstondyng hym of hys ryght,
But delyvyr the cytte to hys syght.
For he dyd them to wytte with owtyn bade,^d
He wolde not goo er he hyt hadde,
But or he paste farre in space,
Wynne hys ryght thoroughe Goddys grace.
To that the cytte gaf non answere,
But prayde oure herrowdys furthe to fare.
They made a maner skorne with hyr honde
That they there shulde not longer stonde.
   Gonnys they schott with grete envye,

^a Pont de l'Arche.
^b Thomas Beaufort, the King's uncle, a son of John of Gaunt by Catherine Swynford.
   Omitted in E. Supplied from B.
^d Delay.

And many were smytte pyttyfully.
And they yssuyde owte many fulle kene
On horsbackys with hyr harneys fulle schene.
The Duke of Exceter droffe hym yn agayne,
Of them were takyn and sum slayne.[a]
Whenne that was done with owtyn bode,
To Pountlarge agayne the Duke rode
And tolde the kyng of that proude cytte,
Howe hyt stode and in what degre.

   Nowe to my tale, and ye wylle hede,
I wylle you telle a cursyde deede,
How evylle they wrought there,
To[b] oure kynge com hem by fore.
Subbarbys with owte the towne,
Chyrchys and howse they drewe downe,
And the Porte Synt Hyllary they schende,
A parysche chyrche downe ther rente.
Of Synt Hyllary was that same,
And aftyr hyt þe Porte bare hys name.
At Porte Causses a downe they drowe
A chyrche of Syut Androwe,
And an abbay of Synt Gervays;[c]
There þe Duke of Clarans loggyd was.
And the Porte de Pounte doune they bete,
A chyrche of oure Lady swete,
And othyr of Syut Kateryn, that maydyn meke,
And of Synt Savyoure a nothyr eke;
And of Seynt Mathewe they drewne downe one,
And lefte there of stondyng nevyr a stone ;
At Martyrvyle[d] a doune they mynde.

Nota de malicia eorum.

---

[a] *And there monstryde the dewke agayne,*
   And meny of his men were take and yslayne. B.
[b] Until.
[c] *Synt Jamys.* E., which is clearly an error. B. reads *Synt Gervays*
[d] *Marchyle.* B.

Of Syut Mychelle a chyrche fynde;[a]
And of Synt Poule a nothyr thoo
And mynde dounc[b] a nothyr a lytylle fro.
Hyr heggys, gardons and streys,[c]
They drewe hem into the cytte every pece.
Buschys and brerys and boughys they brende,
And made hyt as bare as my honde.
 Nowe was there a prowde araye
That a boute the cytte gaye.
Welle hyt was ordaynyd for the warre
With alle the fence that myght darre.
The wallys was fulle varyable[d]
And the dychys depe and fensabylle.
The dyche that was the walle aboute
The londe syde whythe oute,
Hyt was depe and also wyde,
A trenche sewynge in every syde.
A trenche hyt was with a depe dyssende
That was made the diche to defende
That noo man shulde come to nere
In hyr donger[e] but they were.[f]
Whoo went that trenche withyn,
With owtyn harme he myght not wynne.
The diche was brode and depe,
And fewe myght fro many man hyt kepe.
The bottom of the diche with yn
Was pyttefallyd ij fote evyr bytwyn,
And every pyttefalle a spere hyghthe

 [a] *Full fyne.* B.
 [b] *And onynde Dame.* E., which is evidently a transcriber's error. B.
reads, *They mynede downe.*
 [c] *her treys.* B.
 [d] *warryable.* B.
 [e] *donge.* E. B. reads *donger.*
 [f] *lest they dede were.* B.

That there schulde stonde noo man to fyght.
And soo, to make hem clere
That noo man a boute them were,
Fro the pyttefalle unto the walle
Hit was hyghe and stowtc with alle.
As thycke of caltrappys hit fulle was sette
As meyschys be yn a nette.
With yn the cytte aftyr [a] the walle
Welle countyrmuryde hyt was welle with alle,
With erthe soo thyke and so brode
That a carte myght goo þer uppon lode.
That poynt they made in there werre
That noo gunne shulde not hym derre.[b]
Hoo soo wylle hem count soo
There ben a hundryd or too.[c]
And also mote I thryffe
There ben portys fyve.
Of tonrys aboute that cytte
Many a schore [d] there yn be;
And every towre from othyr ys
But of vj. rode in space I wysse;
Ande in every toure iij gonnys lay,
For to sebete dyvers waye.
In the myddys of þe walle every towre be twyne
Alle that cytte by-dene,
A grete fouler [e] was layde lowe
Evyn by the erthe that hit myght throwe.
Every towre by twyne þer lay on lofte
viij gounnys smalle þat myght schute ofte,

[a] *afore.* B.
[b] Injure.
[c] *But trewly zytte hade they with them also*
   Of other soteltys meny other mo. B.
[d] Score.
[e] A species of cannon.

And also launcetys layde on hyght
To schute farre at nyght.[a]
And at every warde was there set
A engyne or a trebget,[b]
And on sum warde sete were ij.
Synt Hyllerys warde was one of tho.
Thys they made hyr ordynaunce
With fence of grete substaunce.
And of thys fence leve we talkynge
And talke we more of oure kynge.
      The Fryday be fore Lammasse daye
The kynge remevyde in ryche a raye
To the cytte of grete pryde,
And loggyd hym a lytylle þer be syde.
The Satyrday he sygnyde the grounde
To hys chyftaynys by-fore that cytte rounde.
A cry on Monday he dyd make
That every man schulde hys grounde take.
At the este ende of that cytte
With[inne][c] a howse of Chartere
There loggyd hym oure kynge a non,
And with hym loggyd many one.
Of alle worschyppe he ys a welle;
Hys honoure noo tonge may telle.
Of all pryncys for to a counte,
Sette hym pryncepalle in the frounte.
And at the ende towarde the weste,
Clarence the Duke he toke hys reste.
At an abbay he hym lende,[d]
That was mynyd doune and alle for-sehende,

[a] *Ferre an ney*. B.
[b] Trebuchet, an engine for throwing stones.
[c] Om. E. Supplied from B.
[d] Abode.

At Porte Causse that gate be-fore,
And kepte the Fraynysche men yn fulle sore,
And wan worschippe and grete honoure.
Of Pryncehode he may bere a floure.
Thoughe alle pryncys were i-mette,
Nexte the beste he myght be sette.
At the northe syde by twyne
There was loggyd Excetyr þe kene.
And at the Porte Denys he lay,
Where Freynysche men yssuyde owte every day.
He bet hem yn at every brounte,
And wanne worschyppe as he was wounte.
Of alle pryncys manhode to reporte
Set hym for on of the sorte.[a]
By twyne hym and Clarence[b] thanne,
Erle Marchalle[c] a man-fulle man,
Loggyd hym nexte the castelle gate
And kepythe hyt bothe erly and late.
And forthe in the same way
The Lorde Haryngton he lay.
Talbot from Dennifrount[d] when he come,
He loggyd hym next that gome.[e]
Then Haryngton Syr Wyllam
When he dyde hys retenewe he nam.[f]
The Erle of Urmounde[g] then lay he
Next Clarence with a grete mayne;
And Cornewale that comely knyght

[a] *Set Exseter as for one of the best surcote.* B.
[b] Thomas Plantagenet, the King's brother.
[c] John Mowbray, son of Thomas, first Duke of Norfolk. He was restored to his father's title in 1424.
[d] Domfront.
[e] Man.
[f] Took.
[g] James Butler, fourth Earl of Ormond.

He lay with Clarence bothe day and nyght;
And many knyghtys in a frounte
That nowe come not to my mynde to counte.
From Exceter towarde the kynge
Roos[a] and Wylby[b] were loggynge;
And thenne the Lorde Fe Hewe,[c]
That ys a goode knyght and a trewe;
Syr Wylham Porter thenne lay he
By fore the Porte Synt Hyllare.
Fulle spytefulle werre there was
And ought the cytte yssuyd owte in þat place.[d]
And ofte he droffe hem yn a gayne
Manfully with myght and mayne,
And wanne worschyppe alle wayes.
Moche ys that knyght to prayse.
And whylys Synt Kateryns was yolde,[e]
Of Mortayne the Erle[f] soo bolde,
That abbay and that towne by-twyne,
There he lay and wrought hem tene.
Moche worschyppe there he wanne;
Whyle he levyd he was the man.
The Erle of Saulysbury[g] in that tyde,
He loggyde in that othyr syde.
Syn thys vyage was thus begunne
Moche worschippe he wonne.

[a] John Lord Roos.
[b] Robert Lord Willoughby of Eresby.
[c] Henry Lord FitzHugh.
[d] *For ever they came owte at that same place.* B.
[e] *Was un zolde.* B.
[f] Edward Holland, Earl of Mortayne, who died at this siege. See Williams's "*Gesta Henrici Quinti,*" p. 128, note. It must have been after his death that the title was conferred on Edmund Beaufort, afterwards Duke of Somerset.
[g] Thomas de Montacute, Earl of Salisbury, who was slain at the siege of Orleans in 1428.

A comely knyght, Syr John the Gray,
On the Mounte Synte Mychelle he lay,[a]
That abbay and that towne by twyne,
And wan worschippe with war kene.
Syr Phylyppe Leche [b] thenne he lay
By twyne Sayn water and the abbay,
[c]And kepyd a warde undyr the hylle.
Worschyppe and honoure to hym fylle.
And Carowe,[d] that baron bolde,
Above he lay, and soo he wolde,
And kepte the watyr by the see syde.[e]
There fore hys worschyppe walkys wyde.
And Janygo[f] lay hym a-bove
A grete Squyer for to prove.
And in that othyr syde of Sayne
Lay Huntyngdone,[g] that cytte a gayne,
And helde them yn with manfulle warre
And gate hym worschyppe for evyr more.
Also Nevylle [h] that nobylle knyght,
And Umfravyle[i] that lorde soo lyght,
And Arundelle Syr Rycharde,
With Huntyngdon they lay inwarde.

[a] "And þan Sir John Grey, knyght, with all hys retenue and ordenaunce atte chapell þat is called Mount Seynt Mighell." H.

[b] The prose chronicle in H. calls him "Sir Philip Leche, knyght, the Kyngis tresorere."

[c] The preceding four lines are omitted in B., which thus makes Sir John Gray, and not Sir Philip Leche, keep ward under the hill.

[d] Thomas Baron Carew.

[e] *He kepte a warde as be that syde.* B.

[f] Jenico d'Artas, a Gascon gentleman. For some account of him, see Archæologia, xx. 92; and Williams's *Gesta Henrici Quinti*, 125-6.

[g] John Holland, Earl of Huntingdon.

[h] John Nevill, eldest son of Ralph Earl of Westmoreland, who died before his father in 1423.

[i] Sir Gilbert Umfraville, sometimes called Earl of Kyme.

Thoo Ferres [a] that lorde alle soo
With Huntyngdon he lay tho
At the Porte de Pounte in ryalle a-raye,
And wanne worschippe every daye.
Towarde Pounte del a roche [b] on Sayn,
Oure kynge made a gret chayne.
Thoroughe grete pylys he dyde hyt a-ray,
That no vesselle schulde rove a-way.
As nye the cheyne a brygge he made
To serve for man and hors i-lade.
Thenn every man myght to othyr fare
In hasty tyme yf nede were.
    Sone as Warwyke [c] Domfrount wan
Then to oure kyng a non he cam,
A-non commaundyd hym oure lege
To Calbecke [d] to set a sege,
And when he come the toune be-fore
They dyd trete with owtyn more. [e]
He sought that soverayn Erle unto
That he that dede wolde doo.
He grauntyd hem in compassyon,
And sclyd uppe a condyscyon,
The watyr of Sayn with owtyn lette,
Owre shyppys to passe with oure frette.
Then passyde oure shyppys alle in fere [f]
And keste hyr ancrys Roone fulle nere,
As thycke in Sayn as they myght stonde,
And segydde hyt bothe by water and by londe.

[a] Edmund Lord Ferrers of Chartley.
[b] *Pownte large.* B.
[c] Richard Beauchamp, Earl of Warwick.
[d] Caudebec.
[e] B. adds, in place of the next three lines :—
        " *And as Rone dyde, so thay wolde done,*
          And granted hyt in compocyssyone."
[f] Together, or in company.

And when Warwyke that ende badde made,
To Roone agayne that ryalle rode.[a]
By-twyxte Syut Kateryns and the kynge
He loggyd hym and was byggynge
Tylle that abbay in trety was,
And was yoldyn thoroughe Goddys grace.
Then withyn a lytylle whyle
He loggyd hym at Porte Martynvyle.[b]
Moche worschyppe therefore to hym was
And soo hathe ben in every place.
Saulysbury that was synyde to ryde,
Yet he returnyde and dyd abyde
By Huntyngdon, there lende
Tylle the sege was at an ende.
Glouceter that gracyus home,[c]
From the sege of Chirboroughe he come,
At the Port Syut Hyllarye
Fulle manfully loggyd he.
In caste of stone, in schot of quarelle,[d]
He dradde hym for noo perelle,
But wanne worschyppe with his werre,
And lay hys eumys fulle nerre
Thenne any man that there was
Be xl. rode and more in spas.
Whenn alle othyr pryncys ben tolde
Set hym for one of the bolde.
Of Sowthe folke[e] the Erle so wyght,

[a] *that lorde hym rode.* B.
[b] *Martwyle.* B.
[c] *gome.* B. A *gome* means a man.
[d] Square bullets of iron, with pyramidal heads, discharged by cross-bows.
[e] William de la Pole, Earl, afterwards Duke, of Suffolk. This was the nobleman who negociated the marriage of Henry VI. with Margaret of Anjou, but was afterwards compelled to quit the country, and was murdered at sea in 1450.

And Bergayne [a] that nobylle knyght
With Glouceter [b] bothe they lay,
And wanne worschyppe every day.
And then the pryor of Kylmaynan [c]
Was come with yn the mowthe of Sayn.
At Harflete he londed evyn, [d]
With **xv.** hundryd fyughtyng men,
Welle a-rayde of warre wyse,
As the cuntraye bathe the gysse.
Faste he hyed unto the sege,
And was welle-come unto oure lege.
Then was sayde the Fraynysche kynge
And the Burgaynys caste hyr entrynge [e]
In the northe syde of oure oste,
For cause there was playne [f] moste.
Oure kyng assygnyd a yenne
The priour [g] with hys **xv.** hundryd men
To logge hym in that syde,
For to kepe the wayes wyde.
By the Foreste of Lyones stoute,
To kepe the Fraynysche men owte,
He loggyd hym with owte that woode,
And made wacche and ordynaunce goode
Withowte oure oste iij legys large.
So for to logge hyt was hys charge.

[a] Richard Beauchamp, Lord Abergavenny, afterwards created Earl of Worcester.

[b] Humphrey Plantagenet, Duke of Gloucester, the King's brother.

[c] Sir John Botiller, prior of Kilmainham, head of the Order of St. John of Jerusalem in Ireland. See *Henrici Quinti Gesta* (*ed. Williams*), p. 125, note.

[d] *he londyde then.* B.

[e] *onttrynge.* E.

[f] *plague.* B. An obvious clerical error. The prose chronicle in H. says, "by cause þat þere was lefte entre and most playn grounde."

[g] *pouer*, MS.; but evidently a transcriber's error.

The knyght thenne there-to sent,[a]
And manfully thedyr wente.
Yf the Fraynysche men ofte wolde there that way
The fryste frunt he thought to fray.[b]
Moche worschyppe wanne he there,
And soo he badde done ellys where.
And moche worschyppe there he wan
I wolde you telle but alle I ne can.
Thys was oure sege with ryalle route
Alle the cytte sette aboute.
Nowe of thys cytte wylle y spelle,
And of the Captaynys wylle I telle.
 Monsenyour Gy the goode Botlere[c]
Was cheffe captayne alle in fere,[d]
Bothe in castelle and in towne.
He was a man of grete renowne.
Monsenyour Termagon in that spase,
Captayne of Porte Causse he was.
Monsenyour de Roche alle soo
Of Bevewsyn captayn thoo.
Monsenyour Antoyne, a werryour wyght,
He was leuetenaunt to that knyght.
Herre Chanfewe[e] was captayne
Of the Porte de Pount de Sayne.
Johan Mawtrevers that [nobylle][f] man
Of the Porte of Castelle was captayne.
Monsenoure Pennewys[g] thenne was he
Captayne of Porte Syut Hyllare.

---

[a] *therto did sone assente.* B.
[b] *The furste brownte they thowgte affray.* B.
[c] Guy le Bouteiller.
[d] *i. e.* of the whole company.
[e] *Ehanfewe.* E. *Camfewe.* B. *Chamfewe.* H. and H. 2.
[f] Supplied from B.
[g] *Pemewes.* B. *Peneux.* H.

The Bastarde of Teyne in that whyle
Was captayne of Porte Martynvyle.
And Gaunt Jaket or Jakys [a] of werrys wyse,
He was captayne, and alle so the pryce,
And of alle the skarmoschys that were withowte
Of alle the cytte rounde aboute.
And every on of thes captaynys badde
v. m[l]. men and moo in lade.[b]
And whenn they wolde rayse all the comynaltye,
Many a thousande myght they be.
Men nomberyd them with yn
Whenn oure sege dyde by-gynne
To iij.ccc.m[l]. and ten [c]
Of wymmen, chyldryn, and of men.
O' pepylle hyt was a pronde score,
A kynge to lay a sege be-fore.
And there-to they were fulle hardy in dede
Bothe in foote and eke in stede,
And als prowde men as evyr I saye,[d]
And poyntys of warre many one dyd shewe.
Whenn they yssuyd owt, moste comynly
They come not owte in one party.
At ij gatys, or iij, or alle
Sodynly they dyd owte falle.
And every parcelle there wolde be
A thowsande, or ellys thre,[e]
Rychely arayde at the beste
And there to prowdely and preste.r

---

[a] *Graunte Jakys.* B.   *Graunde Jakis.* H.
[b] Inlaid, *i. e.* provided.
[c] *Unto four hundred thowsande and ten.* B.
[d] *knowe.* B.
[e] *A ten thousand, also mote I the.* B.
[f] Ready.

Hyt was grete lykyng hem [a] to hede;
To counter hem[b] hyt was grete drede,
For the fensce of hem nought at alle,
For moche of the drede come fro the walle;
For schot of goonne and quarelle bothe
Sawe I nevyr gretter wothe.[c]
Evyr as they yssuyd oute and made a fray,
There wolde be schot I dar welle say
A hundryd govnnys at wallys and tourys
With[in][d] the mount of ij halfe hourys.
Of quarellys noo tonge may sowne
That wolde be schot in schorte rome.
Thys they yssuyd owte tho and thoo,
And on the erthe men shulde be sloo,[e]
And othyr whyr with spere and schylde,
Whenn they wolde owte in to the fylde.
[f]Thenn oure kynge lette a diche make
And set ther uppon scharpe poyntyd stake
And heggys a-bove[g] for prykyers owte
Alle that cytte rounde a-boute.
Syr Robert Babthorpe in that space
Countroller unto oure kynge he was;
Bothe hegge and dyche he ordaynyd that,
And moche worschyppe there he gatte.
Then they yssuyd owte ofte on fote,
For in horsse-backe was noo boote.
Bothe in watyr and in londe
Oure men gaffe hem mete at hond.

[a] *hom.* E. *hem for to lede.* B.
[b] *hom.* E. *ham.* B.
[c] Injury.   [d] Om. E.
[e] Slain.
[f] Before this in B. occurs these two lines:—
   " *And than owre kynge a cry lette make
      That every man trewly to wake.*"
[g] *And heggyd hyt about.* B.

And oft oure men were fully slayne,
For rennynge[a] of the walle soo gayne[b]
That was bothe grace and Goddys wylle
Bothe govnnys and quarellys went so thrylle,
Trypget and spryggalde and grete ingyne,
They wrought oure men fulle moche pyne,
And namely to Glouceter that dere,[c]
For he was loggyd them soo nere.
And come tydyngys newe and newe,
The Burgonnys wolde come for rescue.
Suche tydyngys come that cytte tylle
That the bellys they gon rynge fulle schrylle.
Nevyr aftyr tylde ne ronge the sythe þe sege was sette,
Ne aftyr tylle the cytte was gette.
Oure kynge demyd þat Duke of Burgon had ben nere,
And made a fylde with chyftens there.[d]
Sone tydyngys come hyt was not soo.
A-gayne to Parys þe Duke was goo.
Thenn with yn fewe dayes
They say he was at Pounthayes,[e]
And hadde iij.c. thousand[f]
Of fyghtyng men hym sewand.[g]
Oure kynge commaundyd with his crye
In barnys every man to lye.
With owtyn the border of hys oste
He made a dyche of grete coste,

---

[a] *remyge.* MS.
[b] *For they wolde rynne the walles agayne.* B.
that lorde so dere. B.
[d] *Than come ty dynges howe they were nere.*
Than sayde oure kynge wyth mery chero,
" *Felowes, be mery nowe every chone,*
" *For we schalle fygte sone anone.*" B.
[e] *Dounthayes.* MS. *Pownteys.* B. The place is clearly Pontoise.
[f] *four hundred thowsand.* B.
[g] *In good order.* ꝫ

Pyght with stakys that wolde perysce,[a]
With turnepykys, and with many an hers;
Govnnys goode and redy bente,
They were layde in many went.[b]
The countrollers the werke see,
A besy knyght in chevallcre.
And sone they sayde with ynne a whyle,
He come with yn xx myle.
Thys tale was tolde un the Tuysday[c]
That he wolde com [d] on Fryday,
In that cytte was sayde the same;
Thys of hys comyng they hadde game.
And on the Fryday, with owtyn boode,
To Huntyndone oure kyng roode ;
There he ordaynyd at hys a vyse,
A poynt of warre hyt was fully prysse.
He reryd that warde to batelle bonne,[e]
Hyr backys tornyd toward the towne,
In hyr a ray so as they stode;
A nothyr batylle owte of a woode
Musterryd them with batylle sore.
Of Burgayne ys armys sum they bore.[f]
He made the bataylys for to mete,
As they badde fought soo dyd they lete,
To make the cytte to yssue owte,
But they ne durste for they had dowte,
And supposyd hyt was a trayne;
They bode with yn for they wold not be slayne.
    And aftyr that they werryd soore,
    And yssude oute as þey dyd be-fore,

[a] hors to perche. B. þat would perissh. Prose narrative in H.
[b] Passages.
[c] Thursday. B., with which H. agrees.   [d] con, MS.
[e] Ready.   [f] bere, MS.

Fulle myghtyfulle with power stronge,
And a-bode a-pon the Burgonnys longe,
Tylle hyt drewe towarde Crystysmas.
Bp þat tyme there vytayle waxyd scars.
Mete and drynke and othyr vytayle
In that cytte be-gan to fayle.
Save elene watyr they hadde i-nowe,
And vyneger to put there twoe,
Hyr brede was fulle ny gone
And flesche save hors hadde they non.

Nota of the
hunger in
that cytte.

They etete doggys, they ete cattys;
They ete mysse, horse and rattys.
For an hors quarter, lene or fatte,
At c s. hyt was atte.
A horsse hedde for halfe a pound;
A dogge for þe same mony round;
For xxx d.[a] went a ratte.
For ij noblys went a catte.
For vj d. went a mous;
They lefte but fewe in any house.
For brede as brode as my hond
Was worthe a franke, I undyrstond.
Hyt was febyll that they myght fynd,
For hyt was made in syche a kynde,
Ne of melle, ne of otys,
Bot of branne, God it wotys.
Oynonnys, lykys, bothe in fere[b]
Was to hem a mete fulle dere;
There of was a pece at a schelynge.
Welle was hym that myght gete a pyllynge.
A negge at ix d. a nappylle at x d.;
Suche a market was a-monge thes men.

---

[a] *Fourty pens.* B.   [b] together.

There was many a carefulle herte
By-cause hyr market was so smarte.
They caryd not for exspens of goode,
For they myght fynde noo foede
Where on they myght hyr mony were;
And that made them soo fulle of care.
They ete uppe bothe roote and rynde
Of docke of gras * they myght fynde.
Thenne to dye they dyd be-gynne,
Alle that ryche citte withyn.
They dyde faster every day
Thenn men myght them in erthe lay.
There as was pryde in ray be-fore,
Thenn was hyt put in sorowe fulle soore.
There as was mete, drynke and songe,
Thenn was sorowe and hunger stronge.
Yf the chylde schulde be dede,
The modyr wolde not gyf hyt bredde,
Ne nought wolde parte hyt a scheve
Thoughe sche wyste to save hys lyve;
Ne the chylde the modyr gyffe;
Every on caste hym for to leve
As longe as they myght laste.
Love and kyndenys bothe were paste.
Alle kyndenys love was be-syde
That the chylde schulde fro the modyr hyde,
To ete mete that shulde hyt not see,
And ete hyt alle in prevyte.
But hunger passyd kynde and love,
By that pepylle welle ye may prove.
Yet in the wallys they made hyt stoute
For we shulde not wyt with-owte.

dewe of the grasse. B

And sum stale a-way as they myght cache,
And they were takyn ay with-owte wacche.[a]
Alle they us tolde of hyr myschyffe,
And yet we can not them be-leffe,
That they shulde stonde in suche a state
By-cause that hyr warre dyd not a-bate.
   Thenn with yn a lytylle space,
The poore pepylle of that place,
At every gate they were put oute
Many a hundryd in a route;
That hyt was pytte hem to see
Wemme[n] come knelyng on hyr kne,
With hyr chyldryn in hyr armys,
To socoure them from harmys;
Olde men knelynge them by
And made a dolfulle cry.
And alle they sayden at onys thenne,
" Have marcy uppon us, ye Englysche men."
Oure men gaffe them of oure brede,
Thoughe they badde don sum of oure men to dede,
And harme unto them dyd they non,
But made them to the dyche gone.
There they kepte them a baycche
That non of hem shulde passe oure wacche.
Meny of them saydc they hadde levyr ben slayne
Thenn in to the cytte goo a-gayne.
They turnyd thenne with murmuracyon,
And cursyd hyr owne nacyon.
The cytte wolde not lete them yn,
There of I wote they dyd grete syn.
For many one there dyde for colde
That warmythe of howese savyd wolde.

That seson of Crystysmasse,
I shalle you telle a fayre grace,
And a mekenys of oure kynge,
Of goodenys a grete tokenynge.
He sent a-pon Crystysmasse daye
Hys herrowrys [a] of armys in ryche a-raye,
And sayde, by-cause of that hyghe feste,
Bothe to moste and leste,
With yn the cytte and with owte,
That were storles, and vytaylys with-owte,
They shulde have mete and drynke inowe
And save condyte to come there too.
They sayde " Graunt marcy," alle lyghtely,
As thoughe that they hadde sette lytylle þerby,
And unnethe they wolde grannte a space,
The pore to come there to that with-owte was.
ij prestys and iij men hem with [b]
To bryng hem mete they grauntyd grythe;
And yf there come any moo,
Them to slay they swere thoo.
On rowe þe pore were set in sete.
The prystys brought them hyr mete
They ete an dronke and were fulle fayne
And thankyd God [c] with alle hyr mayne,
And as they sette hyr mete to fong
Thys tale was them a-mong:
" A myghty God," they saydyn then,
" Of tendyr bertys ben Englysche men.
" Lo, here oure excellent kynge
" That we have ben so long stondynge,

---

[a] So in E. *herawdes.* B.
[b] *Save to two prestes and no mo hem with.* B. The prose chronicle in H. says, "two prestis and iiij servauntes."
[c] *our kynge.* B.

" And nevyr wold obbey hym to,
" With oure wylle the omage hym do,
" Of us nowe hathe more compassyon
"Thenn bathe oure owne nacyon.
" That God as þou art fulle of myght,
"Graunt hym grace to wynne hys ryght."
Thus the pepylle be-gan to speke.
Thenn to hem thys ij prystys toke.
When they hadde etyn they wente hyr way.
The trewys leste but that day ;
And as the nyght be-gan to come
They hyr way yede sone."

   Thenn wacche and warde fulle strayte
Bothe day and nyght on hem they wayte,
To holde them yn, bothe grete and smalle ;
For hunger brekythe the stone walle ;
And the captaynys of that cytte,
Mayre, burges, and yemonrye,
For nede they muste wante mete,
Conselle they toke that they wolde trete.
A-pon the newe yerys evyn at nyght
At every gate of cytte þer callyd a knyght ;
There was no man that tyme them herde.
With-owte answere forthe they farde,
Save a-pon Huntyng done ys syde,
Whenn they callyd in that tyde,
At the Porte de Pount of Sayne,
They answeryde full sone a-gayne.
A knyght thenn askyd what they wolde.
They sayde for sothe and thus they tolde.
" Speke with a knyght of oure lynage
" Or with sum lorde of Baronage. "

* *For nyzt as the nyght began to store,
So gan azen all that they wore.*   B.

He sayd, " For sothe I am a knyght ;"
And they hym askyd what he hyght.
He sayde " My name ys Umfrevyle."
They thonkyd God and sayde þat whyle,[a]
" Of Normandy the olde blode
" Shalle helpe that we may have a ende goode
" By-twyxte us [b] and thys worthy kynge."
He sayde, " What ys youre wyllynge?"
They saydyn, " With[owte][c] any sporte,
" We have ben at everyche Porte
" Where thys pryncys lyen before,
" And callyde aftyr them sore.
" Fryste at Clarence, that excellent,[d]
" Ought we callyde or we wente.
" Thenn at Glouceter the goode,
" Oftyn callyd and longe stoode.
" Thenn at Exceter we were,
" Fulle many tymys were callyd there.
" At Warwycke warde the Erle so fre
" We callyd moo then tymys thre.[e]
" Alle so at the Erl Marchalle we were,
" There was non that wolde us hyre.
" That we thys callyd yf they do muse,
" We pray you the ye us excuse,
" And pray thes pryncys for Goddys sake,
" That ys Lorde of alle and dyd us make,
" As they byn dukys of dignyte,
" And cheftaynys cheffe of chevalre,
" Unto the kyng pray for us,

---

[a] and the swete Seynt Gyle. B.
[b] you. E. us. B.
[c] Om. E. With owte any more reporte. B.
[d] that lorde so exselente. B.

Here 56 lines have been transposed by the copyist in E., who goes on from this place to the 13th line on p. 25,

" Tolde they thys tydyngys alle in fere."

" That we myght fynde hym gracyus;
" And we wylle you also
" Unt[o] the kyng for us to go,
" Besekyng hym for love of that Kynge
" In vj dayes that made alle thynge,
" With hys wyt and hys a-vyse,
" (Of alle othyr pryncys he ys þe pryce,)
" And also for hys owne prynce hode,
" And for hys moche manhode,
" And he ys kyng excellent,
" And unto non othyr obedyent,
" That levythe here in erthe be ryght,
" But only unto God almyght,
" With-yn hys owne Emperoure,
" And also kyng and conqueroure,
" That he wylle graunte us, of hys grace,
" Save condyte and also space,
" Nought to with-stonde oure offence,
" That we myght come unto hys presence,
" xij of us in one assent,
" Oure wylle to telle and oure entent.
" And with the myght of Goode soo fre,
" May we come onys þat we myght he see,
" We wylle hym say by lytylle instans
" Shalle turne the prynce to grete plesaunce."
Quod Umfrevyle, " Thys I assent."
He toke hys leve and forthe he went
To Clarens þe duke so dere
And tolde hym thys tydyngys alle in fere.
He thonkyd God and Marye eke
That owre enmys were made so meke,
And sayde " We wylle with fulle goode wylle
" Speke for them the kyng untylle."
Lo, so sone he undyrtoke,
And mekenys he nought for soke.

He ys a prynce for to commende,
But fewe in londe suche we fynde;
He ys manfulle whylys þe warre dos laste
And marcyfulle when wer ys paste;
Manhode, mekenys, bothe wyt and grace,
He has, content in lytylle space.
Hym wantyd no thynge þat a prynce shulde have:
Almyghty God moste[a] hym save!
Then Umfrevyle he toke hys leve,
Hys message went he for to meve.
To Glouceter then dyd hee goo,
To Exceter þe Duke alle soo.
Tolde they thys tydyngys alle in fere,
And thanked God of bevyn dyre,
That ther enmys agayne there wylle
For socoure shulde sende tham tylle;
And sayde they wolde for Goddys sake
Helpe a goode ende for to make.
Lo![b] thes pryncys of mekenys
(God save them alle from sekenys!),
Thoughe they hadde sufferde war smarte,
Yet were they marcyfulle in herte.
Thenn Umfyrvyle hys leve there tas,
And passyd forthe on hys pace
To the Erlys alle by name,
And they hym sayde alle the same.
Loo! thes grete men of chyvalrye
Soo sone were in charyte.
There God of Hys grete grace
He them spedde in every place.

---

[a] *mote.* H.
[b] *To.* E

On neweyerysday in the mornynge
Umfyrvyle went unto the kynge,
Alle the mater to hym he sayde.
Lyke as hyt was unt[o] hym layde.
Oure kynge with counselle and wyse
Also by hys owne wyte and vyse,
Graunt the cytte alle hyr wylle,
That xij. of hem shulde com hym tylle.
And of hys lordys everyche on,
A-gayne hyt was nevyr of them non.
Lo! that Prynce pryncypalle,
Of worthynys he passythe alle.
Lo! howe he provyd hym manfully,
And also fulle marcyfully.
Thoughe they had of hys men so many maymyd,[a]
And so gretely hym grevyd,
And put hym unto so grete a coste,
And of hys men so many loste,
And so withstondyng hym of hys ryght,
And then were fallyn in to hys myght,
At hys wylle them to greve,
Yf he wolde venge hym with myscheve.
Then for to lyght so lowe,
Of hyr wylle to wytte and knowe.
Also to graunte them trete,
There was marcy and charyte!
And they so grevysly hym had gylte
And of hys pepylle so many [b] spylte;
He to grannte hem of hys grace
A marcy fulle mete hyt was.

---

[a] *For tho that had hym oft ameved.* **B.**
[b] *sony.* E. An obvious clerical error. B. reads:—
    " *And of hys men meny one spylte.*"

The chylde of God I wote he ys
That dothe þe goode for the mys.
Of goodenys he lackythe noo thynge
That ys semyng for a kynge;
That Cryste for Hys Passyon
Kepe hym in Hys regnacyon l
Whenn he hadde grauntyd as I have tolde,
To Umfrevyle the knyght so bolde,
He askyd " Syr when shalle thys be?"—
" If that they wylle, to morowe," sayde he.
Umfrevyle hys leve there hente,
To the cytte a-gayne he wente,
And when he come unto the gate
The statys * he founde there ate.
He sayde " I have ben at oure kynge
" And he hathe grauntyd you youre wyllyng.
" To morowe by-tyme loke ye be yare,ᵇ
" For xij of you shalle with me fare.
" And sythe ye shalle goo hym to,
" Thys counselle I rede you doo.
" To morowe, I wotte, ye schalle se
" The ryalste prynce of Crystante.
" With suche a prynce yet ye nevyr spake,
" Ne not so sone a worde can take.
" Thynke with herte by fore youre tunge,
" Leste youre wordys ben alle to longe.
" Speke wordys but lytylle and welle hym set
" With that prynce when ye be met ;
" For one worde wrong and owte of warde
" Myght cause you alle to fare fulle harde;
" For-thy of wordys be ye wyse
" And say not withowte a vyse."

* of Rone. B. of the citte. H   ᵇ Ready.

They thonkyd hym alle curtesly,
And sayde, " Mon syr, graunt mercy,
" And ye thus moche good wolde us teche,
" Or that we com unto þat pryncys speche,"
And sayde " A dewe " and went hys waye—
Thys was Sonday and Neweyerysday.[a]
On that othyr day by pryme
Umfrevyle he come that tyme ;
And of the kyngys squyers gente
That tyme with hym a certayne wente,
And many yemen with hym also
Were assygnyde for to go.
They wente to Syut Hyllarys gate,
The xij men come forthe there ate;
iiij knyghtys, and iiij clerkys,
And iiij burgeys wyse of workys;
And they alle were clad in blacke.
Maner they were [b] and fayre they spacke.
When they com unto Chartryte [c]
The kyng hyryng masse was he.
With yn Chartyr howse with yn dyd lyende,[d]
Tylle the masse was at ende.
Forthe come the kynge with owtyn let
Where he had knelyd in a closet,[e]

---

[a] *Onto the Sonday after Newe zere daye.* B. New-year's day, however, was Sunday in 1419 ; so that the reading in our text may be quite correct. In H. the passage stands thus :

> " *He seyde adewe and went his waye.*
> " *The Satirday after Newyeresday,*
> " *At that houre of day at prime,*" &c.

thus omitting the date of the conference with Umfraville, but placing the interview with the King on the Saturday following.

[b] *Comely of chere.* H.
[c] *the house of Charture.* H.   *tho hous of Charite.* B.
[d] *alle they did lende.* H.
[e] A pew.

With a chere so chevetaynelyche
So lyght of loke and so lordelyche.
Solemp with semeland so sad
To se the kynge men myght be glad.
As sone as the Fraynysche men hym se
That lorde be fore they fylle on kne.
He blessyd them with statefulle chere
As he ne wyste what they were.
They inclynyd with meke speche
And a bylle to hym dyd they reche,
An bade a lorde to take the hylle,*
And sumwhat more he turnyd hem tylle.
What hyt ment, as I hyrde say,
A tretys they wolde have by sum way.
They hym be sought for Goddys sake,
That bevyn and erthe and alle dyd make,
Bothe este, west, northe, and soughthe,
That he wolde hyre them speke with mouthe.
And he bade them speke alle hyr wylle,
And they were fayne and knelyde stylle.
They sayde, " We you be seche and praye
" For Hys love þat dyde on Goode Frydaye,
" And for hys Modyrs love so fre,
" Consydyr ye the charyte,
" The pore pepylle that ben with owte
" In youre dychys rounde a-boute,
" That ben there and lacke mete and brede,
" For hunger many on ben dede.
" Have ye pytte thaim uppon
" And graunte them leve for to gone."

---

* *The kynge bade Exsetere loke on that bylle.* B. *He taughte a lorde to take her bylle.* H.

Alle stylle he stode that whyle,
Nothyr dyd he laughe nor smyle,
But with a countenaunsce fulle clere
And with a fulle lordely chere,
Nor to mylde, nor to stronge,[a]
But in a mene withowtyn change.
Hys countenans dyd he not a bate,
But stylle he stode and in astate,
Or hym lyste to geve an answere.
He sayde, " Felowys, hoo put them there,
" To the dyche of that cytte?
" I putte them not there, and Þat wote ye.
" Nothyr hyt was not myn ordynaunce,
" Ne non passe by my sufferaunce.
" Let them fynde that they have sought ;
" They a bode in the cytte whylys they mought.
" And as to you, ye knowe welle thys,
" Ye have offendyd me with mysse,
" And fro me i-kepte my cytte,
" That ys myn herrytage so fre,
" And ye shalle be my lege men."
They answeryd and sayde then,
" Of thys cytte that we here kepe
" We have a charge, and that a depe,
" That us be-toke oure soverayne lege,
" For to defende from saute and sege.
" We ben hys lege men i-bore,
" And also we have to hym swore,
" Also to the Duke of Burgayne fre,
  Of hym a fulle depe charge have we.
" But wolde ye of youre grete grace
" Graunt us leve and space,

" Sum of us to hem for to goo,

" That we myght warne them of oure woo

" And of oure faythe us to excuse,

" Many of us wolde them refuse,

" And to you delyvery youre cytte

" And many of us youre lege men be." [a]

He sayde, " I put you owte of doute,

" My cytte wylly not goo with owte.

" And as touchyng to youre Freynysche lege,

" He wot fulle welle I holde a sege.

" The Duke of Burgayne also

" Welle they wote bothe too;

" And thys whyle that I here have ben

" Ofte massyngers bathe gone us by-twyne

" If them lyste to nyght me nere. [b]

" Welle they wote to fynde me here.

" Welle they wote I wylle not gon

" With owte my ryght for frende ne fon.

" Sythe they hyt longe be fore kuewe,

" To sende them message newe and newe,

" Hyt were to me but novylte; [c]

" To us but superfluyte.

" Suche massage shalle tham non be sent

" Hit ys noo nede ne competent."

Whan he badde gevyn then that answere

Of that mater they spake no more.

They sayde, " Hyt ys fulle lyke to wyn

" Rone cytte with men there yn."

He sayde, " Hyt ys myn owne londe,

" I wylle hyt wyn, thoughe ye hit with stond;

[a] " *And alle zoure owne liege men be.*" H.

[b] *meyze me nere.* H.

to ham no neweltie. B

" And the men that ye so draffe
" Shalle be rewarde lyke as they serve."
With that worde they were a dradde
Then spake a clerke and thys he sayde:
  " Soverayne lorde, yf ye wylle hede,
" In story thus I fynde and rede.
" ij chevetaynys a day had set,
" And with hyr hoste they met;
" Bothe a rayde uppon a fylde
" And bothe ij to batayle yelde.
" The wekyr party with les men yn
" Brought the bygger brede and wyne,
" In tokenyng that they shulde be
" Marcyfulle and of pytte.
" Lo, we brynge you bredde and wyne,
" We brynge you Rone the cytte fyne."
He sayde, " Rone ys myn herrytage,
" I wylle hit have with owtyn fage;[a]
" And for thys tyme I rede you doo
" That marcy may be grauntyd you to.
" And at the reverence of God alle myght,
" And of hys modyr, þat maydyn bryght,
" Of tretys I shalle graunte you space,
" If ye do welle ye may have grace."
Thenn they sayde, " Syr, for charyte,
" Howe wylle ye to oure pepylle see,
" That in the dychys suffer payne
" And for defaute dyen lyke swyne?"
He answeryd with wyt fulle wyse,
And sayde, " Ther on I wylle take a vyse.
" As God me puttys in herte and wylle,
" So wylle I do that pepylle tylle.

[a] Deccit.

" As me my red ys, soo wylle I rewe "—
With that he went and sayde " A dewe."
The Fraynysche men in the same whyle,
Forthe they went with Umfrevyle.
Towarde the cytte as they yode,
They spake of oure kynge soo goode.
They sayde, " He ys, at oure a vyse,
" Of alle erthely pryncys the pryce,
" Takyng rewarde of hys chere,
" And to hys countenaunce so clere;
" To hys person in propyrte;
" To hys fetowrys and hys beute,
" And to hys depe dyscrecyon,
" That he hathe in possessyon,
" And to hys passyng prynce-hode,
" And to hys mykylle man-hode.
" And he ys marcyfulle in myght,
" And askysse no thynge but hys ryght.
'' Thes vertuys ys a grete thynge
" To be withyn an erdely kynge.
" Howe shulde he but wyn honowre?
" Howe shulde he be but a conquerowre ?
" Welle we wote withowtyn wene,
" God hym lovys, and that ys sene."
Thys the Fraynysche men of hym talkyd,
Towarde the cytte as they walkyd.
There leve of Umfrevyle they toke,
And in to the cytte the gon roke.[a]
A pon that othyr day erlyche
Oure kynge made ij tentys uppe to pycche,
One for Englysche, a nothyr for Fraynysche,
Bothe were sette in Glouceter ys trenche.

[a] *Roke*, i.e., return. We still talk of a thing *rocking* to and fro, of *rocking* a cradle, &c.

CAMD. SOC.

Thoughe the stormys were nevyr so grete,
Dry heddyd ther yn myght they trete.
When bothe pavylyons were uppe ryght,
They went to trete with wylle fulle wyght.
Warwyke, that worthy erle so wyse,
For oure parte he was pryce.
Sawlysbury, that erle so trewe,
And alle so the lorde Fehewe,
The kyngys stywarde Hungerforde,—
By name I can noo moo reporte,—
Fro that cytte cam tham to mete
xxiiij men fulle dyscrete.[a]
That was a syght of solempnyte,
To be-holde eyther othyr parte,
To se hyr pavylyons in hir a raye,
The pepylle that on the wallys lay,
And oure pepylle that was with owte,
Howe thycke they stode and walkyd a boute.
Also hyt was solas to sene
The herrowdys of armys Þat went by twyne.
Kyngys, herrowdys, and pursefauntys,
In cotys of armys suauntys,[b]
The Englysche beste,[c] the Fraynysche floure,[d]
Of Portynggale castelle, and toure;[e]
Othyr in cotys of dyversyte,
As lordys berys in hys degre.
Gayly with golde they were be-gon,
Ryght as the son for sothe hyt schone.

[a] xij of the Frensshe that werene discrete.   H.
[b] suauntys, i.e., suitable or appropriate.   H. reads amyᵃuntis.
[c] a beste.   H.
[d] a floure.   H.
[e] Some Portuguese ships were employed by Henry to block up the mouth of the Seine.

Thys syght was bothe joye and chere;
Of serowe and payne the othyr were.
Of pore pepylle there were put owte,
And nought as moche as a clowte ^a
But the clothys in there backe,
To kepe them from rayne I wotte.
The wedyr was unto them a payne,
For alle that tyme stode moste by rayne.
There men myght se grete pytte,
A chylde of ij yere or iij
Go a boute to hegge hyt brede.
Fadyr and modyr bothe were dede.
Undyr sum the watyr stode;
Yet lay they cryyng aftyr foode.
And sum storvyn unto the dethe,
And sum stoppyde of ther brethe,
Sum crokyd in the kneys,
And sum alle so lene as any treys,
And wemmen holdyn in hyr armys
Dede chyldryn in hyr barmys,^b
And the chyldryn sokyng in ther pappe
With yn a dede woman lappe.
There men myght fynde and see fulle ryfe
By twyne ij ded on lyynge on lyve,
And he not wetyng of there dethe,
Soo prevely they yelde uppe hyr brethe
Withoutyn calle or cry,
As they badde slepte soo dyd they dy.
Thes were the syghtys of dyfferauns,
That one of joye and þat other of penaunce,
As helle and hevyn ben partyd a to,
That one of welle and þat othyr of wo.

---

^a *þay hadde on hem unnethe a cloute.* H.
^b Bosoms.

There ne was noo man, I undyr stonde,
That sawe that but hys herte wolde change,
And he consyderyd that syght
He wolde be pensyffe and no thyng lyght.
There myght men lerne alle there lyve,
What was a-gayne ryght for to stryve.
For when hyt lay in there lotte
They were fulle cruelle, God hyt wote,
And marcy wolde they non have,
Nede causyd them aftyr for to crave.
And yet for alle hyr wyckyd wylle
Mercy they were takyn tylle.
    Nowe of the pepylle lat we be,
And of oure tretys talke we.
We than * chalengyde and accused,
And they answeryd and excusyd.
We askyd moche and they proferd smalle,
That was ylle to corde with alle.
So they tretyd a forghtnyght,
And yet a corde they ne myght.
The tretys then they breke in haste,
And bothe tentys downe were caste.
The Fraynysche men them be thought
That hyr owne woo they hadde wrought.
And when they shulde hyr leve take,
They prayde oure men and thus they spake:
" For the love of Alle myghty God
" Contynu youre trewys to nyght for good.
" And yf we calle aftyr speche,
" In that tyme we you be seche,
" That we may have contynuans
" For to hyre oure audyens."

* hem. II.

Oure men sayde, " That we assent."
Bothe tokyn hyr leve and forthe they went.
To the kyng oure party paste,
And tolde with tale fulle stydefaste,
Howe they hadde lefte and in what yssu,
And howe they had contynuyd trewe.
Oure kynge was marcyfulle in herte mode,
That they hadde grauntyd he not withstode.
The cytesyns with sympylle chere
In to the cytte they went yn fere.[a]
Sone in that cytte hyt was spoke
That the tretys was broke.
The poore pepylle alle a boute
On the ryche made a schoute:
" And ye fals tale-tellers,
" And also men quellers,
" Why wylle ye take no rewarde
" To us that suffer now so harde,
" That dye here every day,
" And welle mou [b] þen men telle may,
" Alle hyt rennys uppon youre coste,[c]
" For in youre faute we ben loste.
" We pray to God that ye answere,
" By fore that Lorde that sufferd sore [d]
" At Calverey uppon a roode,
" And bought us with Hys blessyd blode ;
" That ye be gylty in thys cas
" We you apele by fore Hys face.

---

[a] In company.
[b] *Welle we.* H. *Wele þan telle we may.* H. 2.
[c] *And also rennyth upon our coste.* H.
[d] The final words of these lines are transposed in E. as follows:—
    We pray to God that sufferd sore,
    By fore that Lorde that ye answere.

" Wolde ye obey unto oure lege,
" Thenn wolde he sesse of hys sege.
" But for youre goode that ye hyde,
" Youre pompe and youre grete pryde.
" And ye wolde enclyne unto youre kynge,
" Thenn myght he sesse of oure langgynge.
" But ye a corde with youre wylle,
" He shalle com yn thoughe ye nylle.[a]
" Youre styffe gatys that ye steke,[b]
" We shalle them bren and up breke.
" We shalle lat hym in to hys ryght ;
" If ye defende we shalle fyght,
" Levyr then thys to byde here
" And dy for hunger alle in fere."
They sayde, " Suffyr for a whyle,
" For that we doo ys for a wyle.
" We wylle excuse us to that fode [c]
" For to pay but lytylle goode."
Then sembelyd alle in hyr degre [d]
And every one sayde in hys manere :[e]
" No nede ys to counsel to goo.
" There nys no more but on of too ;
" Othyr delyvery up thys clos,
" Or ellys be ded ther ys no choys."
To the Port Syut Hyllary they went,
And callyd owte by one assent.
Thenn answeryd a knyght a non
Was callyd Robert [f] Syr John.

[a] *Righte here anoono we schal zou killo.* H.
[b] Shut.
[c] Person.
[d] *þay semblid þane alle þat cite.*
[e] *in his degre.* H.
[f] *Robesard.* H.

" Syrs," he sayde, " what ys youre wylle?"
They answeryd and sayde hym tylle,
" We you beseche for charyte,
" And for the honoure of oure Ladye,
" For us that ye wylle spende youre speche
" To Glouceter, and hym by seche
" For us to speke to þe kynge, and prayen
" That we myght come trete a gayne.
" We wylle submyt us unto hys wylle
" And alle that longe us tylle,
" Oure persons and oure possessyons,
" And alle dyspose at hys owne dyscressyns."
Whenn thys knyght the Duke hadde tolde,
For them to speke he sayde he wolde.
So he demenyd * unto the kynge
That spas he gate of newe tretynge.
Of Cauntyrbury the Byschoppe fre,
At Syut Kateryns that tyme lay he,
Whenn he hadde knowelege of that care,
In hys herte he tendyrde sore.
To the kyng whyghtely he wente,
And be sought hym with a good intente,
That he myght wende unto that cytte,
For to speke with hyr spyrytualte,
To helpe a fynyalle pes to gete,
To goo and be a mene at that trete.
The kyng hym grantyd a non ryght.
ij pavylyons a non were pyght
With yn the trenche where they hadde ben.
The byschoppe pyght hys owne bytwyne.
So was the state of spyryualte
A mene to make unyte.

* *He mevid it.* H.

They tretyd day, they tretyd nyght,
With candelle and torchys bryght.
    They tretyd iiij dayes in space [a]
And made a nende thoroughe Goddys grace.
Whenn they knewe a conclusyon,
The Fraynysche men made a petyscyon,
Alle there worschyppe for to save,
viij dayes of respyte for to have,
That they myght goo unto þe Fraynysche kynge,
And to the Duke of Burgon sende tydynge
And in what degre they stode and howe,
Bydyng on them to have rescowe.
That was a poynt of chevalrye,
Oure kyng grauntyd with herte fre,
That they myght wyt welle and when
Howe hyt shulde be delyveryd then.
    Nowe to my tale, and ye wylle tende,
I shalle you telle oure cordymente.
In viij dayes, I you tolde,
If noo rescowe unto that holde,
They shulde delyvyr that cytte
And the burgonys [b] Englysche be.
Alle soo to oure kynge, of mony rounde,
To pay hy[m] l. m¹. pounde.
More ovyr they shulde undyr take
A castelle to oure kynge to make
In iij halfe yerys with owtyn let,
Sum sayde, " In faye hyt shalle be set." [c]
And they to have hyr ffranches fre,
By fore as hyt was wounte to be;

---

[a] *in þat place.* H.
[b] *burgesis.* H.
[c] *And upon Soyne it schold be sette.* H.

No man with[ynne] ^a hyr cytte to selle,
But cyttezyns that þer yn dwelle,
And thoo that was a Norman borne,
And Englysche men wolde not be sworne,
Presener he shulde be us tylle,
Oure kynge hym to ponysche at hys wylle;
And alle the sowdyers that were there,
Hyr goode to leve and goo forthe bare,
In hyr dublettys owte of the towne.
Oure kynge gaffe eche on a gowne.
Thys was hys compascyon,
[And made by good discressioun].^b
And Graunt Jakys a non present,
Aftyr rescu he was sent.
Of that massage he was fulle fayne,
To Roone he come not yet a-gayne,
But massyngers thedyr he sende,
Bade them to come of and make an ende,
Dyd them to wyt, with tale fulle trewe,
No rescu was that he of kuewe.
The viij dayes, the sothe to telle,
On the ffeste of Syut Wolstone^c hyt felle.
That was apon a Thursday.
Oure kynge then in ryche aray,
And ryally in hys astate
[As a conquerour there he sate]^d
With[in] a howse of Carteryte.^e
To hym the keys of that cytte
Delyveryd unto hym in fe.

---

^a Om. in E. Supplied from H.
^b This line occurs in H., but is omitted in E. and H 2.
^c Jan. 19th, which fell upon a Thursday in 1419.
^d Supplied from H.
^e *Charite.* H.

Monsenoure Gy the Botlere,
And burgeys of that cytte in feere,[a]
To oure kynge the keys they brought.
To ben hys lege men they hym besought.
To Exceter oure kynge soverayne
Commaundyd the keys for captayne.
Alle so that Duke chargyd he
To go resake that ryche cytte,
And entyr in hys name that nyght,
And synyd with hym many a knyght.
Then Exceter with owtyn boode
Toke hys leve and forthe he roode,
To Bevyse that Port so stronge
That he badde layn be fore so longe.
To that gate fulle sone he cam,
And with hym many a goodely man.
There was neynge of many a steede,
There was shewynge of many a wede,
There was many a getton [b] gay,
Moche ryalte and ryche a ray.
Whenn the gatys were opynd there,
And they were redy in for to fare,
Tro[m]ppettys [c] blewe ther bemys [d] of bras,
Pypys and claryons bothe there was,
As they enteryd they gave a schonte
With a voyce, and that a stoute,
" Syn Jorge! Syn Jorge!" they cryde on hyght,
" Welle come Rone, our kyngys owne ryght!"
The Fraynysche pepylle of that cytte
Were gaderyd m¹. for to see,

---

[a] And the burgesses of that city in company.
[b] A small standard borne by an esquire.
[c] *Trumpettys,* i. e. trumpetters.
[d] Trumpets.

They cryde alle " Welcome," in feere,[a]
" In suche tyme mote ye entyr here,
" Plesynge to God that hyt myght be
" To us bothe pes and unyte."
Of the pepylle, to telle the treughthe,
Hyt was a syght of grete reuthe.
Moche of the folke that were thereyn,
They were but bonys and bare skyn,
With bolowe yeen and vysage sharpe,
Unnethe they myght brethe or carpe;
With wan color as the lede,
Unlyke to lyvys men but unto dede.
Patrons[b] they were quente,
A Colayne kynge[c] aftyr to paynte.
There men myght see an example
Howe lacke of foode makys men fulle ylle.
In everyche strete lay dede,
And sum cryde aftyr brede.
Aftyr longe and many a day
They dyde faster then cartys myght cary a way.
The redy way þer God them wysse,
That they may bylde in blysse!
    Off them y wylle no more spelle,
But of Exceter I wylle you telle.
To the castelle fyrste he roode,
And sythe unto the Portys alle and brode.
Lengythe and brede bothe he met,
And ryche baners up he set.
A pon the Porte Synt Hyllarye,

[a] In company.
[b] Patterns, or workmen's models ; lay figures.
    Disfigurid pateronys and quaynte. H.
[c] *A* king of Cologne ;—alluding to the supposed Three Kings whose sculls are preserved there.

A baner of the Trynyte.
At Bovens[a] he set fulle evyn
A baner of the Queue of Hevyn.
At Martynvyle up he pyghte
Of Syn Jorge a baner bryght.
In the castelle he set to stonde
The armys of Fraunce and of Ingelond.
In the Fryday in the mornynge
Towarde the cytte come oure kynge.
iij byschoppys[b] in hyr a ray,
vij abbottys with crossys gay;
xlij[c] crossys there were
Of rerygyus[d] and seculere.
Alle they went in processyon.
A gayne thys prynce with owtyn towne
Every cros in ordyr they stoode.
He kyste them alle with meke mode.
And haly watyr with hys hande
Gaffe the prymate of oure lande,
At Boveys the Porte[e] so wyde
He passyde yn with owte any pryde,
With owtyn pype or claryons blaste,
Prynce devoutely yn he paste
As j. conqueroure in hys ryght,
Thankyng in hys herte God Almyght.
Alle the pepylle of that cytte,
They sayde, " Welcome, oure lege so fre,
" Welcome in to youre oune ryght,
" As hyt ys the wylle of God Almyght."

[a] *And at the Port Kaux.* H.
[b] *Alle the Bisshoppis.* H.
[c] xliiij. H 2. ; but xlij. E. and H.
[d] Religious, *i. e.* the religious orders.
[e] *And at the Porte Kaux.* H.

With that they cryde alle "Nowe welle," [a]
Al so schyrle as any belle.[b]
He rode a pon a blacke [c] stede,
Of blacke damaske was hys wede.
A paytrelle [d] of golde fulle bryght,
Aboute hys breste hyt was pyght.
The pendauntys dyd by hym downe hange
On eyther syde of hys hors stronge.
Thay that hym nevyr arste [e] se
By hys chere welle wyste that hit was he.
Soo to the mynyster dyd he fare
And of hys hors he lyght there.
Hys chapylle mette with hym at the doore,
And went by fore hym in the floore,
And songe a responde gloryus,
That ys namyd *Quis est magnus ?* [f]
Masse he hyrde and offyrde thoo;
Sethen unto the castelle he dydyn goo.
That ys a pallays in that cytte,
For hyt a place of ryalte.
There he hym loggyd in the toune
With ryalte and grete renoune.
Nowe ys that cytte welle in tryste
Incresyd bothe of mete, drynke of the beste,
Thoroughe the grace of God and of oure lege.
Thys he badde endyd uppe hys sege.
With owtyn fabylle or fage [g]
Thys procesce made John Page,

[a] The French cry of *Noël.*
[b] *Os heighe as þay myzt zelle.* H.
[c] *browne.* H. and H 2.
[d] Breastplate.
[e] *Erst, i. e.* before.
[f] *Quis est magnus Dominus ?* H. and H 2.
[g] Falsehood.

Alle in raffe and not in ryme,
By cause of space he badde no tyme.
But whenne thys werre ys at a nende,
And he have lyffe and space he wylle hit a mende.
They that have hyrde thys redynge,
To Hys blysse He tham brynge,
That for us dyde uppon a tree.
Say amen for charyte.

Amen.

Explicit þe sege of Rone.

VERSES

ON THE

KINGS OF ENGLAND.

LYDGATE'S VERSES

ON

THE KINGS OF ENGLAND.

*Cronycles of alle Kyngys of Englonde aftyr the Conqueste,
as of hyr namys ande where that they bene i-byryede.*

WYLLELMUS CONQUESTOR.

This myghty Wylliam Duke of Normandye,
As bokys olde make mencyon,
By juste tytylle and hys chevalrye
Made kynge by conqueste of Brutys Albyon,[*]
Putte owte Harrolde ande toke possessyon,
Bare hys crowne fulle **xxj** yere,
Beryd at Cane, thys saythe thys croneculere.

WYLLELMUS RUFUS.

Nexte in ordyr by successyon
Wylliam Rufe his sone crownyde kynge,
Whiche to Godwarde hadde noo devocyon,
Destruyd chyrchis of newe and olde byggynge
To make a foreste plesaunte for hontynge.
xiiij yere he bare hys crowne in dede,
Beryde at Wynchester the cronycle ye may rede.

[*] In margin : "*id est*, Englonde."

HENRICUS PRIMUS.

His brother next, callyde the fryste Henry,
Was to London i-crownyde as I fynde,
Whos brother Robert of Normandye
Ganne hym werry, the cronycle makythe mynde,
Reconsylyd alle rancor sette by hynde.
Fulle xxxiij, by recorde of wrytynge,
Yeres he raygnyde, and ys byryde at Redynge.

STEPHANUS.

His cosyn Stevyn, when fryste Henry was dede,
Towarde Englonde ganne crosse the sayle;
The Archebyschoppe sette upon hys hedde
A riche crowne, beynge of hys consayle.
xix yere with sorowe and grete travayle
He bare hys crowne he hadde noo reste,
At Feversham lythe byryde in hys cheste.

HENRICUS SECUNDUS.

Henry the Secunde the sone of the Emperesse
Was crownyd next, a manly knyght
As bokys olde playnely done expresse.
Thys sayde Henry by forwarde force and myghte
Slowe Thomas[a] for Hooly Chyrche ryght.
Yeres xxxv raygnyde as ys i-made mynde,
At Synt Everard beryd as I fynde.

[a] "Bekett" interlined here, in a later hand.

RICHARDUS PRIMUS.

Richarde hys sone next by successyon,
Fryste of that name, stronge, hardy, and notable,
Was crownyd kynge, callyd Cuer de Lyon,
With Saresenys heddys i-servyd at his tabylle;
Slayne at Gaylarde by dethe lamentable,
The space raynyd fully of ix yere;
Hys herte i-beryd in Rone by the hyghe autere.

JOHANNES.

Next kyng Richarde raynyde hys brothe[r] John,
And afftre sone entred in to Fraunce.
He loste alle Anjoye and Normandye a non,
This londe enterdytyd by mys governaunce,
And as hit ys put in remembrance,
xviij yere kynge of this regyon,
And lythe at Worcester dede of pyson.

HENRICUS TERCIUS.

Henry the iij his sone of ix yere
At Gloucester was crownyde as I fynde;
Longe warre he badde with hys baronage
Gretely delytede in almys dede.
lvj yere raygnyd he in dede,
Beryde at Westmynstre by recorde of wrytynge
Day of Syut Edwarde Marter mayde and kynge.

EDWARDUS PRIMUS.

The fryste Edwarde with the shankys longe
Was aftyr crownyde, that was soo goode a knyght,
Wanne Scotlonde mawgre the Scottys stronge,
And alle Walys in the dyspyte of ther myghte,
Durynge his lyffe mentaynyd trought and ryght.
xxxv yere he was here kynge
And lythe at Westmynester, thys noo lesynge.

EDWARDUS SECUNDUS.

Edwarde his sone, callyd Carnarvan,
Succedynge aftyr to make hys allyaunce,
As the Cronykylle welle rehersse canne,
Wedd the doughter of the Kyng of Fraunce;
On Thomas of Lancaster he toke venjaunce.
xix yere he hylde his regallye,
Beryd at Glowcester, as bokys specyfye.

EDWARDUS TERCIUS.

The iij Edwarde, borne at Wyndesore,
Whiche in knyghthode hadde soo grete a pryce,
Enherytyer of Fraunce withouten more,
Bare in his armys quartle the floure delyce,
And gate Calys by his prudent devyce.
Regnyd in Englonde lij yere,
And lythe at Westmynyster as sayþe þe cronaculere.

RICHARDUS SECUNDUS.

The sone of Prynce Edwarde, Kyng Richard þe Secunde,
In whoes tyme was pes and grete plente,
Weddyd Queen Anne as hit ys i-founde,
Isabelle aftre of Fraunce he lystede to see.
xxij yere he ragnyde here, parde;
At Langle byryde fryste, soo stode the cas,
Aftyr to Wymynster his body caryd was.

HENRICUS QUARTUS.

Henry the iiij next crownyd in certayne
A famos knyght and of grete semblesse;
From his exsyle whenne he come home a-gayne
Travaylede aftyr with werre and grete sekenys.
xiiij yere he raygnyde in sothenysse,
And lythe at Cauntreburye, in that hooly place,
God of hys marcy doo of hys soule grace.

HENRICUS QUINTUS.

The v Henry, of knyghthoode lode starre,
Wysse ande manly playnly to termyne,
Ryght fortunate provyde in pes and yn warre,
Gretely experte and marcyalle dyssepleyne,
Spousyde the doughter of Fraunce, Katerynne,
Raynyd x yere, who lyste to have rewarde,
Lythe at Westmynyster, not far fro Syut Edwarde.

Henricus Sextus.

The vj Henry, brought forthe in alle vertu,
By juste tytylle borne by heretaunce,
A forne provyde by grace of Cryste Jesu,
To were ij crownys in Englonde and in Fraunce,
To whom God bathe gevyn soverayne suffycyaunce,
A vertusse lyffe, and chosyn for hys knyght.
Long he hathe rejoysed bothe by day and nyght.

Edwardus Quartus.[a]

[a] There is no stanza added to this title in our MS.; but another copy of
the poem in the Harleian MS. 2251, f. 2 b., ends as follows:—

> " Comforth al thristy, and drynke with gladnes,
> Rejoyse with myrth, though ye have nat to spende.
> The tyme is come to avoyden your distres.
> Edward the Fourth the old wronges to amend
> Is wele disposed in wille, and to defend
> His lond and peple in dede with kynne and myght.
> Goode lyf and longe I pray to God hym send,
> And that Seynt George be with hym in his ryght ! "

CHRONICLE

OF

WILLIAM GREGORY SKINNER.

GREGORY'S CHRONICLE.

Here folowythe the namys of the Baylyes and Sheryfys* of Lon- don in the cytte of Kynge Richarde the Fryste aftyr the Conqueste of Englonde that was crownyde the thyrde daye of Septembre the yere of owre Lorde M¹ c iiij˟˟ and ix. Ande that yere be ganne the ordyr of Sent Tonyes of Prews, the yere of oure Lorde *ut supra* M¹ c iiij˟˟ x. The namys of the Baylyes and Sherevys:—

Henricus Cornyll Rychardus Ryvers	Anno primo.
Johannes Harlyon Rogerus Duke	Anno secundo.
Wyllelmus Haveryll Johannes Boqueynte	Anno tercio.

And that yere Kyng Richarde made a grette ffeste ande a solempne at Londyn, whithe grete justys and turnementys whythe alle the chevalrye of Englonde and of othir londys. Also that yere he wente ovyr see yn to the Hooly Londe, and he toke the grete cytte of Aerys and slowe many Sarezenys. Ande that yere the Byschoppe of Covyntre put owte the Pryer of monkys, and put ther on secular chanons.

Nycholaus Dukette Petrus Newlynne	Anno quarto.
Rogerus Duke Richardus fiz Aldyne	Anno quinto.
Wyllelmus fiz Isabell Wyllelmus Arnulphi	Anno sexto.

* It is right to state that the list of City Officers in this Chronicle is not altogether trustworthy; but instead of correcting individual inaccuracies in footnotes we reserve our remarks on this subject for an Appendix.

Ande that yere Kynge Richarde come home warde yn to Englonde fro the Hooly Londe ande was take prysener by the Duke of Ostriche & ladde to the Emperoure and raunsomyde.   Ande his raunsum drewe to so moche that every chyrche yn Englonde gave every othyr chalys.   Ande monkys ande othyr howsys of relygyon solde hyr bokys to paye hys raunsome.

Robertus Besaunte   } Anno septimo.
Jokelle le Josowe

Gerardus Antyoche   } Anno octavo.
Robertus Duraunte

In that yere, the yere of oure Lorde M^l c iiij^{xx} xviij be ganne the Ordyr of the Trenyte.   Ande the same yere was Wylliam with the Longe Berde hangyde ande drawe for erresy.   And that same yere, aftyr þe Puryfycacyon of oure Lady, the kynge toke the castelle of Notyngham and descretyde John hyse brothyr.   Ande that yere Kynge Rycharde was crownyde at ȝenne at Wynchester.

Rogerus Blountte   } Anno nono.
Nycholaus Dukette

Ande that yere Kynge Rycharde wente yuto Normandye ande gaffe batylle unto the Kynge of Fraunce.

Constantinus Arnulphi } Anno decimo.
Robertus le Bele

Ande in that yere the kynge come homewarde, ande at the Castelle Gaylerde in Normandy he was schottyn thorowe the hedde whythe a quarelle ande loste ther hys lyffe.   But yet or he dyde he wan the castelle.   And his body ys beryd at Pount Ebraunt,[a] in Normandy, by hys fadyr.   The obyte of the same Kynge Rycharde ys the syxtye [b] daye of Aprylle, the yere of oure Lorde M^l c iiij^{xx} & xix.

---

[a] Fontevraud.   [b] So in MS., meaning the 6th.

Here be ganne fryste the Mayrys of Londyn.

The namys of Marys and Sherevys of the cytte of Londonne in
the tyme of Kynge John, the yere of oure Lorde M¹ c iiij** & xix,
crownyde at Westemynyster.

Arnulfus fiz Arnulphi } Anno primo.
Rychardus fiz Barthi

Ande that yere Kyng John loste alle Normandye ande Angoye.

Robetus Deserte   } Anno secundo.
Jacobus fiz Barthyn

Wyllelmus fiz Alysic } Anno tercio.
Symon de Aldermanburye

Ande that same yere, by concyderacyon of worthy men of the
same cytte of Londone, ther were chosyn xxxv, ande sworne to
up holde and mentayne the cytte whythe the Mayre and Baylys.

Norman Blunden   } Anno quarto.
John Ely

And that yere were grete tempestys of wedyr ande raynys,
thoundyr and lyghtenynge, and hayle stonys the grettenys of
eggys fylle downe a monge the rayne, where of treys and vynys,
cornys, ande alle maner of frute were gretely dystryde.   Al so there
were sene fowlys ande bryddys fleynge in the ayre, berynge fyre
on ther mouthys that brente many howsys ; thys was the yere of
oure Lorde M¹ cc & ij.   Ande the same yere Englonde was
enterdytyd, and other yerys be forne ande aftyr, vilj yere durynge,
for the kyngys trespas.

Walterus Browne   } Anno v°.
Wyllelmus Chambyrlayne

Thomas Havyrylle   } Anno sexto.
Hamonde Bronde

And that yere of oure Lorde M¹ cc iiij be gan the ordyr of
Fryer Prechourys; and that yere was a fulle stronge wynter ande
sharpe, and that enduryd fro Newe yere ys day tylle the Anunu-
cyacyon of oure Lady nexte sewynge.   Ande that yere were the

plays holdyn and motyde at the Towre of London.   Ande that yere were sene two fulle monys in the fyrmament.

John Walhame	} Anno vij°.
Rycardus Wynton	

And that yere was Harry Oysyll hangyd.

Johannes Holylonde	} Anno viij°
Edmundus fiz Gerardi	
Serle, Mercer	} Anno ix°.
Henricus de Sancto Albano	
Rogerus Wynchester	} Anno x°.
Edmundus Hardell	

Ande that yere be ganne a generalle entyrdith thorowe alle Eng-londe.   Here was borne Harry, the sone of Kyng John.

And here beganne the fryste Mayre of London, etc.

Henricus filius	Petrus Bukke
Alwynne, Maior	Thomas fiz Nele
London' primus	Anno xj°.

Ande that yere was Syut Maryes Overay be gunne.

Petrus Josowe	} Anno xij°.
Willelmus Blunte	

Nota bene.—Harry Alwyn was Mayre stylle v yere sewynge.

Ande in thys yere was thys londe reconsylyd a yenne.   And the same yere was London Brygge be gunne of stone oon arche.

Adam Whytteby
Stephin Grace.

Ande the nexte yere aftyr by one Serle Mercer, and Wylliam Alduan the moste parte the yere of oure Lorde M¹ cc x.   And that yere a man of Ambigensis was brent.   And that yere was Castylle Baynard destryde.

Henricus filius Alwyny,	{ Joscus filius Pers	} Anno xiij°.
Mayre of London	John Gerlando	

Ande the same yere was a grete devysyon in þis londe by twyne John.
the kynge ande his lordys. And Lowes the kyngys sone of Fraunce A.D. 1211-16
was wagyd with many Fraynysche men, and they dyd moche harme
in thys londe. And Kyng John fledde to Berandowne. Alle so
the towne of Sowtheworke and London Brygge and a grete party
of London was brente uppon the day of Syn Lenarde the Translacyon, &c.

The same Harry Mayre of London.

Rafe Holylonde Constantine Joswe	Anno xiiij°.

And that yere dyde Harry fiz Alwyn, the firste Mayre of London.

Rogerus fiz Alcyne, Mayre of London	Martyn fiz Alesye Petrus Batte	A° xv.
Serle, Mercer. Mayre of London	Salman Basynge Hugo Basynge	Anno xvj°
Willelmus Ardelle, Mayre of London	John Travers Androwe Newland	A° xvij°.

Ande this yere uppon the vygylle of the Puryfycacyon of oure
Lady the kyng passyd ovyr the see into Pycardy. Also the same
yere, the x day of May, the baronys entryd in to London, and that[a]
was on a Sonday. And thenne be ganne the warre that was i-callyd
Barownys warre. And thenne was the Mayre putt downe by the
Baronys, and made Serle Mercer Mayre viij dayes. And thys
warre duryd alle the yere of Johnne Travers and Androwe New-
lond with ynne wrytynne. Ande the same yere nexte be sayde by
fore the yere of our Lorde M¹ CC xiiij be ganne the ordyr of Freer
Menourys. And the xvij yere of the regyne of the kyng, the sayde
Kyng John[b] dyde, and ys berryd at Worsester.

Jamys Alderman, Mayre fro
the Trynyte Feste forthe, &c.

---

[a] *thas* MS.   [b] *John* repeated in MS.

The namys of Mayrys and Sheryvys in the tyme of Kyng Harry the thyrde, the yere of oure Lorde M̷ cc and xv that was crownyd at Gloucester, and ix yere of age.

| Jamys Aldyrman a parte
Salamon Basyng a parte | } | Mayrys of London. |
| Ricardus Sumpturer
Wyllelmus Blome Travers | } | Anno primo. |

Ande that same yere was Walys enterdyte and Loudwyke the kyngys sone of Fraunce went home a yenne in to Fraunce with hys mayne and he hadde of the kynge a M̷ marke of sylver.

| Serle, Mercer,
Mayre of London
two yere | { Thomas Bukrelle
Raffe Eylonde | } Anno ij°. |
| | John Vyele
John Spycer | } Anno iij°. |

Ande that yere the kyng hadde of every plowe londe ijs. Also that same yere Syn Thomas of Canterbury was translatyde. And the same yere Kyng Harry was crownyd at Westmyster.

| Serle, Mayre of
London, Mercer | { Rycardus Wynbyldene
John Vyele | } Anno iiij°. |
| | Ricardus Renger
John le Joswe | } Anno v°. |

Custace Menke[a] the cros of Broumholme, and that yere the plees of the crowne were motyde at the Towre of London. Ande the same yere was þe Castelle of Bedforde besegyd, and that duryd fro the Assencyon of owre Lorde to the Assumpcyon of oure Lady nexte aftyr; and that day by grete crafte and stronge sawte hit was i-wonne and dystryde and nevyr bylde more, be cause hyt was rebylle a yenste the kynge. Al so that yere the ordyr of the Freer Carmys be ganne, the yere of oure Lorde M̷ cc and xx. Al soo the same yere a Syn Lukys eve or day, ther blewe a grete

---

[a] So in MS. The chronicler doubtless intended to have mentioned the bringing into England of the Cross of Bromholm, of which Matthew Paris gives an account in the year 1223. To that year of our Lord it is also assigned in the text of the Chronicle of London, printed by Nicolas, which a good deal resembles our present Chronicle; but still under the same mayor and sheriffs, and in the 5th year of Henry III.

wynde owt of the northe est, and that wynde caste downe many Hen. III.
A.D. 1220-8.
howsys, styplys, turretys, and chyrchys, and treys.   Ande the same
tyme were sene in the ayre fyre dragons and wyckyd spyrytys a
grete nombre.

| Serle, Mercer, Mayre of the cytte of London | Ricardus Ronger Thomas Lamberte | Anno vj°. |

And that same yere was grete persecusion resyd by one that was
callyd Water Bokerell, soo that Constantyne Arnulphus was hongyd
on the morowe aftyr the Assumpcyon of oure Lady.

| Ricardus Ronger, Mayre of London | Wylliam Jowner Thomas Lamberte | A° vij°. |

Ande that yere the kyng had purposyd hym to have do kaste
downe the wallys of London.   Ande the same yere the ordyr of
Fryer Menours came fryste in to Inglonde, and a man * that faynyd
hym selfe Cryste at Oxynforde, he was cursyde at Aldermanbery at
London the yere of oure Lorde M¹ cc xxij.

| Ricardus Ronger, Mayre of London | John Travers Andrew Bokerell | Anno viij° |
| | Rogerus Duke Martyn fiz Wylliam | Anno ix°. |

Ande that yere the plees of the crowne were holdynne at the
Towre of London, and John Herlyon faylyd of his lawe for the
dethe of Lamberte of le Legys, etc.

| Rycardus Ronger, Mayre of London | Rogerus Duke Martyn Wylliam | Anno x°. |
| Rogerus Duke, Mayre of London | Stephanus Bukler Henricus Colleham | Anno xj°. |

Ande the same yere the Sheryvs of London ande of Myddelsex
late to ferme the Shervys ᵇ of London for iij c pounde ᶜ by yere, and
that was grauntyd the xviij day of Feverer the yere a fore sayde.
Ande þe same yere hit was grauntyd by the kynge and hys consayle,
that alle the werys that stode in Temys sholde be dystroyed and

---

* Here in the margin of the MS. is written " Nota bene," in another hand.
ᵇ Meaning the Sheriffwick.　　　　　ᶜ Fabyan says 400l.

nevyr more aftyr stonde in Temys. Alle so the same yere the kyng grauntyd to the cytsynnys of London that they shulde[a] in alle the kyngys londe, as welle be yende the see as on thys syde the see; yf any man toke any of[b] the Shervys of London shulde take stresse of hem of the same countres were they myght be founde in any place of London. Alle so the xvj day of Auguste the same yere was i-grauntyd to the cytsyns of London wareyne.

Rogerus Duke, Mayre of London	{ Stephyn Bukrelle { Henrycus Cobham	} Anno xij°.

Al so that yere, the vij day of Junij, the lyberteys and the franches of London were radyfyde. Alle so the kyng grauntyd that every Sheryffe sholde have two clerkys and two othyr servauntys and no moo for that offyces. Alle so that yere was ordaynyd þat the towne sholde have a comyn sele, and tha shulde be yn kepynge of two aldermen and two comeners of the same cytte; and that hit shulde not be wernyd nor denyde to poore men, nothyr to comyners of the sayde cytte whenne they had nede ther too yf hyt be resonabylle axyde, and that nought be take for the sayde sele.

Roger Duke, Mayre of London	{ Walterus Wyncester { Roberte fiz John	} Anno xiij°.
Roger Duke, Mayre	{ Ricardus fiz William { John Wodeborne	} Anno xiiij°.

Ande the same yere was i-geve a decre by the Mayre and Aldermen of London, with the counselle and comynne assent of alle the cytte, and sworne on the Evengely or Gospelle, that fro thens forwarde they shulde nevyr suffer Shrevys to abyde in here offyce but oone yere aftyr that day.

Roger Duke, Mayre	{ Mychell de Sancta Elena { Watkyn Denfylde	} Anno xv°.

Ande that same yere the sayde Roger was putt downe of hys offysse. And that same yere was dyscorde by twyne the kynge and Hew de Burgo. And that same Hew was takyn at Brent-

---

[a] So in MS. The words " pass toll free " should be supplied.

[b] So in MS. The writer should have said, " of their goods."

woode and brought unto the Towre of London and put in
preson.

| Andreas Bokerclle,
Mayre of London | { Henricus Eldymenton
{ Gerardus Batte | } A° xvj°. |

Ande that yere was grete harme done in London of fire by
Dame Johne Lamberte.

| The same Androwe,
Mayre of London | { Symond Marys
{ Rogerus Blounte | } Anno xvij° |

And that yere was consecrate Saynt Edmonde of Pounteney,
Archebyschoppe of Canterbury, and that revokyd the fore sayde
Hewe of Burge.

| The same Androwe,
Maire iiij yere
sewynge | | Anno xviij°

Anno xix° |

Ande that yere was Qwene   And here was
the Statute Merton made.

| Ricardus Roger,
Mayre of London | Henricus Cobham
Jordan Covyntre
John Tesalano
Gerad Cordawner | Anno xx°.

Anno xxj". |
| Wyllelmus Joynor,
Mayre of London | John Wylhale
John Goundris
Remoud Bughey
Raffe Asshewy | Anno xxij°.

Anno xxiij°. |

Ande that yere was borne Sir Edwarde Kynge Harrys firste sone.
And that same yere was Poulys chyrche in Londyn i-halowyde.

| Gerardo Batte,
Mayre of London | John Gysors
Mychell Cony | Anno xxiiij° |
| Remonde Bounghey,
Mayre of London | John Vyalle
Thomas Durysyne | A° xxv° |

Ande that yere dyde Saynt Roger, Byshoppe of London. And
Wylliam Marche was drawe and hanggyd at Tyburne.

The same Remonde,	John fiz John	Anno xxvj°.
Marye[a] of London	Raffe Asshewy	

And that yere the kyng wente unto Burdowes.

Raffe Asshewy,	Hew Blounte	A° xxvij°.
Mayre of London	Adam Basynge	

And that yere the kyng com home from Bordowys a yenne. And that yere the plees of the Crowne were holdyn at the Towre of London. Ande Wylliam of Yorke, Rychard Paslewe, Herry Bas, and Geron of Gayton, were justysys.

Mychell Tony,	Raffe Spycer	Anno xxviij°.
Mayre of London	Nicholaus Batte	

Ande the same yere Michell Tony and Nicholaus Batte were convycte in a perjury be fore the kynge on the Sacramentys in presens be fore alle the Aldyrmen, werefore the same Michell was put downe of his mayrelte and the sayde Nicholas of his sheryvehode.

	Robertus Cornill	Anno xxix°.
John Gysors,	Adam Benle	
Mayre of London	Symon fiz Marie	Anno xxx°.
	Laurence Frowyke	

Ande that yere was translatyd Saynt Edmounde of Pounteney, and a newme[b] of blode was put in Saynt Thomas of Acris tylle the feste of Saynt Edmounde next sewynge. Ande that day the kyng whithe a ryalle processyon hit was brought to Westmyster.

Perys Alein,	John Vyale	Anno xxxj°.
Mayre of London	Nicholaus Batte	
Mychell Tony,	Nicholaus Jocy	Anno xxxij°.
Mayre of London	Galfrydus Wynton	

---

[a] So in MS.

[b] So in MS. The word is unintelligible, and a blank has been left for it in the old English Chronicle in MS. Cott. Vitellius A. XVI., which at this period follows the text of our Chronicle pretty closely. The Chronicle in Julius B. 1. mentions the matter as follows:—" This yere was Seint Edmond of Pountney translatid, et uen' (renarum?) sanguis depositus fuit in hospicio Sancti Thomæ apud Conductum usque ad festum Sancti Edwardi; quo die dominus Rex cum honorabili processione venerabiliter apud Westmonasterium deposuit."

Roger fiz Roger, Mayre of London	Raffe Hardelle John Telasano	Anno xxxiij°. Hen. III. A.D. 1248-58.
John Norman Maire of London	Humfray Basse William fiz Ricum	A° xxxiiij°

Ande that same yere on Saynt Symon and Judys day there was a grete wynde, and dyd moche harme in many placys of Englonde.

Adam Basynge, Mayre of London Laurens Frowyke, Mayre of London	Nicholaus Bate, sheryffe, Anno xxxv°	

Ande that yere, the yere of oure Lorde M¹ cc. l., be gan the ordyr of Frer Austynys.

John Telasano, Maire of London	William Durham Thomas Winborne	A. xxxvj°.
Nicholaus Batte, Maire of London	John Northamton Nicholaus Pykarde	A° xxxvij°.

Ande that yere the kynge grauntyde the viij day of Juni that the shrevys of London sbulde yerely be a lowyde in the Chekyr by ther offyce of ther sherevchod vij li. And alle so whanne the mayre ys chosyn that he shalle be presentyd to the Baronys of the Chekyr, and there to take his othe.

Richardus Hardylle, Mayre of London v yere togedyr	Raffe Aswy Robertus Bylton	A° xxxviij°
	Stephynne Doo Henricus Walmonde	A° xxxix°
	Mychell Bokerell John Lymnour	A° xl°.
	Ricardus Ewylle William Aswy	Anno xlj°
	Thomas fiz Ricardus Robert Catylleyne	A° xlij°.
Johannes Gysours, Maire of London	Johannes Adriam Robertus Cornille	Anno xliij°.

Ande that same yere, the yere of oure Lorde M^l cc and viij,[a] there fylle a Jwe into a gonge [b] att Tewkysbury uppon a Satyr day, and he wolde not be drawe up owt of the gonge for reverens of hys Sabat day. And Syr Rychardus of Clare, Erle of Gloucester, hirde there of and wolde not suffer hym to be drawe uppe on the Sonday for reverens of the hyghe holydaye, and so he dyde in the gonge. And that yere a quarter of whete was worthe xxiiij s. of sterlyngys.

| Wyllyam fiz Ricum, Mayre of London ij yere | Adam Brownenge Henricus Covyntre John Northamton Rychardus Pykarde | A° xliiij°. Anno xlv°. |
| Thomas fiz Thomas, Mayre of London | Robertus Tayler Richardus Walbroke | A° xlvj° |

Ande that same yere be ganne the Baronys warre ayenne, and durynge that werre there were many worthy lordys slayne. And moche myschyffe and sorowe was that tyme in thys londe.

| The same Thomas Mayre stylle | Robertus Mounpelers Obertus Sowtheworke | A° xlvij°. |

Ande the same yere was Northamton towne takyn, ande many of the men of the towne that were there yn were slayne, for they badde ordaynyd wylde fyre to have brente the citte of London.

| The same Thomas Mayre | Gregorye Rokisle Thomas Forthe | Anno xlviij°. |

And that yere was the batylle of Lewys, and then was the kynge and his sone takynne.

| The same Thomas Maire of London | Edwardus Blunte Petrus Armiger | A° xlix°. |

Ande the same yere was the batelle of Evysham.

| William fiz Ric, Mayre of London | John Lynde John Walrent | Anno l° |

And the same yere be ganne the Emperowre of Tarteryn for to

---

[a] So in MS., instead of 1258.   [b] A jakes.

reygne, that was callyd the Grete Cane. The yere of oure Lorde Mᶦ cc lxvij.

| Alein Sowthe, Custos of þe citte of London ij yere to gedyr | John Adrian
Lucas Batyngcort | Anno lj°. |
| | Walterus Hervy
WyllyamDuryseyne | Anno lij°. |

Ande the same yere Octobon, the Legate, hylde a conselle at Syn Poulys at London.

| Henricus fiz Thomas, Mayre of London | Thomas Basynge
Robert Corinhylle | liij°. |

Ande the same yere the **xxvj** day of Marche was ordeynyd by the kynge and his consell that noo cyttezen of London shulde goo owte of the cytte to mete with noo maner of vytayle comynge unto the cytte, nothyr by londe nothyr by water, unto the tyme that they come to the cytte, on payne of presonnement. The yere of oure Lorde Mᶦ cc lxix.

John Adryan, Mayre of London	Walterus Plotte John Taylour	A° liiij°,
	Gregory Rokysle Henricus Waleys	A° lv°.
Syr Watyr Hervy, knyght, Mayre of London	John Bedell Richardus Parys	A° lvj°.

Ande that same yere dyde Kyng Harry the iij, and was beryd at Westemyster.

Deus misereatur.

The namys of mayrys and sherevys yn the tyme of Kyng Edwarde the sone of Kyng Harry. The yere of owre Lorde Mᶦ cc lxxij.

| Syr Water Hervy, Mayre of London | John Horne
Water Potter | Anno primo. |

Ande that yere Lewynne, the Prynce of Walys, he rebellyd a gayne Kynge Edwardo. And the kynge scomfytyd hym in the batayle and toke hym.   And he gave hym grace, and he swore that he shulde nevyr rebelle a yenste the kynge more aftyr that tyme.

| Henricus Waleys, | Nicholaus Wynchester | A° ij°. |
| Mayre of London | Henricus Covyntre | |

Ande that yere the kyng grauntyd unto the Mayre of London for to chastys bakers and myllers whenne they trespasse.   That ys whenne that bakers make there brede aftyr the whyte that ys ordaynyd by the mayre and a sysyd, and the myllers for stelyng of corne. And that yere Lewys Prynce of Walys rebellyd a yenne, and was take and scomfyte.   And yet the kynge gave hym grace the ij tyme.

	Lucas Ratyncourte	A° iij°.
	Henricus Frowyke	
	John Horne	Anno iiij°
Gregory Rokeley,	Raffe Blount	
Mayre of London	Robert Aras	Anno v°
	Raffe Feverrer	
	John Adryan	A° vj°.
	Water Englysche	

Ande that yere the corte was remevyd from Westmyster unto Schrovysbury fro the feste of Saynt Mychelle un to Synt Hyllarys daye nexte folowynge, and then remevid a yenne to Westemyster. And that yere was the batelle of Evysham the xiiij day of Auguste, the yere of our Lorde M¹ cc lxxviij.[a]

| Gregory Rokysley, | Robertus Basyng | A° vij°. |
| Mayre of London | William Maserer | |

Ande that yere the Kyng of Scotlond com unto þe Parlment of Kyng Edwarde holdyn at Westemyster.   And at the feste of Saynt Martyn the same yere there were Jwys a reste for treson, and othir certayne goldesmythys.   And uppon the Monday next aftyr the Epiphanye iij Crysten men, Englysche, and cc and iiij schore Jewys, were drawe and hangyd.   And that yere was the chyrche of Frere Prechourys in London be gonne.

[a] So in MS., though the battle of Evesham has already been noticed under its true date in the 49th year of Henry III., A.D. 1265.

			Edw. I. A.D. 1280-8.
Gregory Rokysle, Mayre of London	Thomas Boxe Raffe More	A° viij°.	
	William Farindon Nicholaus Wynchester	A° ix°.	
Henricus Waleys, Mayre of London	William Mascrer Ricardus Chikwelle	A° x°.	

Ande in that yere the kyng segyd the towne and castelle of Berwyke. And in short tyme he wanne hyt bothe the towne and the castelle with a sawte. And that tyme were slayne xxv M^l Scottys and viij c.

Harry Waleys, Mayre of London	Raffe Blounte Aukyn Betnell	A° xj°.

Ande that yere was borne Edwarde of Carnarvyan. Ande that yere Prynce Lewyn of Walis rebellyd a yenne þe iij tyme a yenste the kynge, and the kyng toke hym ande lette smyte of hys hedde the ix daye of Feverer, the yere of oure Lorde a M^l cc iiij schore and iij.

Harry Waleys, Mayre of London	Jordon Goodeschepe Martyn Box	Anno xij°.

And that yere was the grete condytte in Chepe made.

Gregory Rokysle, Mayre of London, unto the feste of Petyr and Poule; and thenne was he put downe and Raffe of Sandewyche made Mayre of London tylle the Monday aftyr the Puryfycacyon of owre Lady nexte aftyr, ande John Bryton chose Mayre of London to the feste of Sayntt Margarete the nexte yere folowyng. Stephynne Cornehylle and Roberte Bokysby Sherevys that yere folowyng. Anno xiij°

	Anno xiiij°
Raffe Sandewyche, Mayre of London	Anno xv°
	Anno xvj°.

Wylliam Byton
John de Cantysbury   } A° xvij°.

Fullo de Sancto
    Edmundo   } A° xviij°.
Salaman Lancastre

Ande in thys yere alle the Jewys that dwellyd yn Englond were exilyd and drevyn owte of the londe. Ande for to have that done the Comyns of the Reme grauntyd to the kynge the xv parte of hyr mevabylle godys.

Thomas Romayne
Wylliam de Lyre   } Anno xix°.

Raffe Blounte
Hamonde Box   } Anno xx°.

Ande that yere the kyng presonyd Edwarde his sone of Carvarvyan. And aftyr he exilyd hym for dyvers traytours that he mentaynyd a yenste the kyng hys fadyr.

Harry Belle
Elysse Russelle   } Anno xxj°.

Ande the same yere, the morowe aftyr the feste of Saynt Barnabe, thys Raffe Sondewyche was putt downe. And John Bryton was made Wardyn of the citte of London.

John Brytton, | Robert Rokysle
  Mayre of London | Martyn Aumbre   } A° xxij°.
    or Wardon | Harry Box
                    | Ric. Glowcester   } A° xxiij°.

Ande that same yere, the yere of oure Lorde M¹ cc lxxx & xvij, Kyng Edwarde toke the Castelle of Edyngborow, in Schotlonde. And in that castelle he foundo the regaylle of Schot londe, that ys to wytte, the kyngys see, hys oronne of golde, and his septour, the which regaylle the kyng offerde up to Saynt Edwarde schreyne at Westmyster, the xvij day of June, &c.

John Bryton, | Thomas Sowthefolke
  Mayre of London | Adam de Fullam   } A° xxv°.

	John Stroteforde	A° xxvj°.	Edw. I. A.D. 1297- 1307.
	Wylliam Strateforde		
Henricus Waleys, Mayre of London	Ric. Bosham Thomas Tely	A° xxvij°.	
Eleys Russelle, Mayre of London	John Armenters Herry Fyngrey	A° xxviij°.	
	Lucas Haveryng Ric. Chaunpyn	A° xxix°.	
John Blounte, Mayre of London	Robert Caller Petrus Besynhe	A° xxx°.	
	Hugo Pentre Symon Parys	A° xxxj°.	
John Blounte, Mayre a yenne.	William Combermartyn John Burforde	A° xxxij°.	
John Blounte, . Mayre of London	Rogerus Parysche John Lincolne	A° xxxiij°.	

Ande that yere Wylliam Waleis, that was sworne lige man to the Kynge of Inglond, he made hym selfe Kynge of Schottys, and rebellis a yenste the Kyng of Inglond. And he was take and brought unto the Towre of London, and there he was jugyd that he schulde he [a] trawe, hangyd, and quartryd and hys bowyllis i-brente before hym, &c.

The same John Blounte, Mayre	Galfridus Conductu Symon Bolete	A° xxxiiij°.
The same John Blounte, Mayre	Wylliam Cosyn Raynolde Thundrylle	Anno xxxv°.

Ande the same yere deyde Kyng Edwarde þe friste, and ys beryd at Westemyster the vij day of Juylle, that ys the yere of oure Lorde M¹ ccc vij.

The namys of Mayrys and of Sherevys of the cytte of London in the tyme of Kyng Edwarde of Carnarvyan, that was crownyd the kalendys of Marche the yere of oure Lorde a fore sayde.

[a] So in MS.

| John Blount, Mayre of London | Nicholaus Pycok Nygellus Drewry | A° primo. |

And that same yere the kyng weddyd the kyngys doughter of Fraunce, dame Isabelle Phylyppe. And the same yere profecyde the Chanon of Brydlyngton.

| Nicholaus Faryndon, Mayre of London | William Basynge John Butteler | Anno ij°. |
| Thomas Romayne, Mayre of London | Roger Palmer Jamys Edmunde | Anno iij° |

Ande that yere the kyng lette to frem the Sherevys of London and of Myddelle sex for CCCC li of starlyngys by yere. Alle so the same yere of oure Lorde M CCC x the ordyr of Templers were dystroyde thorowe alle Crystyndom in on day, the whiche ordyr be ganne the yere of oure Lorde M¹ iiij schore & xviij. Alle so the same yere be ganne the ordyr of Powlys, that ben callid Crowche Frers.

| Ricardus Bosham, Mayre of London | Symon Creppe Pers Blackeney | Anno iiij°. |
| John Gysors, Mayre of London | Symon Merwoode Ricardus Wylforde | Anno v° |

Ande that yere was borne Kynge Edwarde the iij at Wyndsore, the whiche was callyd Kyng Edwarde of Wyndesore.

| John Kysors, . Mayre of London | Johm Lambin Adam Litkyn | Anno vj°. |
| Nicholaus Faryndon, Mayre of London | Adam Burton Hugo Gayton | A° vij° |

Ande that yere, the yere of our Lorde M¹ ccc xiiij, Kyng Edwarde went to Schotlonde whythe a ryalle power at the feste of the Natyvyte of John the Baptyste. And the Shottys gaffe hym batayle and dyscomfyte hym and slewe many of hys men. Ande the kynge fledde awaye.

| John Kysors, Mayre of London | Stephyn Habyngdon Hamondc Chikewelle | A° viij°. |

And that yere ther was a fole that was callyd John Canne, and he claymyd to be Kyng of Inglonde, sayng that he was the kyngys sone, and, of negligens of his norys, wylle that he was yn hys cradylle ther come a sowe into the howse, and alle to rent hym and hys norys druste nott telle that, and toke a nothyr yong chylde that was a water berrers chylde, in[a] kepte hyt in stede of hyt, and put me in othir mennys kepyng for to norysche, and soo he was dyssayvyd of hys kyngdome; and Edwarde take for kyng that was the water bererrys chylde and namyd hym Edwarde, and to make that knowe he shewyde clothys with bloode of hys hurtys. Alle so he sayde that the maners of Kyng Edwarde acordyd to the maners of his fadyr the water berer. For in as moche he sayde that he usyd erly werkys of kynde, and for suche sayyngys he was jugyd false and was hangyd at Northe hampton. And yet sum men be levyn hys wordys.

| Stephyn Habyngdon, Mayre of London | Hamon Goodeschepe William Redynge | A° ix°. |

Ande that same yere, the yere of owre Lorde M¹ ccc xvj, on Mydde Lent Sonday, the towne and the castelle of Berwyke was loste by the treson of Perys of Spaldyng that was keper of the sayde castelle and towne. And alle soo the sayde yere grete derthe of corne thoroughe alle Inglonde, for a boschelle of wete was worthe v s.

| John Wengrame, Mayre of London | William Causton Ricardus Balaunser | Anno x°. |

Ande that dyrthe duryd of corne and vytayle that for hunger pepyle yetyn houndys, cattys, and horse, for be fore there was grete morayne of bestys of oxyn, kyne, and shippe.[b]

| John Wengame, Meyre of London | John Pryoure William Furneyse | A° xj°. |

And that yere the Schottys dyd moche harm in Inglonde with fyre.

| Nycholaus Farindon, Mayre of London | William Proudham Raynolde at the Condyte | A° xij°. |

[a] So in MS.
[b] In the margin in another hand is written " Nota the hunger in Hynglonde."

John Poyntélle
John Darlynge
} A° xiij°.

Ande in that yere Syr Thomas of Lancaster was be hedyd the
xx day of Aprylle, the yere of oure Lorde M^l ccc xxj.   And that
yere was the rysyng of erlys and baronnys of thys londe, and they
toke Syr Pers of Cavyrston, the kyngys sworne brother, and smote
of his hede.   And sone aftyr the kyng dyd be hedde iiij schore
lordys in a day for the dethe of the sayde Pers, by consello of Syr
Hew Spenser.

Hamond Chickewelle, | Symon Habyngdon
    Mayre of London | John Preston
} A° xiij°.

Nicholaus Farindon, | William Proudeham
    Mayre of London | Raynolde at þe Condite
} Anno xiiij°.

Hamonde Chyckewelle, | Ric. Constantyne
    Mayre of London | Ric. Habeneye
} Anno xv°

Ande the same yere there of oure Lorde M^l ccc xxij the sonne
was turnyd in to the color of bloode, and duryd from the morne
tylle xj att the clocke in the laste day of October.

The same Chyckewelle, | John Grauntham
    Mayre of London | Roger Ely
} A° xvj°.

Nicholaus Farindon, | Adam Salusbury
    Mayre of London | John Oxynforde
} A° xvij°.

Hamond Chickewelle, | Benet Fullam
    for a parte | John Cawston
} Anno xviij.

Rycharde Betayne, | Gybon Mordon
    for a parte | John of Coton
} A° xix°.

Ande that yere the Quene com a yenne yn to Inglonde whythe
Edwarde hir sone by the helpe of the Erle of Henowde.   And
that yere Mayster Watyr Stapylton, Byschoppe of Execeter ande
Tresourer of Inglonde, was be hedyd at the Standerde of Chepe.
Alle so the same yer the kyng was put in to the castelle of
Barkcley.   And that yere by the assent of alle the lordys of thys
reame, spyrytualle and temporalle, and by alle the comyns of the
saydo reame, he resynyd, and Edwarde his sone, of Wyndsorc, was

crounyd at Wcstemyster at the age of xv yere. Ande that same yere Syr Hewe Spenser the eldyr was take, and he was take and drawe and hangyd at[a] quarteryd at Brystowe, and his hede smete of and sett uppe att Wynchester. And the same yere the kyng by conselle of his modyr went into Walys, and many lordys whithe hym, and there he toke Syr Hewe Spenser the yonger in the montaynys, and Mayster Robert Boldete, and moo othyr of hir assent, and they ne wolde nevyr ete mete ne drynke aftyr that day. And at Herforde they were drawe and hangyde and quartyrde and bchedyde, and Sir Hewe Spenser the yongcr al so.

Here folowythe namys of Marys and Shcrevys in the tyme of Kyngc Edwarde the iij, that was crownyd at the feste of the Conversyon of Syn Poule. The yere of oure Lorde M¹ ccc and xxvj at Wynchester, the yere of hys age xv.

Rycardus Beteyne,	Ric. Rotinger	
Mayre of London	Roger Chaunceler	Anno primo.

Ande that yere, the yere of oure Lorde M¹ ccc xxvj°, were sene in the firmament ij monys. And alle so that tyme there were two Popys. And in that yere, the vj day of Marche, the kyng confermyde the lyberteys and the franches of London. Ande he grauntyd that the Mayre of London sbulde be on of þe Justysse of Newgate; alle so he grauntyd that sherevehodys sholde goo to ferme for ccc li. be yere, as hyt was yn olde tyme. Ande alle so the kyng grauntyde that the cytsynnys of London sbulde not be chargyd with no man that flede to holy chyrche, nor they shulde not be constraynyde to goo owte of the cytte of London to noo werre, but yf thaye wylle hem selfe. Also the kynge grauntyde the same tyme that the lyberteys and franches of the cytte shulde nott aftyr that tyme for noo cause [be][b] takyn away in to the kyngys honde. Al so that same tyme Southeworde[c] was [granted] to the Sherevys of London for to have to ferme.

---

[a] So in MS. [b] Omitted in MS.
[c] Southwark.

Hamonde Chyckewelle, | Harry Darcy
Mayre of London | John Hadden   } A° ij°.

Ande that same yere, the xxj day of September, Kyng Edwarde
the Secunde was slayn yn the castelle of Barkely by treson of Syr
Roger Mortymer.   And that yere the kyng helde a Parlyment at
Notyngham.   And in the fyrste yere of Kynge Edwarde the iij,
aftyr the feste of the Trynyte, the Schottys come in to Inglonde in
to the parke of Stanhope.   And ther they were vyseryde for
knowynge, and storyd them with vytayle thorowe the treson of Syr
Roger Mortymer.   And in the secund yere of Kyng Edwarde the
iij Davyd Brus, Kyng of Schottys, weddyd Dame Jone, the
kyngys doughter of Inglonde, by conselle of the sayde Mortymer.
And the kynge was governyd alle to gedyr by the same Mortymer.
And by the counselle of the sayde Mortymer the kynge ma a
chartoure to the Schottys.   And the tenoure of the chartoure ys
unknowe to Englysche men yet.   And that same yere the kyng
weddyd Dame Phylyppe, the kyng ys doughter of Fraunce, the
Erlys doughter of Henowde.

John Grauntham, | Symon Fraunsces | A° iij°.
Mayre of London | Harry Thonbyrmartyn |

And that yere the kyng wente into Fraunce to make omage to
the Kynge of Praunce for the Duche of Gyene and for the Counte
of Pountyf.

Symon Swanne, | Ric. Lacer | Anno iiij°.
Mayre of London | Ric. Gysers |

Ande that same yere the fryste be gotyn sonne of Kynge Edwarde
the iij was borne at Wodestoke in the feste of Vite et Modeste.
And that yere Edmond of Woodestoke, Erle of Kent, was be hedyd
at Wynchester.

John Putteney, | Robert Ely | Anno v°
Mayre of London | Thomas Harrewode |

And the same yere Edwarde Baylolle, the sone of John Baylolle,
sum tyme Kyng of Schottys, whythe home many lordys of Inglonde,
went with in to Schott londe.   And at Dounfrymylyn they aryvyd

faste uppe be the Abbey. And there ij M¹ Englysche men scom- fytyd xl M¹ Schottys. And the same Syr Roger Mortymer was hangyd uppon a comyn galowys of thevys of Synt Androwys eve, the yere of oure Lorde M¹ccc & xxx.

| John Putteney,
Mayre of London | John Mokkynge
Androwe Awbrey | Anno vj°. |

Ande that yere the kyng layde sege to the towne and castelle of Berwyke. And on Saynt Martyn ys evyn they come thedyr a grete nombyr of Schottys for to have brokyn the sege. And the kyng and his mayne fought with hem, and slowe viij earlys and M¹ccc knyghtys and squyers of Schottys, and many fotte men; of Englysche men were slayne but a knyghet, and a squyer, and xij fotte men. Ande on Saynt Margaretys day the towne and the castelle was i-yolde to the Kyng of Englonde.

| John Preston,
Mayre of London | Nicholaus Pyke
John Hosbonde | Anno vij° |

In that yere the kyng slowe many Schottys, and wanne the Castelle of Kylburge.

| John Pounteney,
Mayre of London | John Hamonde
Wylliam Haunsarde | Anno viij°. |

Ande that same yere the kyng of Schotlonde came to the Newe Castelle uppon Tynde. And at the feste of Syn John the Baptyste he dide omage unto oure Kyng of Inglonde. And the same yere the Duke of Bretayne dyde omage to the kynge for ᵃ the Counte of Regemounde,ᵇ the yere of our Lorde M¹ccc xxxiij.

| Radulfe Cotymger,
Mayre of London | John Kenton
Water Turke | Anno ix°. |

And that yere was grete dethe of men and morayne of bestys and grete rayne. And that yere a quarter of whete was worthe xj schelyngys.

| The same Radulfe
Maire of London | Water Mordon
Ricardus Upton | Anno x°. |

ᵃ *Omage to the kyng for,* repeated in MS.   ᵇ Richmond.

Edw. III.
A.D. 1335-40.

Ande that yere the kyng went ovyr the Schottys see. And he toke the Erle of Moryf and many othyr of the wylde Schottys, and warryd apon the wylde Schottys and slowe many of them.

| John Pounteney, | William Byrkyllysworthe | A° xj° |
| Mayre of London | John Northehale | |

And that same yere, in the mounthis of Junij and Julij, in dyvers partys of hevyn apperyde the starre comate, id est a blaṣyng sterre. And that yere was grete plenty of vytayle, and a quarter whete was at ij s. at London, and a fat oxe for vj s. viij d., and vj pejonys for a peny; nevyrtheles ther was grete scharsyte of mony that tyme. Al so that yere deyde Syr John of Eltham. Alle so the kyng grauntyd that yere that the ṡargentys of the mayre and sherevys schulde bere by fore them macys of sylveı and ovyr gylte with the kyngys armys in that one ende and the armys of London in that othyr ende.

| Harry Darcy, | Water Nele | Anno xij°. |
| Mayre of London | Nicholaus Grene | |

Ande that yere the kyng made of the Counte of Cornewale a duchye, and gave hyt too Edwarde hys eldyste sone with the Erledome of Weste Chester.

| The same Harry | William Pountefrete | Anno xiij°. |
| Mayre of London | Hew Marberer | |

Ande that yere the kyng and the quene saylyde yn to Brabayne.
Nota partus
Lyoneli.
And in the towne of Andeworpe the queue chyldyd Syr Lyonelle. And that yere the kyng made fryste clayme unto the crowne of Fraunce yn Braban.

| Androw Awbry, | William Thorney | A° xiiij°. |
| Mayre of London | Roger Forsham | |

Ande that yere the kyng helde a Parlement at Weste myster. And he askyd to be gyune hys warrys the v parte of the mevabylle goodys of Inglonde, and the costome of the wollys, and ix sheffe of every corne, and hyt was grauntyd hym. And that yere þᵉ kyng changyd hys armys. And that same yere the kynge made the coyne of the nobylle, halfe nobylle, and farthynge.

| The same Androwe, Mayre of London | Adam Lucas Bartholow Mareys | Anno xv⁰. | Edw. III. A.D. 1340-6. |

Ande that yere the kyng fought in the Swyn whythe Fraynysche men at Scluse. And there were slayne of Fraynysche men **xxx** thoughesaund. And they toke **ccc** and **x** grete shippys. And the same yere the kynge be ganne the seege [of]* Turney, and the towne of Saynte Amandys was destroyde. And that yere the kynge come home a yenne in to Inglonde a Synt Androwe ys evyn, and come by the nyght in to the Towre of London. And he toke many lordys and put hem in preson. And al so the same **xv** yere was the fyrste yere of his rayne of the kyngdome of Praunce, þe yere of oure Lorde M¹ ccc and **xl**.

| John Oxynforde, a parte of the yere Symon Fraunches, a parte of þe yere, Mayres of London | Ricardus Berkyng John Rokysle | Anno xvj⁰. |

| Symon Fraunches, Mayre of London | John Lowkyn Ricardus Kyllingbury | Anno xvij⁰. |

Ande that same yere was the grete turnement att Dunstapille of alle the chyvalry of Inglonde ande of gentellys. Alle so that same yere there was a grete erthe quake.

| John Hamonde, Mayre of London | John Sywarde John Aylsham | Anno xviij⁰. |

Ande that yere the kyng at a Parlement at Westemyster he made Edwarde hys yldyste sone Prynce of Walys.

| The same John Hamonde, Mayre of London | Geffray Wychyngham Thomas Leggy | Anno xix⁰ |

Ande that yere the kyng be ganne the Rounde Tabylle at the castelle of Wyndesore, that ys for to saye, þe ordyr of the Knyghtys of the Gartyr.

| Ricardus Lacer, Mayre of London | Edmounde Hemnale John Glouceter | A⁰ xx⁰. |

* Omitted in MS.

Edw. IH.
A.D. 1346-8.
And that yere the kyng saylyd to Bretayne and in too Gyene, and come a yenne the same yere.

Geffrey Wichyngham, ⎰ John Coydon   ⎱ A xxj°.
Mayre of London   ⎰ Wylliam Clopton ⎱

And the same yere the kyng wentte unto Normandye. And the xij day of Juylle the kyng faught whythe the Normandys at the Brygge of Cadona, and there was take the Erle of Eue, the Lorde of Tankyrvyle, and C. knyghtys, and men of arms vij C., and many of the comyns of Normandy were slayne. The yere of grace M^l CCC & xlvj. And the same yere there went owte a maundement fro the Emperowe of Tartery into alle his londe that every man schuld usyn what lawe and beleve that he wolde soo that he worschippe noo ydollis but only every lyvyng God. Al so the same yere of oure Lorde M^l CCC xlvj was the batelle of Cresse, the xxj day of August. In the same batelle was slayne the Kynge of Beme, the Duke of Lorayne, the Erle of Launson, the Erle of Flaundrys, the Erle of Bloys, the Lorde Arcourte, the Lorde Almarle, the Erle of Maners, and many othir baronys and knyghtys the nombyr of xv C and xlij. And King Philippe of Fraunce fledde. And the iij day of September next folowyng be ganne the sege of Calys, and that contynuyd unto the iij day of Auguste next sewyng. And al so the same yere the Kyng of Schotlonde, Davyd, was take at the batelle of Dyrham the laste day of October; and he was ramsomyd at C M^l marke for to pay hyt in x yere.

Thomas Legge,   ⎰ Adam Bramson   ⎱ A° xxij°.
Mayre of London   ⎰ Ricardus Basyngstoke ⎱

Ande that yere, duryd the sege of Caleys, Kynge Phylyppe of Fraunce come downe the xxvij day of Juylle whythe a grete hoste, and purposyd for to have remevyd the sege; and proferde batelle to Kyng Edwarde, Kyng of Inglonde, and a sygnyd the day a place. And the Kyng of Inglonde acceptyd hit whythe a gladde chere. And Kyng Philippe,[a] and Kynge Phylyppe,[a] knewe that he

* So in MS., repeated.

wolde kepe his day, and he brent his tentys by nyght, and went Edw. III. A.D. 1348-53
hys waye cowardely; and the pepylle in to the towne seyng noo
comfort of rescuse, the yelde the towne to the kynge whythe the
castelle.   And at Myhelmas nexte folowynge the kyng come unto
Inglonde.

| John Lowkyn, | { Harry Pykarde | } Anno xxiij°. |
| Mayre of London | { Symon Dolsle | |

Ande that yere wa[s] a grete morther of pepylle, and pryncepally
a mong the Sarsonys that un nethe ther lefte the x. man on lyve.
Alle so that same yere hit raynyd the moste parte from Mydsomer
unto the feste of Crystys masse nexte sewynge aftyr.

| Wylliam Turke, | { Adam Bury | } Anno xxiiij°. |
| Mayre of London | { Raffe Lynne | |

Ande that yere was the grete pestelance at London, and thorowe
alle Inglonde, and duryd from the feste of Synt Michelle unto
the monythe of Auguste next folowyng, the yere of oure Lorde
M¹ ccc xlix.

| Ricardus Kilbngbury,ᵃ | { John Notte | } A° xxv°. |
| Mayre of London | { William Worceter | |

Ande that yere the kyng faught whythe Spaynardys uppon the
see by syde Wynchelsee, and slewe many of them, & toke many
vessellys of hem.

| Androw Awbry, | { John Wrothe | } A° xxvj°. |
| Mayre of London | { Gybon Steyndrope | |

And that yere, the yere of oure Lorde M¹ ccc and lij, the kyng
made newe mony, that ys for to saye grotys ande j d of two pensse,
the whiche was lasse by v s. in the pounde thenne olde sterlyng
was.

| Adam Fraunseys, | { John Pecche | } Anno xxvij°. |
| Mayre of London | { John Stodyd | |

Ande that yere was a grete dyrthe of corne ande of alle maner
of vytayle in somer tyme.   And that was callyd the dyre somer.
And that yere was a grette drought that laste fro the begynnynge

ᵃ So in MS.   The name is Kislingbury or Kilsingbury in other Chronicles.

of Marche unto the laste ende of the monythe of Juyll, the yere of oure Lorde M¹ ccc liiij.

<table>
<tr><td>The same Adam
Mayre of London</td><td>{ John Wolde
  John Lytylle</td><td>} Anno xxviij°.</td></tr>
</table>

And the same yere, at a Parlement at Westemyster, the Erle of Lanchaster, Harry, was made Duke of Lancaster, the fyrste Duke that was made at Lancaster.

<table>
<tr><td>Thomas Legge,
Mayre of London</td><td>{ Wylliam Totnaham
  Ricardus Smarte</td><td>} A° xxix°.</td></tr>
</table>

And that yere Kyng Edwarde and Kyng Philippe of Fraunce were sworne to kepe pesse. And the Kyng of Inglonde schulde have in pesse, with owte omage doynge, alle the londys of Gyan,

Aungoye, and Normandye, and alle that longyd to hym by hys herytage. Al so that yere the kyng remevyd the stapellys of the wollys owte of Flaundrys in to dyvers placys of Inglonde, that was to Westemyster, Cantyrbury, Chychester, Brystowe, Lyncolne, and Hulle, the yere of oure Lorde M¹ ccc lv.

<table>
<tr><td>Symon Fraunseys,
Mayre of London</td><td>{ Thomas Brandon
  Thomas Foster</td><td>} A° xxx°.</td></tr>
</table>

Ande that yere dyde the Kyng of Praunce, Phylippe, and John his yldyste sone was crounyde. Ande the same yere Kyng Edwarde wente to Calysse and so forthe unto Fraunce to mete whithe Kyng John that un goodely badde broke the pesse. And whenne Kyng John wyste that the Kyng of Inglonde was come he with drowe hym and made his pepylle to cary a way alle maner of vytayle, that Kyng Edwarde shulde have no maner of freschynge for hys mayne. Al so the same yere the Schottys wanne the towne of Berwyke a yenne, but nought the castelle, for hyt was kepte with Englysche men. And that yere was grauntyd unto the kynge þe costome of the wollys, xl schelyngys of sacke for þe tyme of vj yere folowynge.

<table>
<tr><td>Harry Pykarde,
Mayre of London</td><td>{ Ricardus Notyngham
  Thomas Dolsell</td><td>} A° xxxj°.</td></tr>
</table>

Ande that yere Syr Baylolle, Kyng of Schotlonde, gave up the croune of Schotlonde unto Kynge Edwarde at Rokysborowe, and the towne of Barwyke was delyveryd a yenne unto the Kyng of Inglonde. Also the same yere of oure Lorde M¹ccc lvj, the **xxix** day of Septembre, was Kyng John of Praunce takyn at the basteyle of Peyters, and Syr Philippe his sone with hym, the Erle of Pountyf, the Erle of Eue, þe Erle of Longevyle, the Erle Tankyrvyle, and viij erlys moo, and iij byschoppys. And there were slayne the Duke of Burbone, the Duke of Docens,* Constabylle of Fraunce, and the Byschoppe of Chalons, and many moo grete lordys. And the were M¹ M¹ viij° personys, of the whyche were M¹ M¹ knyghtys and squyers; ande the Dolfyn fledde. And this batylle dyd Edwarde Prynce of Walys.

John Stodey,	Sthevyn Cauwndysche	Anno xxxij.
Mayre of London	Bartholomewe Frostyng	

Ande that yere the kyng cam home and brought with hym the Kyng of Fraunce whythe alle hys presoners of lordys and knyghtys, and thys was the xxiiij day of May that they come to London and so to Westmyster. And that yere were ryalle justys in Smethefylde, there beyng iij kynges, the Kyng of Englond, the Kyng of Fraunce, ande the Kyng of Schotlonde, and many othyr dyvers lordys of othyr londys

John Lowkyn,	John Bernes	Anno xxxiij°.
Mayre of London	John Burys	

Ande that yere the kyng hylde hys feste ryally of Syn Gorge at Wyndesore, and ther was the Kyng of Praunce and the Kyng of Schottys.

Symon Donfylde,	Symon Radyngton	Anno xxxiiij°.
Mayre of London	John Chichester	

Ande that same ye[re], the xiiij kalendys of Juylle, Sir John of Gaunte, Erle of Richemounde, weddyd Dame Blanche. Alle so the same yere Kyng Edwarde saylyd in to Praunce, by cause that Charlys Regaynt of Fraunce badde movyd and steryd warre a gayne the Kynge of Inglonde. And the same yere of oure Lorde M¹ccc lx. ande the xiiij day of Aprylle, the morne aftyr Estyr daye that yere,

---

* The Duc d'Athènes or Duke of Athens.

the kynge with hys hoste lay aboute Parys.   And that day was a
foule derke day of myste, rayne, and hayle, and soo bytter colde that
men dyde for colde, where fore yet in to thys day hyt ys i-callyd
Blacke Monday next aftyr Estyr day.

John Wrothe,	John Deynys	Anno xxxv⁰.
Mayre of London	Water Berney	

Ande that yere were rovers apon the see undyr the governayle
of the Erle of Syn Poule.   And the fyrste day of Marche they
dystryde the Rye and Hastynge ande many moo townys by the
see syde, and slowe many menne.   And that yere the pesse was
made by twyne Kynge Edwarde and Kyng John of Fraunce, the
x day of May.   The Kyng of Inglond sende hys bassetours to take
the othe of the Regayunt of Praunce, Charlys, the whiche othe was
doo undyr this forme: Charlys dyd do syng a masse solempny;
and whenne that Agnus Dei was thryesse i-sayde layde his ryght
honde uppon the patent, were uppo lay Goddys owne precyus body,
and his lyfte londe on the Masse Boke, sayng on thys wyse, "We
sweryng uppon this holy precyus Goddys body, and uppon the
Ewangelys, fermly and trewly to holdyn and mentayne pesse and
concorde by twyne us two kynges, and in no maner for to do the
contrarye in no maner wyse."   And that same yere men, bestys, treys,
and howsys were smyght fervently with lytthenyge, and sodenly
i-peryschyde.   And they fonde[a] in mennys lyckenys splatt men
goyng in the waye.

John Pecche,	Wylliam Holbeche	A⁰ xxxvj⁰.
Mayre of London	Jamys Tame	

Ande that same yere, uppon the kalende of Julij, ther fylle a
blody skynne[b] in Burgayne, and a bloody crosse apperyd in the ayre
from the morne unto myd day, the whyche crosse aftyr mevyd and

---

[a] *they fonde.*   The Chronicle in Vit. A. XVI. reads "the Fend."   The Chronicle
published by Nicolas says, "And the devell in mannes lyknes spak to men goynge
be the weyo."

[b] *skynne.*   Evidently a transcriber's error.   Harl. 565 has "a blody reyne," and
no other authorities.

fylle doun into the see. Al so that yere Prynce Edwarde weddyd the Countasse of Keutt. And the same yere was the secunde pestylence, in the whiche Syr Harry, Duke of Lancaster, deyde ynne, and Syr John Erle of Rychemounde was made Duke of Lancaster. And that yere be-ganne the grete company in to Fraunce. Ande the grete wynde, the yere of oure Lorde M¹ ccc lxj.

| Sthevyn Caundische, | ⎰ John of Synt Albonys | A° xxxvij°. |
| Mayre of London | ⎱ Jamys Androwe | |

Ande that yere Syr Lyonelle, the kyng ys sone, was made Duke of Clarence, and Syr Edmounde of Wodestoke was made Erle of Chambryge, the yere of oure Lorde M¹ ccc lxij.

| John Notte, | ⎰ Ric. Croydon | Anno xxxviij°. |
| Mayre of London | ⎱ John Hyltofte | |

And that yere ther come iij kyngys in to Inglond for too speke with Kyng Edwarde; that ys to say, the Kyng of Fraunce, the Kyng of Schottys, and the Kyng of Syprys.

| Adam de Bury, | ⎰ Symon Mordon | Anno xxxix°. |
| Mayre of London | ⎱ John de Metforde | |

And the same yere the same Adam was mayre unto the xxviij day of Janyver. And thenne John Lowkyn chosynn mayre. And that yere was the batelle of Orrey in Bretayne. And the same yere deyde Kyng John of Praunce in the Savey be-syde Westmyster. And that yere was a grete froste, and duryd fro the feste of Synt Androwe tylle the xiiij day of Feverere next folowynge.

| John Lowkyn, | ⎰ John Brykylysworthe | Anno xl°. |
| Mayre of London | ⎱ John Irlande | |

Ande the same [yere]* Edwarde, the fyrste sone of Prynce Edwarde, was borne on the vij kalnd of Feverer. And at that age of vij yere he endyd his lyffe. Alle soo the same yere was grete batelle of sparowys in dyvers placys of Inglonde, where the bodys were founde dede in the feldys with-owte nombyr. Al so the same yere men and bestys were grettely infectyd with pockys, wher fore they dyde, bothe men and bestys.

---

* Omitted in MS.

| John Lowkyn, | { John Warde | } Anno xlj° |
| Mayre of London | { Wylliam Dykman | |

And the same y[e]re Rycharde, the sone of Prynce Edwarde, was
borne in Burdox, the yere of our Lorde M¹ ccc lxiiij.

| Jamys Androwe, | { John Corgolde | } Anno xlij°. |
| Mayre of London | { Wylliam Dykman | |

And that yere, the yere of oure Lorde M¹ ccc lxviij, in the
monythe of Marche, apperyd S[t]ella comata, ydest, a blasyn sterre.
And that yere was the batelle of Nezers[a] in Spayne, and there
Prynce Edward scomfyte the Bastarde of Spayne,[b] and restoryd
Kyng Petyr into hys realme a yenne, that was put ewte by the
sayde Bastarde. And there was take the Erle of Dene, Syr Olyvyr
Claykyn, and many mo knygtys and squyers, by syde fronkelaynys.

| Symon Mordon, | { Adam Wynbyngham | } Anno xliij°. |
| Mayre of London | { Robert Gyrdeler | |

Ande that yere Syr Lyonelle Duke of Clarence saylyd ovyr the
see unto Meleyne, and at the feste of the Natyvyte of oure Lady he
dyde. Ande the same yere dyde Dame Blanche, and she ys beryd
att Syn Poulys at London. And that yere was the thyrde pestylaunce.

| John Chichester, | { John Pyelle | } Anno xliiij° |
| Mayre of London | { Hewe Holbeche | |

Ande that same yere a buschelle of whete was worthe xl d.
And that yere dyde Quene Phylyppe, the yere of oure Lorde
M¹ ccc lxix.

| John Bernes, | { William Walworthe | } A° xlv° |
| Mayre of London | { Roberte Gayton | |

Ande that yere the Duke of Lancaster saylyd ovyr the see and
roode thorowe Fraunce, and Syr John Hawkewode floryschyde in
Lombardy. And that same yere the prynce come home a yenne
owt of Spayne in to Inglonde. And he lefte by hynde hym in
Gascoyne the Duke of Lancaster and the Erle of Cambryge.

[a] Najara.   [b] Henry of Trastamare.

John Bernis,   { Robet Hatfylde   } Anno xlvj°.
Mayr of London   { Adam Staple

Ande that yere the Chaunceler and the Tresyrer of Inglonde were put downe of hir office; and they were byschoppys bothe; and the prevy seele and secular lordys were putt in the same offyce.

John Pyell,   { John Philpote   } A° xlvij°
Mayre of London   { Nicholaus Brembre

Ande that yere was John Northewode slayne on the Blacke hethe at a wrastelynge, wherefore there rosse moche dyssencyon a mong certayne craftys of the citte. Al so the same yere the Duke of Lancaster and the Erle of Cambryge com home in to Inglonde owt of Gascoyne. And the same yere the duke weddyd the doughter of Kyng Petyr of Spayne. Alle so the same yere there were ij cardenellys sent fro the Pope for to trete for the pesse of ij realmys of Inglonde and of Fraunce. And that yere ther was a batylle on the see by twyne Englysche men and Flemmyngys, and xxv shyppys ladyn with baye salte were take from the Flemmyngys. And that yere the Erle of Penbroke was take on the see with Spaynardys on Synt Johnys Even the Baptyste.

Adam de Bury,   { John Awbry   } A° xlviij°
Mayre of London   { John Feffyde

And that yere the Duke of Lancaster saylyd in to Flaundrys and paste by Parys by Burgayne, and atte Praunce unto Burdox with owte any with stondyng. Al so the same yere Alysaundyr Nevyle was made Archebyschoppe of Cantyrbury, and Thomas Arundelle was made Bischoppe of Ely, and Mayster Harry Wakefylde Byschoppe of Worceter.

Wylliam Waworthe,   { Richardus Leyonys   } A° xlix°
Mayre of London   { Wylliam Wodhous

Ande the same yere the towne of Bryggys in Flaundrys tredyd of dyvers artyculys be twyne the Pope and Kyng Edwarde. And that yere was tretyde pesse by twyne Inglonde and Praunce.

John Warde,   { John Hadley   } A° l°.
Mayre of London   { William Newporte

Ande that yere Edwarde the Lorde Spencer dyde and is buryd
at Teukysbury.

| Adam Stapille, | { John Northehampton | } A⁰ lj⁰. |
| Mayre of London | { Robert Launde | |

Ande that same yere the sayde Adam was mayre tylle unto
the xxj day of Marche, and thenne was he put downe, and
Nicholaus Brembre chosse mayre, and toke his othe at the Towre
of London.

And the same yere on Trenyte Sonday deyde Prynce Edwarde
at Westmyster, and his body buryd at Cantyrbury.

| Nicholaus Brembre, | { Androw Pickeman | } A⁰ lij⁰. |
| Mayre of London | { Nicholaus Twyforde | |

Ande that yere was grauntyde unto the kyng that every person,
man and woman, that was of xiiij yere of age and more shulde[a]
paye to the kynge iiij d., and every man of hooly Chyrche xij d.
that was a vaunsyd man, and that othyr þat were not a vaunsyd
iiij d. Freers were only owt takynn. And that same yere
Richarde, the sone of Prynce Edward, was made Prynce of Valys.
And that same yere the Cardynalle of Inglonde was smyte with a
palsey, and loste hys speche. And on Mary Magdelene ys day he
dyde. And the same yere the xij Jovis Aprylys, Syr John Myn-
styrwode, knyght, was beheddyd. And that same yere, the xij
kaulendys of Julij, deyde Kynge Edwarde at Shene, and ys buryd
at Westmyster, the yere of oure Lorde M¹ ccc lxxvij.

The namys of mayrys ande sherevys in the tyme of Kynge
Richarde the Secunde, that was crownyde the xvij kalend' of the
monythe of Auguste, the yere of our Lorde M¹ ccc lxxvij.

Nicholaus Brembre,	{ Androw Pyckeman	} A⁰ j⁰.
Mayre of London	{ Nicholaus Twyforde	
John Phylpott,	{ John Bosham	} A⁰ ij⁰.
Mayre of London	{ Thomas Corwaleys	

---

[a] *shulde*, repeated in MS.

Ande that yere Roberde Rawde[a] was slayne in the chyrche of Wystemyster the yere of oure Lorde M ccc lxxviij.

| John Hadle, | { John Hylsdon | } Anne iij°, |
| Mayre of London | { William Baret | |

And that same yere there cam galeyys of warre to Gravysende and brente a grete quantyte of the towne. And that yere [was][b] on Kirkeby hangyd, W. Baret the sheryve.

| Wylliam Walworthe, | { Water Dogete | } Anno iiij°. |
| Mayre of London | { William Knyghtkete | |

Ande that yere, the yere of oure Lorde a M ccc ande iiij schore, uppon a Corpuscrysty day, cum many dyvers pepylle owt of Keutt and owte of Esex unto þe cytte of London, and brent the great maner and place of Savey in Flete Strete and a parte of the howse of Syn Johnys at Clerkyn welle be syde Smethefylde, and drewe downe the maner of Hybery. And on the morowe aftyr they went unto the Towre of London and fette owte the Archebyschoppe of Cantyrbury, and the Pryor ot Syn Johnys, and Freer William Apilton a Fryer Mynor, and they smote of her heddys at the Towre Hylle. And Richard Lyonys and many moo of the Flemmyngys were by-heddyd in dyvers placys of London. And at Synt Edmonde ys Bury they be-heddyd the Pryur of Bury and Syr Symonde Caundische, Cheffe Justyse of Inglonde, and many moo of othyr pepylle. And thys was callyd " the hurlyng tyme." And that tyme was Syr Wylliam Walworthe made a knyght in Smethe Fyllde for that he slowe the chefteyn of hem the whiche that were rysers, that was called Jacke Strawe. And there were made moo knyghtes that there namys folowyn here: Syr Nicholaus Brembre, John Philpotte, Roberd Launde, and Syr Nicholaus Twyforde. And this was callyd " the hurlyng tyme."

John Northehampton,	{ John Rotte,	}
Mayre of London	{ John Hende,	} Anno v°.
	{ Sherevys	

---

[a] Robert Hawle, or Hauley, according to all other authorities
[b] Omitted in MS.

Ric. II.
A.D. 1382-7.

Ande that yere come Queue Anne unto Inglonde and was weddyd unto Kyng Rycharde.   Ande that yere was the erthe quake, the yere of oure Lorde a M^1 CCC iiij schore and ij, the xxj day of Maye.

John Northehamton, Mayre of London	⌐Adam Wamme ⌊ John Sely	} A° vj°.

And that yere went the Byschoppe of Norwyche unto Flaundrys; and the xxv day of Maye the Flemmyngys gaffe hym batayle faste by Dunkyrke, and there were slayne xj M^1 Flemmyngys.

Nicholaus Brembre, Mayre of London	Symon Wynchecombe John More	} A° vij°.
	Nicholas Exton John Frosche	} Anno viij°.
	John Organ John Chyrcheman	} A° ix°

And that yere Kyng Rycharde went unto Schotlande.   And there were i-made ij dukys, the [Duke]ᵃ of Glouceter and the Duke of Yorke.   And the Erle of Oxynforde was made Markys of Devylyn.

Ande the same yere the Erle of Arundelle faught uppon the see a-pon oure Lady day in Lent whythe the Flemmyngys, and he badde the better of hem, and he toke many shippys.   There was a shippe i-callyd Mewys Colman, in the whiche schippe was the Amyrelle of Praunce and many moo ᵇ gentellys.   Also that same yere the Duke of Lancaster whythe hys wyffe Dame Constaunce saylyd yn to Spayne for to chalenge his herytage that was hys wyvys ryght.

Nicholaus Exton, Mayre of London	⌐Wylliam Venour ⌊ Hewe Fastolfe	} Anno xj°.

Ande that yere was a gaderyng of lordys, but of certayne, as Syr Thomas Woodestoke Duke of Glouceter, Syr Harry Erle of Derby, Syr Richarde the Erle of Arundelle, and Syr Thomas Erle of Warwyke, and Syr Thomas Erle of Nothyngham, the whyche

---

ᵃ Omitted in MS.   ᵇ *mo* repeated in MS.

appechyd Robert Devyr, Erle of Oxynforde, whom Kynge
Rycharde hadde made fyrste Markys of Dorsett and aftyr Duke
of Yrlond, and he fledde into Yrlonde, and al so he fledde into
Loveyne in Brahan and there he deyde. Al-so Syr Mychelle of Pole,
the Erle of Sowghtfolke, fledde into the same place, and there he
dyde. And Syr Alysaundyr Nevyle fledde into Schotlonde, that
was that tyme Archebyschoppe of Yorke, and Syr Robert Tre-
vylyon, Cheffe Justys of Inglond, and Syr Nycholle Brembr,
knyght, were drawe and hangyd, and Syr John Bechampe, and
Sir Jamys Berners, and Syr Symon of Bevyrley were be-heddyd
at the Towre Hylle. And Syr John of Salusbury was drawe and
hangyd, and Robert Belknappe, John Holte, John Gray, Wylliam
Borughe, Robert Folthorpe and John Lokton, Justyse, were exylyd
into Yrlond, there for to abyde and dwelle alle ther lyvys.

| Nicholaus Twyford, | Thomas Austyn | A° xij°. |
| Mayre of London | Adam Carlylle | |

| Wylliam Venour, | John Walkote | Anno xiij°. |
| Mayre of London | John Loveye | |

Ande that yere were grete justys of warre in Smethefylde in the
monythe of May by-twyne the Erle of Nothyngham and the Erle
of Morycke, Schottys, and the Lorde Wellys and Davyd of Lyndesay,
Schottys, and Syr Nycholle and John Browne, Schottys.

| Adam Bamme | John Fraunseys | A° xiiij°. |
| Mayre of London | Thomas Vyvente | |

And that yere the goode man at the sygne at the Cocke in Chepe
at the Lytyll Condyte was mortheryd in hys bedde be nyght, and
therefore hys wyffe was brente, and iiij of hys men were hangyd at
the Tyborne.

| John Hynde, | Harry Vanner | A° xv°. |
| Mayre of London | John Schadworthe | |

Ande that yere the mayre and bothe[a] sherevys were dyschargyde
of ther offycys by-fore the feste of Synne John the Baptyste at
Notyngham. And Syr Edwarde Dalyngryge, knyght, was made

---

[a] *hothe*, MS.

Ric. II.
.D. 1392-4.
wardyn by the kynge unto the fyrste day of Jule, the yere of the
raygne of the kyng xvj the begynnynge. And thenne was Syr
Bawdewyn Radington, knyght, i-made Wardyn and Custos of
London unto Syn Symons day and Jude. Thenne by þᵉ lyscensse
of the kynge the cytte chosse a̅ newe Mayre of London, anno xvj,
non sherevys.

Wylliam Stawnden.	Gybon Mawfylde	A° xvij°.[a]	
Thenne he was chosse	Thomas Neuton		Sherevys.
Mayre of London.	Gybon Mawfylde	A° xviij°.[a]	
	Thomas Neuton		

Ande that yere was made a grette translacyon of byschoppys in
thys realme. Syr Thomas Aryndylle, Archebyschoppe of Yorke, was
made Chaunceler of Inglonge,[b] and Wylliam, the Byschoppe of
Salysbury, was made Tresyrer of Inglonde, whos servandys of the
sayde tresyrer raysyd a grete debate and dyscensyon in the citte of
London, that was in Flette Strete, for an hors i-lost, where fore the
tresurer complaynyd unto the kyng uppon the cytte, thorowe
whiche informacyon and procuryng of the tresuer the kyng dyd
sesyn the franches ande þᵉ lyberteys of London fro them, and
remevyde the courte unto Yorke fro the feste of Syn John þᵉ
Baptyste unto Crystysmas next folowynge.

John Hadle,	Ric. Wedyngton	A° xvij° c
Mayre of London	Drewe Barentyne	

Ande that yere, the vij day of June, the yere of our Lorde
M¹ ccc iiij[d] schore and xiiij, Queue Anne at Schene dyde, and ys

---

ᵃ These figures are erroneous. William Stawnden was elected mayor in the
sixteenth year according to what has just been stated in the text ; and both he and
the two sheriffs, whose names are given opposite, held office for one year only. This
error has disturbed the numeration of the years which follow in the MS., which,
however, we have corrected in the text.

ᵇ So in MS.

ᶜ From the 17th to the 21st year of this reign each year is wrongly numbered in
the MS , except the 18th, which, strangely enough, is given correctly. Thus the 17th
is numbered xix°, the 19th xxj°, the 20th xxij°, and the 21st xxiij°. The 22nd is
numbered correctly, notwithstanding that it follows the year numbered xxiij°.

ᵈ " viij schore," MS. which of course is an error.

beryd at Westemyster. And that same yere, at Mychelmas, Kyng ^{Ric. II.} ^{A.D. 1394-7.}
Rycharde went fyrste unto Yrlonde.

| John Frossche, | Wylliam Brampton | A° xviij°. |
| Mayre of London | Thomas Knollys | |

And thys yere the kyng come unto Yrlond.

| Wylliam More, | Roger Eleys | A° xix°.[a] |
| Mayre of London | Wylliam Shyryngham | |

Ande that yere, at the feste of Alle Halowe tyde, the kyng
weddyd Dame Isabelle the kyngys doughter of Fraunce at Calys,
and the vij daye of Janyver nexte she was crownyde at Westemyster. And at hyr comynge to London the Pryor of Typtre, in
Essex, and vij mo pers'onys of men and wemmen were thruste to
dethe a-pon London Brygge in the grete presse, for ther was a
fulle grete prece in that same tyme.

| Adam Bamme, | Thomas Wylforde | A° xx°.[a] |
| Mayre of London | Wylliam Parker | |

Ande that same Adem Bamme mayr stylle tylle the vj day of
Junij, and thenne he dyde. Ande Richarde Wedynton was chosse
for the resydewe of the yere. And the xviij day of the same
monythe waste the Duke of Glouceter a-reste.

| Rychardus Wedyngton, | John Woodecocke | A° xxj°.[a] |
| Mayre of London | William Asckeham | |

Ande the same yere, the nexte Sonday aftyr the Translacyon of
Syn Thomas [b] of Cantyrbury, that was viij day of Juylle, the kyng
commaundyd alle hys mayne for to mete with hym at the Mylys
Ende; and so they dede. And thenne he roode forthe unto Plasche;
and there he restyd the Duke of Glouceter erly in the mornynge,
and the Duke of Arundelle, and the Erle of Warwyke, and the
Lorde E. Cobham, and Syr John Cheyne; alle thes were a restyde
the same tyme, and the Duke of Glouceter was sende unto Calys in
to preson ; ande at Saynt Bartholomewe ys tyde nexte aftyr the
Erle Marchelle was sende unto Calys to hym. And on the morne

---

[a] See note [c] on page 94.

[b] *Syn Thomas.* These words are struck through with the pen by a later hand.

Ric. II.
.D. 1397-8.

hyt was Sonday, and that daye men sayde that he [die]de,[a] but
Gode wote howe, but dede he was. On the morne aftyr Hooly
Rode day, the kyng made a grete justysse be-syde Kyng ys towne
uppe Temys ; and on the Sonday aftyr the Erle of Derby helde
his feste in John Roetis Place, in Flet Strete. And the xxj
day of September be-ganne the Parlement at Westemyster. And
there was made a grete hale in the palysse, and[b] there ynne the
Parlyment was holde. And that day the knyghtys of the shyre
were i-chosyn, ande sherevys chosyn hyr Speker, wyche name
was Syr John Buschey; and every man was commaundyd for
to leve his bowe and his arowys at home in hys inne. And
on the nexte day was the Parlement playnely be-gunne. And
on the Wanysday nexte aftyr was askyd as for þe clargy a
procter for to speke for hem in the Parlyment, for they myght
nought be in that place there as jugement' shulde be gevyn
for treson of felony. And thenne they chosynne Syr Thomas
Percy, and so schulde they have for hym a proctoure in the Parlyment for evyr more for poyntys of tresoune and felony. And
the Fryday aftyr was the E[r]le of Arundelle att hys aunswere ;
and that day was geve juggement on hym, that he shulde be
drawe, hanggyd, ande i-quarteryd, and be-heddyd. But at the
prayer of lordys the kyng relessyd hym, and commaundyd that he
shulde be ladde thorowe London unto the Towre Hylle from Westemyster, and there hys hedde to be smytte of. And so hit was. And
thenne was the body ande the bedde borne unto fryer Austynnys,
and then hit was byryde. And on the Fryday next aftyr was Syr
Thomas Mortymer jugyd unto the same dethe that the Erle hadde,
but that he com yn whythe yn vj monythys. And the Sonday
hylde the Duke of Lancaster hys feste in the byschoppys place of
Durham. And the Monday aftyr was the Lorde Cobham accusyd.
And the Thursday aftyr helde the lordys a Prevye Conselle; and
on the morne aftyr was the Erle of Warwyke at hys answere, and

---

[a] The beginning of this word is defaced and illegible.
[b] and. The MS. has " in " instead of " and " by an inadvertence of the scribe.

was juggyd unto the same dethe jugement that the Erle of Arundelle badde, but he submyttyd hym so louly unto the kyngys grace and to his plesaunce, that the kyng gaffe hym grace and lyffe, and sende hym unto the Towre a-yenne. And the Satyrday was the Parlyment enjornyde unto Shrouysbury. And that day there were made v dukys and a duches, and a markes, and iiij erlys, the whiche namys folowyn aftyr here: Syr Harry Erle of Derby made Duke of Herforde, Edwarde Erle of Rutlonde Duke of Arundylle, Thomas the Erle Marchelle made Duke of Northe folke, Syr John Holand Duke of Exceter, and the Erle of Kentte made Duke of Surreye. And the Countesse of Northefolke i-made Duches of Northefolke, the Erle of Somersett Markys of Dorsett, the Lorde Spencer i-made Erle of Glouceter, the Lorde Nevyle i-made Erle of Westemorelonde, Syr Thomas Percy Erle i-made the Erle of Worceter, and Syr Wylliam Schroppe i-made Erle of Wyldschyre. Ande the Sonday aftyr helde the kynge hys feste, and the Monday was the torment of the Lorde Moumbrey at the Whytte Freerys in þe cytte of London ys subbarbys. And every nyght durynge the Parlyment the kyng was wacchyde, on lorde with his mayny one nyght, and anothyr lorde anothyr nyghte, duryng alle the Parlyment. And that same yere the kyng [a] and the Duke of Herford, and the Duke of Northefolke, shulde have foughte at Covyntre; but whenne that they were ensemblyd in the place afore the kynge, ande he toke hit uppon hys juggement, and a non in the same place they were hothe exylyde, but Harry Duke of Herforde but for x yere, and the Duke of Northefolke for a hundryd wynter.

Alle so the same yere Thomas Aroundelle the Arche Byschoppe of Cantyrbury was exylyde, and Syr Robert Waldon was made Arche Byschoppe of Cauntyrbury. And thenne the kyng, thoroughe wyckyd consayle, deseneyreyd [b] the heyrys of the

[a] We ought certainly to read "And that same year of the king, the Duke of Hereford and the Duke of Norfolk," &c.

[b] i.e. disinherited.

CAMD. SOC.

Ric. II.
A D. 1398.

lordys that were exilyde and done to dethe be fore tyme. And
thenne he sende unto Rome to have the statutys and the ordy-
nannee made in the Parlyment that was begunne at Westemyster
and i-endyd at Shrouysbury confermyde[a] by the Poope;[b] hyt was
donne ande grauntyd by the Poope,[b] and by hym conformyd, the
whiche was pronounsyd at Powlys Crosse and at Synt Mary
Spetylle by fforne and in audyence of pepylle. Alle so the kyng
thorowe conselle that was not goode he hadde the cytte of London
and many othyr cytteys and townys in grette hate and in indygna-
cyon, and were endytyd as for rebellys; and he toke hym to
Cheschyre men, þe whiche were most famulyer with hym, wherefore
the cytesynnys of London and the pepille of the sayde townys and
schyrys endytyd, as hit ys i-sayde byfore, were fulle bevy and in
grete hevynes of herte. Where fore the sayde cyttesynnys of London in plesauns of the kynge and by conselle and helpe of Syr
Roger Walden, Archebischoppe of Cauntyrbury, ande Syr Robert
Baybroke, Byschoppe of London, putte a supplicacion unto the
kyng, of whyche the tenoure folowyth.

To oure[c] excellent ryght dowtfulle soverayne and fulle gracyus
lorde the kynge.[d]   Fulle mekely and lowly besekynge,[e] youre
humble legys, spyrytualle and temporalle, the Archebyschoppe
of Cauntyrbury ande the Byschoppe of London, mayre, sherevys,
and aldyrmen, with alle othyr spyrytualle and temporalle lordys
and gentelys, and comyners of youre citte of London.   And[f]
for as moche and[g] fulle grette and sorowfulle malyce, trespassys,

---

[a] confernyde, MS.

[b] The word " Pope " is smeared through with a pen in these places.

[c] youre, MS., which is certainly an error.   This petition is given more accurately
in the Chronicle in Julius B. i., which we refer to in the footnotes following by the
letter J.   There is another copy in Vitell. A. xvi., which we refer to as V.; but it,
also, is very corrupt.

[d] Our MS. here runs on as if the sentence were continued.

[e] bisechen, J.

[f] And. J. reads " that," continuing the sentence.

[g] and. as, J.

and wyckyd conjecturys [a] have ben procuryd, don, and evyl don
to youre royalle mageste, the [b] grete and perpetualle confusion and
repreffe to the sayde evylle doers, and grette vylony and shame
of alle the dwellynge with yn the sayde cytte, as welle innocentys
as knowynge thereof [c] as of othyr; [which] [d] wyckyd doers, for
the [e] trespas have deservyd harde and wyckyd [f] chastemente and
punyschement, ne were þe hye benyngnyte of youre [g] douthefulle
lorde, fullefyllyd whithe alle grace, wylle nought procede ayenste
them aftyr hyr desertys, whyche yf ye shulde agayne them
procedyn hit shulde ben hyr dystruccyon, and nott with owte
cause, of grette multitude of youre pepylle whithe owt nombre.
Ples hit to youre excellent and doughtfulle ryalle mageste gracyusly
to consydyr the grette repentaunce of youre mysdoers, ande hyre
benynge desyre that they have to aske mercy, ande to redresse
hem to alle maner of reformynge hem aftyr hyr power, as
moche as hyt may ben in any wysse possyble, here exees, folys,
and defautys abovyn sayde. And of the abundaunte wylle [h] of
grace were of the Almyghty Kynge, exempler of alle marcy
and grace, [where of] [i] hathe indeuyd you, to receyve hem to youre
mercy ande grace, and hoolye for to forgevyn alle the malefesourys
or evylle doers of hem dwellynge in the same cytte, because of hem
have trespaisyd to youre ryalle excellente mageste before sayde.
And youre humbylle legys wylle submythem [k] to doen, beryn, and
a-boye [l] alle maner of thynge that shalle in any maner plesyn
the same youre royalle mageste. And ovyr that youre humbylle
legys wylle submyt them, and besekyn that they may ben ressayvyd
to grace, by Roger Walden, Byschoppe of Cauntyrbury, Syr

---

[a] *conjecturys*. Conjecturacions of somme men, and of many evil doers of the seid
cite, J.

[b] *the*. to, J.   [c] *there of*. they of, MS.; thereof, J.

[d] Omitted in MS. J. reads "which malfaisours or evil doers."

[e] *the*. J. reads "here," *i. e.* their.   [f] *wyckyd*. lither, J.

[g] *youre*. you oure, J.   [h] *wylle*. welle, J.

[i] *where of*. Not in J., and clearly superfluous.

[k] So written as one word.   [l] *a-boye*. obeie, J.

Ric. II.
A.D. 1398.

Roberd [Braybroke] [a] Byschoppe of London, Rycharde Wedyngton, Mayre of London, &c., sufficiantly enformyd, and havyng
ful ande [b] suffycyente auctoryte and pouer for [al] [c] youre humble
legys of the sayde cytte, and in hyr name to sweryn and trewly
for to holdyn, kepe, and observe, leyn, [d] and mentayne, with
alle hyr power, whythe owte fraude or maligne, [e] alle the statutys,
stabylmentys, and jugementys don and yevyn in youre hye Parlyment, be gunne at Westemyster the Monday nexte aftyr the feste
of the Exaltacyon of the Hooly Crosse, the yere of youre gracyous
raygne xxj, and fro thens endyde at [f] Schrouysbury unto the
qu[i]nsyn of Syut Hyllarye thenne nexte folowynge, and there
termynyd ande endyd; and alle othyr statutys, ordynauncys, and
stabilymentys sythe hyder to done and madyn with owttyn evyr
to comyn, don, [or] [g] procure anything there a-yenne in any
maner, to that ende that they shalle mowe ben putt thorowe
youre grace owt of alle suspecyon, ande to [ben] [g] holdyn as they
deservyn [h] above alle thynge youre trewe legys for the love of God
and the werke of charite. In wyttenys of this thynge, and for the
thyngys above sayde, welle and trewly to holdyn, kepynne, observe,
and mentayne for alle dayes whythe [al] [i] hyr power in the maner
as hyt ys a-bove sayde, whythe owte evyr to done or procure [k] the
contrarye, to lyvyn ande dyyn youre sayde humbyll legys, of whom
here namys severally ben undyr wrytynge, as welle for them selfe as
in the name of the resydewe of the same cytte to thys supplycacyon
have sette hir selys, that ys to say, we Roger Walden, by the grace of
Gode Archebyschoppe of Cauntyrbury, Prymate of alle Inglonde,
Robart Baybroke Byschoppe of London, and Richard Wedyngton,

---

[a] Supplied from J. and V.

[b] *sufficiantly—ful ande.* These words are supplied from J., being omitted both
in our MS. and V. In the former the words following, viz., "suffycyente auctoryte,"
are absurdly made to begin a new paragraph.

[c] Supplied from J.   [d] *lowen,* J.; *loven,* V.
   malengyne, J. and V.   [f] *ended at.* ajourned to, J.
[g] Supplied from J.   [h] *desiren,* J.
[i] Supplied from J.   [k] *procure.* procerne, MS.; procure, J. and V.

Ric. II.
A.D. 1398-9

Mayre of London, Wylliam Askeham, John Woodecocke, Scherevys of London, the cytte forsayde, &c. And then anon, aftyr the presentacyon of the sayde supplycacion, there were made many blanke chartours, and alle þᵉ men of any crafte in the citte, as welle servauntys as maysterys, were chargyd for to come to the Yelde halle to sette hyr sclys to the sayde blanke chartours. And soo they dyd also for the moste parte of Inglond, and no man wyste what hyt mente.

Drewe Baryntyne, Mayre of London { John Wade, John Warner } xxijᵒ Anno.

Ande that same yere Thomas Aryndelle, the sone and ayre of the Erle of Arundelle, whiche þat aftyr the dethe of hys fadyr was dwellyng in howshold with Svr John of Holon, Duke of Exceter, and holde at non reputacyon but in grete repreffe and dyspyte and moche dysseysse, prevely thorowe helpe of Wylliam Schotte, mercer of London, in a gromys wede he saylyd ovyr þᵉ see and came unto hys onkylle, the Archebyschope of Cauntyrbury, that was that tyme in Coleyne. Al so the same yere dyde Syr John Ganute, Duke of Lanchaster, and ys beryd at Poulys at London. And that yere Kyng Rychard saylyd the secunde tyme in to Yrlonde sone aftyr Estyr. And he hadde with hym Harry, the eldyste [son]e of the Dukys of Herford, the whiche Harry was made knyght in Irlonde. And in the begynnyng of xxiij yere of the raygne Harry, Duke of Lancaster, that was exilyd whithe the Archebyschoppe of Cantyrbury and hys owne sone Thomas, and the sone of the Erle of Arundelle, londyd in the northe contre at a place callyde Raynspouer be-syde Weldynton, to whom there come hastely Syr Harry Percy of Northehumbyrlonde, and Harry Percy hys sone, and many othyr lordys, and thenne the Duke of Lancaster whithe alle othyr lordys went strayt unto Brystowe, and there they fonde Syr Wylliam Schroppe, Treserer of Inglond, and Syr John Busche, and Syr John Grene, the whiche were brought by fore the Duke of York, that tyme beynge Levtenaunte of Inglonde, and there they were be heddyd. And thenne was Syr

John Solake a-restyd at Westemyster, the dene of the kyngys chapylle, and putte in preson in Luddegate, and othir certayne monkys of the Abbey of Westemyster were a-restyd al so. And the same yere were a-restyd Syr Wylliam Baggot, knyght, in Irlonde, faste by Deuelyn, and he was brought unto London and putte in preson in Newgate. And that same yere was Moraunte, fyschemanger, i-slayne at Syut Mary at the Hylle be-syde Byllyngysgate.

Thes benne the namys of Mayrys and of Sherevys of the cytte of London in the tyme of Kyng Harry the iiij that was crownyd at Westemyster the xiij day of October, the yere of oure Lorde Mᶜ ccc lxxxxix.

| Thoma Knollys, | { William Walderne | } Anno primo. |
| Mayre of London | { Wylliam Hyde | |

Ande that same yere, a-non aftyr Crystysse masse, was be-heddyd at Sussetyr the Erle of Kentt, and the Erle of Saulysbury, and the Erle of Oxynforde, and Syr Thomas Blounte, and Syr Raffe Lumney, Syr Benet Cely, knyghtys, and Syr Thomas Wyntyrsylle, sqwyer; also Syr John Holand, Erle of Huntyngdone, was beheddyd at Playsche in Exsex, and the Lord Spenser was be-heddyd at Brystowe;[a] and a-non aftyr dyde Kyng Rychard and was beryd at Langley. And that same yere Syr Barnarde Brokers was heddyd at Tyburne, and Syr Thomas Celley, knyght, and Mawdleyn ande Ferby, clerkys, were drawyn and hangyd at Tyburne. And that same yere the kynge roode in to Schotlonde. And there he[b] be-ganne the werre at Walys by Gwyn Glandowre, squyer, ayenste the Kyng of Inglonde, Harry the iiij, &c.

| John Fraunseys, | { John Wackeley | } Anno ijº. |
| Mayre of London | { John Obete | |

---

[a] The Chronicle in Vitell. A. xvi. has a curious variation here. Instead of the foregoing clause it reads: "And Sir John Holand, Duke of Excestre, was take in Essex atte Putelwelle in a mille, and he was bebeded atte Bristowe."

[b] *he.* This word is clearly superfluous.

Ande that yere a quarter of whete was worthe xvj s. The secunde yere. And thenne that yere Syr Wylliam Sawtre, preste, was brente ynne Smethefylde for eresy.

And that yere, the xiij day of September, the yere of oure Lorde M¹ cccc and ij, was the batylle at Halydon Hylle, at the whyche batylle was takynne the Erle Douglas, the ᵃ Erle of Fyfe, and many moo othyr knyghtys and squyers.

John Schadworthe,   William Fremyngham   Anno iij°.
Mayre of London   William Venoure, junyor

Ande that same yere was Dame Jone, Duches of Bretayne, i-weddyd to Kyng Harry the iiij. Also thys yere there was a sterre that was callyd Comata, idest a blasyng sterre, and he shewyd in the weste, and he duryd v wekys and more. Al so the same yere the Priour of Launde and Syr Roger of Claryngdone,ᵇ knyght, and hys men, were drawe and hanggyd, and viij Freers Minors whythe them, at Tyburne, and Syr Roger Walden, the byschoppe, and Rychard Clydrowe were i-quytte by a queste of men of London. Ande that yere was the batyle at Humbyldon Hylle.

John Walkotte,   Richardus Merlowe   Anno iiij°.
Mayre of London   Robert Chycheley

And that yere, the yere of our Lorde M¹ cccc iiij, was the batylle of Shrouysbury, that was uppon Mary Mawdelyn Evyn, in the whyche bataylle Syr Harry Percy was sayle,ᶜ and Thomas Percy was i-takynne and kept iij dayes aftyr, and thenne he was drawe, hanggyd, quarteryd, and be-heddyd; and the quarters was sende one unto London Brygge. And in the same bataylle was the Prynce shotte thorowe the bedde with an arowe, and the Erle of Stafforde was i-slayne in the kyngys cote armure undyr his baner, and many mo lordys and knyghtes lost there lyvys, and squyers and many a goode yemon. For hit was one of the wyrste bataylys that evyr came to Inglonde, and unkyndyst, for there was the fadyr a-yenst

---

ᵃ *the.* ther, MS.

ᵇ *Claryng done,* MS., the last two syllables being disjoined.

ᶜ *sayle.* So in MS., but the reading ought certainly to have been *slain.*

the sone and the sone ayenste the fadyr, and brother and cosyn a-yenste eche othyr.

| William Askam, | { Thomas Faukener | } Anno vᵒ. |
| Mayre of London | { Thomas Polle | |

And that yere Serle, that was one of thoo that mortheryd the Duke of Glouceter at Calys, was takyn in the Marche of Schotlond, and was brought unto London, and was hangyd at Tyburne.

| John Hynde, | { William Lowthe | } Anno vjᵒ. |
| Mayre of London | { Stevyn Spylman | |

Ande that yere Syr Thomas the kyngys sone was Amerelle of the See, and he wente unto Flaundrys and brent bothe in Cachante and in Flaundrys, ande londyd at Scluse and gaffe there to a stronge sawte. Alle so he toke carrekys of Jene and brought them unto Wynchylse, and they were brent thorowe mysse gover naunce and moche of the goode ther ynne. Alle so the same yere Syr Richard Schroppe, Archebyschoppe of Yorke, and the Lorde Mombray, were be-heddyd at Yorke.

| John Woodecocke, | { Wylliam Crowmer | } Aᵒ vijᵒ. |
| Mayre of London | { Harry Barton | |

Ande that yere alle the werys bytwyne London and Mydway were drawe downe by the conselle of the kynge and of the mayre of London, and of the comyns of the same cytte, for they dyd moche harme in the ryver of Themys, for they dystroyed moche yonge frye, for the pepylle gaffe hit hir hoggys, and soo uncomely devouryd hyt.

| Rychard Wytyngdon, | { Nicholaus Wotton | } Aᵒ viijᵒ. |
| Mayre of London | { Geffray Booke ᵃ | |

Ande that yere the Erle of Kent weddyd the Erlys doughter of Mylaync, at Synt Mary Overeys in Sowtheworke, the xiiij day of Juylle. And that yere deyd Syr Robert Knollys, and ys byryd at the Whytte Freers at London.

ᵃ Should be Broke or Brooke.

Wylliam Stawndon,	Harry Pomfrett	
Mayre of London	Harry Halton	} Anno ix°.

Ande that yere the Erle of Northehumberlond ande the Lorde Bardoffe were take in the Northe countre ande be-heddyd and quarteryd; and the hedde of the erle and the quartyr of the lorde were brought unto Londyn Brygge. And that yere was a grete froste, and that duryd xxv wekys and more. Alle so the same yere the Erle of Kentt was slayne at the castelle of Bryake whythe a stone.

Drewe Barentyne,	William Norton	
Mayre of London	Thomas Duke	} A° x°.

Ande that yere was the grette playe at Skynners Welle in London. Ande that yere there were grete justys in Smethefylde by twyne the Erle of Somersett and the Synyschalle of Henowde, and Syr John Corwayle and Syr Rycharde of Arundelle, and the sone of Syr John Chenye, and othyr Fraynysche men dede the dedys of armys there.

Richardus Merlowe,	John Lane	
Mayre of London	Wylliam Checheley	} A° xj°

And that yere ther was an heretyke, that was callyd John of Badby, that be-levyd nought in the Sacrament of the Auter, and he was brought unt[o] Smethefylde for to be brent, and bownde unto a stake; and Syr Harry Percy* of Walys conselyd hym to holde the very ryght beleve of Hooly Chyrche, and he shulde faylle nothyr lacke noo goode. Al so the Chaunceler of Oxynford, on Mayster Corteney, informyd hym in the faythe of Holy Chyrche, and the Pryour of Syn Bartholomewys brought the hooly sacrament with xij torchys and brought hyt before hym. And hyt was askyd howe that he be-levyde. Ande he answeryd and sayde that he wyste welle that hit was hooly brede, and nought Goodys oune blessyde body. And thenne was the tonne putt ovyr hym ande fyre put unto hym; and whenne he felde fyre he cryde marcy. And a-non the prynce commaundyd to take a wey the fyre, and hit was don soo anon. And then the prynce askyd hym yf that

---

* *Percy.* A clerical error. "Harry Prince of Wales" is the reading in other Chronicles.

he wolde for-sake hys heresy and be-leve on the faythe of alle Hooly
Chyrche, and he wolde gyffe hym hys lyffe and goode i-nowe
whyle he levyd; but he wolde nought, but contynuyde forthe in
hys heresye.   And thenne the prynce commaundyd hym up to be
brende at onys, and soo he was.   And John Gylott, vynter, he made
ij wevers to be take, the whyche folowyd the same waye of heresy.

And the same tyme was the hurlynge in Estechepe by the lòrde
Thomas and the lorde John, the kyngys sone, &c.

Versus { Hereticus credat ne[a] perustus ab orbe recedat;
{ Ne fides[b] ledat [Satel][c] hune baratro sibi predat.

Thomas Knollys,   ⌠ Thomas Pyke   ⌡ A° xij°.
Mayre of London   ⌡ Thomas Penne   ⌠

Ande that same yere there com inbassetours to the kynge from
the Duke of Burgeyne for to have men sowdyd whithe hym ayenst
the Duke of Orlyauns, but the kynge wolde not graunte hym non.
And they spake unto the prynce, and he sende thedyr the Erle of
Arundelle and Syr John Oldecastelle, Lorde of Cobham, and many
mo knygtys and squyers of thys londe.

Robert Checheley,   ⌠ John Raynewelle   ⌡ A° xiij°.
Mayre of London   ⌡ William Cotton   ⌠

And that yere, the xij day of October, the yere of oure Lord
M¹ cccc and xj, ther was in Temys iij flodys in oo day.   And
that yere the Lorde Thomas, the kyngys sone, was made Duke of
Clarence, and that yere there com inbassetours fro the Duke of
Orlyaunce unto the kyng for to wage men ayenst the Duke of
Burgayne, and þᵉ kyng sende thedyr the Duke of Clarence and
othyr certayne lordys; and at the feste of Syut Laurence they
londyd at Hoggys.   And the same yere the kyng let make to be
smetyn newe nowblys, but they were of lasse wyght thenne was
the olde nobylle by the paysse of an halpeny wyght, soo that a

---

[a] *no.* ve in MS., struck out and corrected into " ne."

[b] *fides.* So in our MS. and in Harl. 565. J. reads *fidos,* which of course is better
grammar. Fabyan has *fidem.*

[c] *Satel, i. e.* Satan. The word is omitted in our MS., but occurs in all the similar
MS. Chronicles, and in the first two editions of Fabyan.

nobylle shuld wey but iiijd. and halfe a peny, and that l. nowblys Hen. IV.
A.D. 1412-13
shulde make a pounde of Troye wyght.

| Wylliam Walderne, | Raffe Lubnaham | A° xiiij°. |
| Mayre of London | William Sevenok | |

Ande that same yere the kyng dydo at Westemyster, the xx day
of Marche, the yere of oure Lorde M¹ cccc and xij; and he ys
byryde at Cauntyrbury be-syde the schryne. And that same yere
Syr John Olde Castelle was a restyde at Wynsore and sende to the
Toure of London for poyntys of heresy that he was accusyd of;
and at the Frere Prechourys he was examnyd by fore alle the
clargy of thys realme, spyritualle and temporalle and relygyous,
and he was sent unto the Toure a-yenne; and sone aftyr he brake
owt of the Towre and wentte in to Walys; and aftyr he was take
ayen by the Lorde Powes in the tyme of Rychard Merlowe, as ye
shalle hyre aftyr.

Walderne, mayor, the same xiiij yere of his* fadyr and the fyrste
yere of the sone, ande thys ys rckynde but for oone yere.

Thes ben the namys of Mayrys of London and of the Sherevys Hen. V.
A.D. 1413-15
of the same for-sayde cytte in the tyme of Kyng Harry the v, that
was crownyd the ix day of Aprylle at Westemyster, the yere of
oure Lorde M¹ cccc xiij. And hyt was apon Passyon Sonday,
and that was a fulle wete day of rayne.

| William Waldcrne, | Raffe Lubnaham | Anno primo. |
| Mayre of London | William Sevenok | |

Ande that yere the kyng made to be brought the bonys of Kyng
Rychard to Westemyster, and they were beryd and put in his owne
sepulture, that he let make hym selfe with Queue Anne his wyfe.
ᵇ þis was the laste yere ᵇ of raygne of the fadyr, and the fyrste yere
of the raygne of the sone, Kyng Harry the v.

| William Crowmer, | John Sutton | Anno ij° |
| Mayre of London | John Nichole | |

* So in MS.
ᵇ The words between ᵇ ᵇ are repeated in the MS.

Ande that same yere, on the Twelfe the nyght, were a-restyd certayne personys, called Lollers, atte the sygne of the Ax, whithe owte Byschoppe ys gate, the whyche Lollers hadde caste to have made a mommynge at Eltham, and undyr coloure of the mommynge to have dystryte the kyng and Hooly Chyrche. And they badde ordaynyde to have hadde the fylde be-syde Syn Gylys. But, thonkyd be God Almyghty, owre kyng hadde warnyng thereof, and he come unto London and toke the felde be syde Syn Jonys in Clerkynwelle; and as they come the kyng toke them, and many othyr. And there was a knyght take that was namy[d] Syr Roger of Acton, and he was drawe and hanggyd be syde Syn Gyly, for the kynge let to be made iiij payre of galowys, the whiche that were i-callyd the Lollers galowys. Al so a preste that hyght Syr John Bevyrlay, and a squyer that hyght John Browne of Olde-castellys, they were hanggyd; and many moo were hanggyd and brent, to the nomber of xxxviij personys and moo. And that yere was Tebayne Breste,[a] a preste, slayne in London by a squyer that was callyd Yownser and hys men; wherefore the same Yownser with iij of his men for-swore the lond. And that yere was the Parlyment at Layceter.

Thomas Faukener,	John Michell	
Mayre of London	Thomas Aleyne	Anno iij°.

Ande that same yere was brent in Smethefild John Claydon, schynner, and Rychard Turmyn, baker, for heresye that they were convycte a-pon. Al so the same yere the kyng toke his jornay and wagyd[b] in to Normandy; and the xv day of Juny the kyng roode thorowe London[c] whithe sherevys, aldermen, and alle the comeners brought the kynge at Blacke Hethe; and there the mayre ande alle hys aldermen with alle the comyns toke there leve of þe kynge, and

---

[a] His name is given as Maister "John Tybbay, clerk," in Harl. 565. It is "Tykcy, preest," in Vit. A. xvi.

[b] So in MS., but apparently a transcriber's error for "viagyd."

[c] So in MS.; but doubtless we should supply here, as the beginning of a new sentence, "And the mayor."

the kyng bade the mayre goo home and kepe welle hys chambyr in hys absens, and [yave hym][a] Crystysse blessyng and hys, and he sayde "Cryste save London." And he roode forthe hys way tylle he cam to Hampton, and there he roosteryd hys mayne. And there were certayne persoonys that had caste to slayne oure kynge, but God that knewe alle trougthe, he sende warnynge to oure kyng; and hys enmys, the whiche namys folowy the aftyr, Syr Richarde Camborowe,[b] Erle of Cambryge, Syr Harry, Lorde Scrope, ande Syr Thomas Gray, knyght, with moo of hyr assent, þe whiche persoonys were a-restyde and put in the preson, ande do to dethe. And the xij day of Auguste the kyng saylyd towarde Arflewe, whythe M^l M^l sperys and moo; and the xvj day of the same monythe he londyd at Kytkawys, and the Satyrday he leyde sege unto the towne of Arflewe, and that was the Satyrday nexte aftyr of the Assompsyon of oure Lady; and the sege contynuyd unto the Sonday nexte be fore the feste of Syut Mychelle, on the whiche Sonday the towne of Arflewe was delyveryd uppe to the kyng, that was xxij day of Septembre. But hit ys to wyte that the Tewysday before, that ys to saye the xvj day of the same monythe, at xij of the clocke whytheynne nyght, the lordys that were the capytaynys and governowrys of the towne, that ys to wete the Lorde Gawcorte,[c] the Lorde Tutvyle, and moo othyr lordys, sende owte herodys of armys unto the Duke of Clarens, prayng hym at the reverens of God that he wolde of hys hyghe lordeschippe that he wolde graunte them lyve and leve for to trete whythe what persoonys that the kyng wolde a-sygne unto hem; and the kyng at the reverens of God and at hyre requeste he assygnyde the Duke of Exceter, the Lorde Fchewe, and Syr Thomas Erpyngham, to hyre whatt they wolde say and desyre. And they desyryd that the kyng wolde nought warre on them fro that oure of mydnyght unto the Sonday nexte aftyr the feste of Synt Mychell, and but hyt were

---

[a] Omitted in our MS., but supplied from Vit. A. xvi.
[b] *Camborowe*. Conysborughe in Vit.
[c] *Sawcorte* in our MS. by a misreading; Gawcourte in Vit.

rescwyd by batayle by that day by the Frenysche kyng or by the
Dolfynne, ellys at that daye to delyver the towne unto the kynge,
and they to have hyr lyvys and hyr goodys.   Ande the kyng sende
hem worde yf that they wolde delivery the towne on the morne
aftyr, be the oure of mydnyght a bove sayde, with owte any condyscyon, he wolde accepte hyt, and in non othyr wyse he bade hem
for to trete.   Ande yette the Fraynysche lordys prayde our lordys
that they wolde fochesave to be-seche the kynge at the reverens of
God and of oure Lady that he wolde graunte them respyte fro
the same Twysday at nyght unto the Sonday nexte aftyr tylle one
owre aftyr none; and in the mayne tyme the lordys that were
captaynys of the towne to come to the kynge whithe xxiiij
knyghtys and squyers with hem, of the moste suffycyent men
whithe in the towne, and they to be sworne on Goddys body
opynly before alle the pepylle.   But yf[a] hit soo were that the
Fraynysche kynge or the Dolfynne rescwyde hem by that Sonday
by the owre of none, othyr ellys a-non aftyr none, they for to
delyvery the towne to the kyng and alle hyr bodys and goodys
to don whythe hem what so hem evyr lyste, whythe [b] any condiscyon.
Whythe that the kynge sufferde hem to sende unto Frauns viij
personys owte of the towne lettyng hym wytte in what plytte
that they stode yn, and the kyng grauntyd hem; and uppe the
Wanysday by þe mone the lordys come owte, and xxij knyghtys
and squyers whythe hem; and thenne come the prosessyon solempny
and stately, whithe xxiiij copys of clothe of golde by-fore Goddys
body, whythe many worschipfulle lordys, knyhtis, and squyers,
and othyr multytude of pepylle from þe kyngys tente, solempny
and stately as evyr was done suche a thyng be-for tyme.   But the
kyng was nott here present.   And the Franysche lordys made thare
hyr othys a-pon the sacrament; and, the othys done, the Fraynysche
lordys were brought unto the kyngys tente, and there they dynyd
in the kyngys halle, but in alle thys tyme they sawe nought the
kynge.   And whanne that they hadde etyn they departyd and

---

[a] *But if,* i. e. unless.   [b] *whythe,*   withoute, Vit.

delyveryd to sartayne for to kepe yn ostage tylle the Sonday on none, as hyt was a cordyment i-made before tyme whenne that they toke hyr othys. And the Sonday at the same owre a-signyd the kyng hadde a tente phyght a-pone a hylle be-fore the towne, and there he sate in his estate, ryally, and alle hys lordys aboute hym. And thenne come the Fraynysche lordys, with lxiiij whythe hem of the moste suffycyentt men that were whythe yn the towne, to the kyngys owne propyr person, and delyveryd uppe the keyes of the towne and hyr boodys and hyr goodys to the kynges grace, whithe owte any condyscyon. And thys was the xxij day of Septembre, the yere of our Lorde M¹ cccc xv. And thenne sone aftyr the kynge and hys mayne ostyde from thens xxj dayes thorowe the realme of Praunce towarde Caleys. And the Fraynysche men hyrde telle of his comyng that way, and they brake the bryggys there that the kyng shulde passe ovyr, and in so moche that ᵃ he myght not passe noo way but he moste nedys mete with the Fraynysche oste. And a-pon the Fryday, that ys to saye, the day of Syn Cryspyn and Cryspynyany, alle the ryalle pouer of Praunce come by-fore oure kynge and hys lytylle blessyd mayne. And thenne they sawe the Dolfynne whythe alle the lordys of France were by-fore oure good kynge enbatellyd in iij batellys the number of iij schore M¹ men of armys. And that was the fayryste syght of armyde men that evyr any man saye in any place. And the kyng sawe he myght not passe whythe out batayle, and thenne he sayde unto hys lytylle mayne, "Serys and felowys, yendyr maynye wylle lette us of oure waye, and they wylle not come unto us. But nowe lette every man preve hym-selfe a goode man thys day and a-vance hys baner in the beste tyme of the day and yere." Ande the kyng roode ande hys basnet in hys hede, and alle othyr men wente on hyr foote a-passe in hyr hoole araye and ᵇ Englysche myle or that they assemblyde. And thorowe Goddys grace the kynge made hys way thoroughe the thyckyste of alle the batayle; and ther was slayne on the kyngys syde the Duke of Yorke, the

ᵃ *that* repeated in MS.   ᵇ So in MS.

Erle Southeffolke, and ij knyghtys, and Davy Gam, and of the
gentylle men no moo, and of alle maner of Englysche men hyt
passyd not xxviij personys.   And on the Fraynysche syde was
slayne the Duke of Launsonne, the Duke of Barre, the Duke of
Braban, ande vij erlys, and the Constabylle of Praunce, and the
Senschalle of Henowde, and the Mayster Alblester,[a] and many
moo lordys, and knygtys and squyers v M¹ and moo.   And
there was take the Duke of Orlyaunce, the Duke of Burbon,
the Counte of Rychemounde, and the Counte of Ewe, þe Marchalle
of Fraunsce, Syr Bursegaunte, and many moo othyr knyghtys
and squyers.   And whanne thys was done the kyng bode alle
nyghte in a vyllage faste be-syde ther that the batelle was done.
And on the morowe he toke hys waye unto Calys whythe hys
lordys and hys presoners, whythe hys owne mayne.   And the
xxiij day of November the kyng come unto London whythe alle
hys presoners a bove sayd.   And there he was ressayvyd worthely
and ryally, for the mayre, with alle the aldermen, whythe alle
good comyners, roode and fette hym ynne.   And whythe a ryalle
processyon he was brought ynne; and there was mad, stondyng
apone the brygge, Syn Gorge ryally armyd, and at the Crosse in
Cheppe was made a castelle, and there yn was moche solempnyte of
angelys and virgenys syngyng merely.   And soo he roode unttylle
that he came to Powlys, and there mette whithe hym xvj byschoppys
and abbattys whithe processyon and sensyd hym, and brought hym
uppe in to þo qwere whythe devoute songe, and there he offerde and
the Franysche lordys alle soo.   And thenne he rode forthe unto
Westemyster; and the mayre and hys bretheryn brought hym there.

Ande thys same yere be-ganne the generalle Conselle at Custaunce
of alle clargye and of alle maner of nacyons.

Nicholaus Wotton, | William Cambryge | A° iiij°.
Mayre of London | Alayne Everarde |

And in that same yere, onne the morne aftyr Syn Symonnys day

---

[a] Thomas Arblastier. He was one of the retinue of Sir William Bourchier.
See Nicolas's Battle of Agincourt, 360.

and Jude, that the mayre shulde ryde to Westemyster for to take hys othe, come tydyngys to London of the batayle a-bove sayde by the Byschoppe of Worseter,[a] that tyme beyng Chaunceler, for he come to London erly in the mornynge, and warnyd the mayre. And thenne thorowe London they lette rynge the bellys in every chyrche and song *Te Deum;* and at Powlys, at ix of the clocke, the tydyngys were oppynly proclaymyd to alle the comeners of þe cytte and to alle othyr strangerys. And thenne the Quene,[b] and alle hyr byschoppys and alle the lordys þat were in London that tyme, wentte to Westemyster on hyr fete a prosessyon to Syut Edwarde ys schryne, whythe alle the prestys, and clerkys, and fryers, and alle othyr relygyous men, devoutely syngynge ande saynge the letanye. And whenne they hadde offerde, the mayre com home rydynge merely whythe alle hys aldermen and comeners as they were i-wounte for to doo.

Le Feste de Sentt Gorge a Wyndesore.

Ande thys yere com the Emperowre of Almayne[c] in to London be-fore the Feste of Synt Gorge. Ande the feste was deferryde unto hys commynge, and that was done solempny at the castylle of Wyndesore. And at the prosessyon the kynge went a-pone the upper-moste syde of the emperowre, and soo alle the masse tyme he stode a-bove the emperoure. Ande at the mete the kyng sate on the ryght syde of the emperoure, and the Duke of Bedforde sate on the lefte syde, and the Chaunceler of Inglonde and the Byschoppe of Devylyn sate on the left syde, and the Duke of Bryga and a-nothyr duke of the emperours sate on the kyng ys syde; and alle thosse vij satte on oo syde of þe table. And the fyrste sotellete of the fyrste cours was howe Oure Lady armyd Syn Gorge and a aungylle doyng on hys sporys. And the secunde sotellete was Syn Gorge rydynge and fyghtyng whythe a dragon

---

[a] Should be Winchester. Henry Beaufort, Bishop of Winchester, afterwards Cardinal. The title is given correctly in Vit

[b] Joan of Navarre, widow of Henry IV.   [c] Sigismund

whythe hys spere in hys honde. And the iij sotellete was a castelle, and Syn Gorge and the kynges doughter ledyng the lambe in at the castelle gatys. And all thes sotelleteys were servyd be-fore the emperoure and the kyng and noo ferther; ande othyr lordys were servyd with sotelleteys aftyr hyr astate and degre. And that same yere come the Duke of Holand into London, but he was nought at the feste a-fore sayde. And the emperoure lay at Westmyster alle the wyle that he was here for the moste party, and the Duke William of Holand in the byschope ys place of Ely; and sone aftyr Mydsomer the kyng went to Caleys whythe the emperoure, and the duke saylyd home ayenne and mette whythe kyng at Caleys. And the Duke of Burgayne and the Counte of Charlys sone come to Gravelynge; and the kynge sende thedyr the Duke of Glouceter hys brother and the Erle of Marche to abyde there in ostage, wylys that the Duke of Burgayne come to Calys to speke with the kynge; and in the myddys of the ryver the lordys mette togedyr. And the dukys sone of Burgayn ressayvyd oure lordys and led hem in to Fraunce, and the Erle of Warwyke ressayvyd the Duke of Burgayne ande brought hym to Calys, and there they badde a conselle twyne hem two; and thenne he toke hys leve of the kyng. And the Erle of Warwyke brought hym unto Gravelyng water and in to the same place there as they mette at the fyrste metynge; and there every party toke hyr leve of othyr. And thenne the kynge retornyd ayenne into Inglonde and the emperoure saylyde unto Holande and so passyd forthe in to Constaunce.

Alle so that same yere the Duke of Bedforde and the Erle of Marche, on oure Lady Day the Assumpsyon, they fought whythe viij grete carykys of Jene and whythe l. othyr shyppys, and they toke hem whythe hyr patronys and drownyde a grette hulke of the contre of Flaundrys.

Harry Barton,	Robert Wedyngton	
Mayre of London	John Covyntre	Anno v⁰.

Ande the same yere, on Syn Petrys eve and Poule, the Erle of

Huntyngdon whythe oþyr certayne lordys faughtyn whithe carykys of Gene, and dyscomfyte hem, and toke iiij of þᵉ grettyste of them and hyr patronys. And the amerelle of hem was the Duke of Burbone, and he was take whithe hem whythe alle the tresoure that sholde have wagyd hem for halfe a yere. Al so the same yere the kynge saylyd unto Normandye the second tyme, ande he londyd on Lammas day by-syde Tooke in Normandye. And the same tyme the kyng wanne the towne of Tooke and assaylyd the castelle, the whyche castelle on Syn Laucrens evynne was yolde unto the kynge, and he gave hyt unto hys brother the Duke of Clarens whithe alle the lorschippys dependaunt there too; and thenne the Duke of Clarens roode forthe to Cane whythe othyr lordys whythe hym. And one oure Lady evyn, the Assumpcyon, he mustryd hys men by-fore the towne of Cane; and the xij day of August the kyng layde sege to Cane, and that contynuyd tylle the day of the Natyvyte of oure Lady nexte folowynge; uppon the same day the towne whythe grete sawte was yoldyd and wonne. And thenne the kyng layde sege unto the castelle, and that in shorte tyme was yoldyn unto the kynge; and whylys the kyng boode in Cane, the Duke of Clarens roode to Bayeux and wanne that. And the same yere the kyng wanne Argentyne, bothe the towne and the castelle. And the kyng wanne Alansonne and many moo stronge castellys and townys and stronge abbeyes.

Ande the same yere, a-pon Estyr daye at aftyr none, the Lorde Stronge and Syr John Trusselle, knyght, fylle at debate for hyr wyvys in the chyrche of Syn Donstonys in the Este, evyn at the prechyng tyme. In the same fraye Thomas Pedwardynne, fysche-monger, was slayne as he wolde have lettyde hem of hyr fyghtynge, and many men were i-hurte; and therefore the chyrche was suspendyd. Ande thenne was the Lorde Stronge a-restyde and brought unto the Counter in the Pultrye, and the Sonday nexte aftyr he was cursyde in every chyrche in London, whithe boke, belle, and candelle, in one houre of the day. And aftyr he dyde hys penaunsse opynly thorow London for hys trespas ayenst Hooly

Chyrche.   And that yere was a dyre yere of whete, for a buschelle was worthe ij s.

| Rycharde Merlowe, | Harry Rede | A° vj°. |
| Mayre of London | John Gedney | |

Ande the same yere, *scilicet*, in anno v^{to},[a] the general conselle was endyd, and a unyte made in Hooly Chyrche, and oo pope chosynne at Custaunce on Syn Martyns daye, by comyn assente of alle the generalle counselle, the whyche was callyd Pope Martyn the fyrste.[b] Alle so the same yere Syr Johnne Oldecastelle was take in the Marche of Walys and brought unto Westemyster in a chare, and there he was juggyde to the dethe; and thys was hys juggement, that he shulde be ladde thorowe London in the same chare unto Towre Hylle, and there to be layde on a hyrdylle and drawe to Syn Gylys galowys, and there to be hanggyd and brent.   And so he was hanggyd by a stronge chayne.   For there was the Duke of Bedforde, the Duke of Exceter, and alle the lordys of thys londe that were þat tyme a-bowte London, tylle that they badde sene hys juggement.

Ande the same day the person of Wortham, theffe, and hys peramowre was broughte unto Westemyster Halle.   And he was sente to Newgate, and there he dyde.

Ande that same yere the kyng layde sege unto Faleys the fyrste day of Novembre, and that sege contynuyde unto the xx day of Decembre, the yere of grace M¹ cccc xvij.   Thenne the towne dysendyd for to trete whythe the kynge, and the kyng commyttyd the trety unto Thomas Erle of Saulysbury, and to Harry Lorde Fehewe, and to Syr Johnne Cornewale, and to Syr Wylliam Haryngdon, knyghtes and commyssyoners for hys partye; and as for the party of the towne, Syr Wylliam Molene,[c] Syr Gylberte

---

[a] Notwithstanding that the mayor and sheriffs for the sixth year are given at the head of this chapter, almost the whole of it is devoted to events of the fifth year omitted in their proper place.

[b] Should be Martin the *Fifth*.

[c] *Molene.*   Melone in Vit.   The name is Moulhou in Rymer.

Hen. V.
A.D. 1417-18

Mounstrewys, lorde of Fayete,[a] capytaynys of men of armys, and of the schotte whythe ynne the towne of Faleys, and whythe [them] [b] a pon the same trete, the lord of Gamulle;[c] which [d] parteys entretid[e] ande a cordyd uppon the artyculys and poyntmentys aftyr folowyng.

Fryste, that hit ys accordyd that the secunde day of Janyver next folowynge they shulde yelde uppe þe towne be-for sayde of Faleys, whythe ynne the houre of terce, into the hondys and power of oure soverayne lorde the kynge, or in to the hondys of hem be hym commyttyde and assygnyde, yf soo be that they be nott rescwyde be batayle of the kynge hyr lorde, or Dolfyn, hys eldyste sone, or by the Constabylle of Fraunce. And on that the kyng [to][f] setten or do settynne in the fore sayde towne suche [g] warde and kepynge as hit schalle lyke hym.

Alle so hit ys accordyd that alle the strongers that benne in the fore sayde towne of Faleys, the whyche before thys tyme hathe ben founde agayne, and in the rystynge of, the kynge in tyme sythe hys fyrste comynge to hys Duche of Normandye, were hyt at Cane, or in any othyr of furtheresser, or that have benn with the kynge, or with any of hys subgettys in hys commaundementys, that alle suche strangerys shulle put hem only in the kyngys grace and mercy of oure soverayne lorde the Kyng of Inglonde.

Alle so hyt ys accordyd that they shalle delyvery and yeldyn uppe [h] alle the presoners, Englysche or any othyr, holdyng of owre lege lorde the Kyng of Inglonde, the whiche that [i] have benne

<hr>

[a] *Fayete.* Our MS. reads, *lorde of feyfty capytaynys;* but Vit. more accurately, "lord Fayete, capteyns."   [b] Omitted in MS.; J. reads "hem."

[c] *the lord of Gamulle.* This reading is taken from J. The name is written in the same way on Norman Roll, 5 Hen. V., m. 2, from which the treaty is printed in Rymer, and perhaps it may be read, as Rymer reads it, "Gauville." Our MS. reads absurdly, "they of Gaunte." Perhaps the person intended was the Sire de Graville, who a few months later (4 July, 1418) disputed with the English the passage of the Seine at Pont de l'Arche.—Williams's "Gesta Henrici V.," 122

[d] *which.* with, MS.   [e] *entretid.* encreayd, MS.; corrected from J.
[f] Supplied from J.

[g] *suche.* The MS. reads "whiche," an evident error, which is corrected from Vit.
[h] "the town and," V.   [i] *that.* there, V.; that there, J.

presoners be fore [a] the fyrste daye a fore sayde, ande at the same
daye of thys present trete, and [that] [b] non appechementt ben put up
on none of hem by hyr maysterys nowe at that thys tyme [nor in
tyme] [c] to come, be hyt sommaunce [d] requyrynge or askyng in any
maner [matier] [e] what soo evyr hyt be, but fynallye the for sayde
maysterys shalle aquyntyn, renownsyn, and relessyn to hyr presoners
hyr troughthys, hyr behestys, and hyre othysse, whyche that [the
seid presoners mowen have made to heir maisters in eny maner, and
that] [e] whythe owte fraude or malyngyne.

Alle so hyt ys accordyd that the fore sayde capytaynys shulde delyvery owte of the towne of Faleys in to the hondys of the commys-
senaryours of oure soverayne lorde the Kyng of Inglonde, al thoo
that were borne in Inglonde, Walys, and Yrlonde, or Gascoyne,
whiche be-fore thys tyme have holde whythe the party of Inglonde,
and for thys presentt tyme ben in thys sayde towne of Faleys
contrarye ayenste the kyng and hys parteyes.

Alle so hyt ys accordyd that non of the captaynys, nor burgessys,
nor non othyr of the towne, shalle geve nor suffer for to be gevyn
to hem of the castelle of Faleys any strengthe of men, of armys, or
of schotte, nor maner of socoure of armyrowrysse or artury, schottys,
powder, gonnys, or any othyr comfort durynge the for sayde trete.

Alle so hyt ys accordyd that noo captayne, ne none sowdyer,
burgeys, ner comyner, nor non othyr beynge whythe yune the
sayde towne of Faleys, shalle ressayve or suffer to be ressayved or
drawyn owte of the castelle the captayne of the same castelle nor
non othyr of the same garysonne thereynne beynge at [f] thys present
tretys. [g] Ande alle soo they shulle nott drawe any [h] of hem of the
castelle undyr the coloure of thys presentt tretye.

Ande uppon thys our soverayne lorde the kynge of specyalle grace

---

[a] *be fore* repeated in MS.   [b] Supplied from J.

[c] Omitted in MS.; supplied from J. and V.

[d] J. reads, "be it to sommone, requiren, or asken."

[e] Omitted in MS.; supplied from V.   [f] *at.* and, MS.; at, J.

[g] *tretys.* tymo, J.; trete tyme, V.

[h] *any.* J. reads, "ony goodes of them of the castel undre the colour and shadowe
of her owne goodes of the towne, ne undre the colour of this present trete."

hathe grauntyd unto the forsayde captaynys, sowdyers, and othyr of the sayde towne, hyr horse, harneys, and alle hyr othyr goodys what evyr hyt be, owte-take artury, shotte, powders and gonnys, arblastrys, and bawderykys for arblastrys, whyche that shalle abyde stylle in the same towne, and alle wey for to sen that the straungers of whyche the seconde artycule makythe menęyon, nor shalle not emynucyon[a] the pryvelegys and the benvfytys of thys presentt artyculys.

Alle the for sayde captaynys have sworne a-pon hyr honowre that durynge the for sayde trete that they shalle not makyn nor suffyr to be made any brekyng, wastynge, nor be putt nor done a waye any of suche artyculys, shotte, or any othyr thyng be-fore sayde.

Alle so hit ys accordyd that durynge the fore sayd trete noo maner of poyntment of the wallys of the towne shalle be made, but the wallys shalle be leve stylle lyke as they ben foundyn the fyrste daye of this present trete.

Alle so hyt hys accordyd that noo sowdyer nor stranger in the towne of Faleys shalle not make noo robory nor pylyage on the burgeysys of the towne of Faleys in noo maner, ande yf any suche evylle doers ben founde, that thenne the captaynys of men of armys and of shotte do ther on justyfyynge and execusion, or ellys that alle suche evylle doers shalle forfete hyre benyfys and hyr saffe-condyte.

Alle so hyt [is][b] accordyd that the sayde captaynys nor non othyr of the same towne shalle nought bere away, nor purlayne, nor suffer to ben i-purlaynyd or doo a-waye, any ornamentys, jewellys, or relyqwys of Hooly Chyrche, be they of the same towne or of any othyr relygyous owte of þe towne, that perchaunce were brought unto the towne for dowte of warre or othyr wyse i-brought unto the towne.

Alle so hit ys accordyde that the for sayde captaynys nor non

[a] *emynucyon.* enjoie, J. A blank is left for the word in V.
[b] Omitted in MS.

othyr of hyr feleschyppe shalle nought ledyn nor bere, nor suffer
for to be borne nor lede, owte of the townye of Falcys, noo maner
of goodys undyr the colowre of appyontementt, but oonly hyr owne
propyr goode.

Alle so hyt ys accordyd that alle the capitaynys whythe hem of
alle hyr company shalle a-voyde the towne of Faleys the secunde
day of Janyver abovyn sayde by the sonne goynge downe, but yf
that they were rescwyd as hyt ys a-fore sayde. And oure soverayne
lorde the Kynge of Inglond of hys specyalle grace hathe grauntyd
to alle and to every burgeys of the towne of Faleys, that wylle
dwelle and abyde stylle in the fore sayde towne, there to a-byde
and dwelle, sykerly and surely and fully, whythe owte any enpechy-
mcnt uppon hem to putte in body or in goodys, mevabylle or
unmevabylle, as herytagys nor possessyons whythe ynne the fore
sayde towne, but pessabylly rejoysynne as hyr propyr goodys at
thys tyme and in tyme to come, as they myght done before the
yelding upe of the same towne; be so alle way that they so wyllynge
to dwelle and byde in the same towne be come legys and obedyaunte
to oure soverayne lorde the Kyng of Inglonde and hys ayrys.

[a]Alle so hyt ys accordyd that noo captayne, sowdyer, nor burgeys,
nor comyner, nor non othyr whithe ynne the sayde towne of Faleys,
shalle nought ressayvynne, nor suffer to ressayvynne, nor drawyn of
the castelle of Faleys the captayne ther of, nor non of there garysons,
nor non at thys tyme there abydynge [in][b] the for sayde chastelle, nor
noo maner of goodys to hem longyng undyr colowrc and shadowe of
goodys of the towne, nothyr undy[r] coloure of thys presente trete.

Alle so hyt ys accordyd that hangyng thys prescntte trety and
appoyntement noo maner of warre shalle be made by-twyne hem
ande the oste of oure soverayne lorde the Kyng of Inglonde and
hem of the towne of Faleys.[c]

---

[a] This is a repetition of a former article which will be found in its right place on
p. 118.   [b] Omitted in MS.; supplied from J.

[c] J. adds, " forseen alwoys that it be understanden that tho castel of Faloys, no
non theryn, be comprohendid ne taken in this present abstinence."

Hen. V.
A.D. 1417-1

Alle so hyt ys accordyd that the forsayde lordys and capytaynys of the towne of Faleys shalle take and delyvery xij of the jentyllyste knyghtys and squyers notablys in ostage, the whiche shalle be delyveryde a-yenne at the daye that the forsayde lordys and capytaynys havyng fully hyr poyntys.[a] And for thys trete and appoyntment welle and trewly [to][b] ben holdyn on oure parte, the forsaide Thomas Erle of Salysbury, Harry Lorde Feehewe, John Cornewale and Wylliam Haryngdon, knyghtys, unto thys sedylle (id est a bylle) of poyntmentt have sette to oure selvs for the grete[c] affyrmacyon of trought. Gevynne be-fore the towne of Faleys, the xx day of the monythe of December and the yere a-fore sayde.

The whyche towne in maner and forme as hyt ys be-fore sayde was yoldynne to our soverayne lorde the kynge of Inglonde þᵉ seconde daye of Janyver as hyt was before lemytyd, ande the castelle be lefte stylle un-y[o]ldon unto the fyrste daye of Fevyrer;[d] the whyche castelle was yoldynne the seconde dave of the monythe a-bove sayde, and delyveryd in maner and forme a-fore-saydc, &c.

Ande thenne the Kyng of Inglonde lette parte his oste to prynces thens on dyversse wayes; that ys to saye, on party toke my lorde the Duke of Clarens whythe many fulle worthy lordys whythe hym, and he gate many townys and castellys and stronge abbeys. And the Duke of Glouceter toke a nothyr partye of the oste, and whythe hym the Erle of Marche, the Lorde Graye, the Lorde Clyfforde, Syr Watyr Hongerford, stywarde of the kyngys howse, whythe many othyr knyghtys and squyers; and he gate, or he layde sege to Chyrborowe, xxiiij townys and castellys. And sone aftyr Ester he layde sege to the towne of Chyrborowe, and contynowyde unto Mychelmasse, and thenne the towne and the castelle was yolde unto hym. Ande the iij party of the oste the kynge

Hen. V.
A.D. 1417-19.
delyveryde unto the Erle of Warwyke and othyr lordys whythe
hym.   And they gate many stronge townys and castellys and abbeys.

Here begynnythe the vj yere.

Ande aftyr Ester the kyng layde sege unto Lovers ande wanne
hyt, and aftyr that he wanne Pountte Large.   And the kynge
layde sege unto the cytte of Reyne,[a] and that contynuyd tylle the
xxiiij[b] day of Janyver nexte aftyr.

| Wylliam Sevenoke, Mayre of London | John Bryon Raffe Barton John Pernys | A° vij. |

The same John Bryan scheryve unto the ix day of Octobre, and
thenne he dyde; and thenne John Pernys was chose sheryve for
the yere.   And fro that day of Saynt Edwarde contynuyd the sege
of Rone unto the xxiiij[b] day of Janyver, as hyt ys by-fore sayde; at
the whiche day they of the cytte desyryd to trete.   And the kynge
commaundyd the Erle of Warwyke, and the Erle of Salysbury, the
Lorde Fehewe, Syr Watyr Hungerforde, Gylbert Houmfryvyle,
John Vasquyes de Almada, and Robert[c] Knyght, to trete whythe
hem.   And for the party of Roone [these folowyng]:[d]

Fyrste, hyt ys accordyd that Syr Gy Butler, captayne of the
cytte of Roone, with the consentte of the nobylle cyttezyns and
of othyr dwellynge and beyng in the same cytte and castelle a-bove
sayde, whythe owt fraude or malyngnynge, what tyme aftyr the
myddys of the xix day of thys present monythe of Janyver, oure
sayde lorde the kynge wylle that the cytte and the castelle too
hym or to hys be delyveryd undyr maner and in forme whythe
ynne wrytte.

Alle so hyt ys accordyd that the day and the howre[e] of that of
the nobylle cyttezyns and othyr whatt soo evyr they be dwellynge

---

[a] Rouen.   [b] Should be the 13th.
[c] *Robert.* Robesard, J.
[d] [*these folowyng*].   Omitted in MS.; supplied from J.   Nevertheless it is clear
there is a further omission, even in J.
[e] *howre.*   The *h* of this word is struck out in all these places.

and beynge in the fore sayde cytte and castelle shalle submyt hem in alle thyngys to the grace of oure excellent lorde the kyng.

Alle so hyt ys accordyd that fro thys howre [a] unto the reale and effectualle [yeldyng] [b] of the sayde cytte and castelle, none of forsayde noble cyttezyns othyr othyr [c] being in the same cytte and castelle shalle nought goo owte of the sayde cytte and castelle with owte specyalle lyscens of oure excellente lorde the kynge. [d]

Alle so hyt ys accordyd that fro thys howre [a] unto the delyverans of the cytte any [e] of þe parteys shalle abstayne hem from alle goodys [f] of werre to make a yenste the othyr partys of hem. Alle so hyt ys accordyde that the noble cyttezcyns and othyr beynge in the cytte and castelle shalle paye to oure fore sayde lorde the kynge ccc M[l] scwtys of golde, where of alle way ij of hem shalle be worthe an Englyscke noble, or in stede of every scwte xxx grete blankys wyte, or xv grotys; of the whyche ccc M[l] scwtys that one parte shalle be payde unto oure soverayne lorde the kynge, or unto hys deputys, whythe yune the cytte of Roone be-fore sayde, the xxij day of thys present monyþe of Janyver, and the othyr halfe payde to oure sayde lorde or to hys deputys in the feste of Syn Mathie the Apostylle nexte to come, that shalle be the xxiij [g] day of Feverer, whythe owte any delay i-badde, &c. [h]

Alle so hyt ys accordyde that every subgett of oure sayde lorde the kynge that nowe ben or were presoners to any person in the sayde cytte or castelle, and hyr pleggys, shall be utterly fre as a-yens thes personnys, and the summys that they ar boundyn ynne, at the day of thys present trete and accorde.

---

[a] See note [*], p. 122. [b] Omitted in MS ; supplied from J.

[c] So in MS. The first "othyr" seems to mean "or."

[d] This clause is repeated in the MS. with the variation, "non of the fore sayde cyttezyns or othyr."

[e] any. every, J.

[f] goodys. Evidently a transcriber's error for dedys. J. reads dede.

[g] xxiij. Should be 24th. See Rymer, ix. 665.

[h] Here several articles are omitted which may be seen in Rymer. They are given in the English in J.

Hen. V
A.D. 1419.

Alle so hyt ys accordyde that alle and every soudyer and stranger beynge in the sayde citte and castelle shalle swere on the Evaungelys of God be-fore there departyng, that they shall not bere armys a-gayne oure sayde lorde the kynge or any of hys, unto the fyrste day of Janyver nexte to come, for no maner maundement þat to hem of any maner person in contrary may be done or ennyode.[a]

Alle so hyt ys accordyde that alle and every jewelle, relykys, and othyr goodys longgyng to the abbaye of Syut Kateryne, whythe ynne the same cytte and castelle, beyng alle hoolly, shalle be delyveryd unto hym whom that the Kyng of Inglonde deputyn or ordeyn hem to ressayve aftyr the delyveraunce of the sayd cytte.

Alle so hyt ys accordyde that the fore sayde noble cyttezyns and othyr whythe in the sayde cytte and castelle beyng, shalle make the same cytte and castelle be-fore the sayde xix daye of this present monythe of Janyver suffycyantly and honestely to be made clene, and alle so honestly and diligently that alle the dede bodys newe dede or to ben dede in to that daye of delyveraunce of the cytte honestely and dylygently shalle ben beryd.

Alle soo hyt ys accordyd that the for sayde noble cyttezyns and alle beynge in the sayde citte and castelle anon shalle receyve[b] and don entre in to the same cytte and castelle alle and everyche beynge in the dychys[c] of the sayde cytte that for penurye[d] went owte of the same cytte whom[e] they shalle be holde to fede unto the xix day of Janyver above sayde, as they wylle answere unto Gode and the kyng; and owte takyn them they shalle not ressayve non othyr personnys in to the same cytte or castelle unto the forsayde day with owte specyalle lyssens of oure moste dowtfulle lorde the Kyng of Inglonde. But yf hit happe any massyngere or harowde of armys

[a] enjoined.

[b] *receyve.* resome, MS.; recoyvo, V.; receyven, J.

[c] or about diebes, J.

[d] *penurye.* fomurye, MS.; penurie, J. Vit reads "fero."

[e] *whom.* whanne, MS.

Hen. V
A.D. 1419.

of the adversy party of the kynge to come to the partys of þᵉ gatys
or dychys of the sayde castelle and cytte . . . . . .ᵃ

Whiche ᵇ artyculys and appoyntmentys, as hyt ys before sayde, alle
and every chone in maner as hyt ys accordyd, the forsayde captaynys
and the noble cyttezyns ande othyr whythe ynne the sayde castelle and
citte being, welle and trewly whythe owte any fraude or malygny ᶜ to
holdyn ande observe and kepe they be-hote, ande thoo two be kepte
and fullefyllyd they bynd them soo, but yf yt be falle oure sayde
moste doughtefulle lorde the kynge, that God for bede, to ben ovyr
come in the batayle to hym i-made by Charlys hys adversarye of
Fraunce or the Duke of Burgayne, be-fore the for-sayde [xix] ᵈ day
of thys present monythe of Janyver; for to sen ᵉ alle way that [if] ᵈ
hyt be falle the forsayde Charlys adversary, othyr the Duke of
Burgayne, or any othyr, to come to the sege of oure kynge to remoeve ᶠ
fro the forsayde cytte, that nothyr the fore sayde captayne nor non
of the cyttezyns, sowdyers, othyr othyr ᵍ beyng whythe ynne the for
sayde cytte or castelle, shalle goo owte, nor noo maner helpe they
shalle delyverye nor lene to hem, so azens oure lorde the kynges
comyng in nomaner a wyse.

Alle so, that alle thes maner of poynttementysse, covenauntys,
and accordys, and every poyute as hyt ys a fore sayde, welle and
trewly and unbrokyn to be kepte; and for the more surete of the
same covenauntys and accordys, the for sayde captayne, the noble
cyttezyns, and othyr above sayde shalle ben takyn in thys tyme
anone into the hondys of oure lorde the kynge iiij schore notable

---

ᵃ The conclusion of the sentence is omitted not only in our MS. but also in J.
and V. In the Latin it is, "ipse in ipsa non recipietur, seu providebitur eidem per
dominum nostrum Regem de salvo conductu."

ᵇ *Whiche.* The MS. has "with the" written as if it were the continuation of the
previous sentence.

ᶜ *malygny.* malengyne, J.

ᵈ Omitted in MS.; supplied from J.

ᵉ *for to sen, i. e.* foreseen, provided.

ᶠ *remoeve.* remayne, MS., corrected from J.

ᵍ See page 123, note ᵃ.

plegys, where of xx^{ty} shalle be knyghtys and squyers, ande the reme-naunte cyttezyns of the same cytte, att hyr owne eoste to be sustaynyd. For the party sothcly of oure moste doutefulle lorde ande kynge a-fore sayde, gracyusly and benyngly consederynge the meke submyttynge and yeldynge of the sayde citte and castelle above sayde, he bathe grauntyde that alle and everye person of what a-state or degre that he be of condycyon with ynne the sayde castelle [and cite] [a] beyng, [excepte] [a] sartayne personys with ynne expressyde, that wylle be-come legys and subgctys to oure lorde the kynge, and fro hensforthe wylle dwelle undyr his obessauns, they shalle have there herytagys and goodys, mevablis and unmevablys, whythe ynne hys duche of Normandy constitute; and whiche that benne afore the day and date of thys present letters by oure fore sayde lorde the kynge to [b] othyr personys have nought be yovyn and grauntyde, excepte armours artyrlys a-bove sayd; makyng and doyng [for] [a] hyr herytagys, and for hyr unmevabylle goodys to oure for sayde lorde the kynge, the services [c] ther-of dewe and consuete, or to swere to whom suche maner of servyce of the graunte of oure lorde the kynge ought too long.

Alle so hyt ys agrauntyd of oure lorde the kynge ys be-halve, that alle the cyttezyns and dwellers of the cytte of Roone that nowe be, or in tyme to come shalle be, [and] [d] shall have alle ande every franches, lybertes, and prevelegys þ^e whiche of worthely mynde be progenys of oure lorde the kynge, of kyngys of Ing-londe, dukys of Normandye, to hem and to hys sayde cytte were grauntyde, in possessyon where [of] [a] they were the fyrste day that oure lorde the kynge a-fore sayde come by fore the sayde cytte; and alle so of more large grace of hys benyngnyte hathe grauntyde, that the same cyttezyns and dwellers of the citte shalle have alle the lyberteys, and franches, and prevelegys, where they were in pos-

---

[a] Omitted in MS.; supplied from J.
[b] *to.* and, MS.; corrected from J.
[c] *services.* sermoys, MS.
[d] This word is clearly superfluous.

sessyons on the fore sayde fyrste day of comynge of oure lorde the kynge before the cytte, of the grannte of hys progenytourys of kyngys of Praunce that were before tyme of Phylyppe Valeys, adversarye of oure lorde [the kyng].[a]

[Also it is grauntid and accordid in our lord] the kyngys behalve, that alle the strangers, sowdyers, and othyr in the fore sayde citte and castelle, beynge at thys tyme nought wyllynge to be come leges of oure lorde the kyng, the for-sayde citte so yoldynne as hit ys before sayde, to departe, levynge to oure sayde lorde the kyng all hyr armowrys, hors, artylyrs, and othyr thyngys, harneysse, and goodys, excepte the Normandys that wylle nought be lyges of oure lorde the kynge, þat thoo alle shalle a-byde presoners of oure lorde the kyng.

Alle so hyt ys grauntyd in oure lorde the kynges behalve, that the werre and alle so schrewde speche that duryng the sege the folke and pepylle nemnyd, of what condycyon that they ben, ayens hys ryalle soveraynyte, or whythe defame lyppys have spoke, oure moste soverayne lorde the kyng, of strenyger the day of parte [b] mekely shalle be forgevynne, owte take the personys that above in specyalle ben exceptyd.[c]

Alle so hyt ys accordyd in oure lorde the kyngys be halve, that the for sayde soudyers and strongers be-fore thys presentt trete and accorde, wyllyng for to departynne, oure lorde the kyng shalle ordaynne and make a sykyr and saffe condyte in form consuete.

And so the fore sayde cytte was yoldyd to oure soverayne lord the kynge uppon Synt Wolstonys day.[d]   And aftyr that he gatte many townys and castellys, as hyt sballe aftyr thys be wretyn alle the processe.

---

[a] The end of this sentence and the beginning of the next are omitted in our MS., which runs on without a break from the word "lorde" to "the kyngys behalve' us if it were one sentence.

[b] *of strenyger the day of parte.* of steryng the day of pietie, J.   These are strange corruptions.   The Latin has *ex instinctu Divinæ pietatis.*

[c] They are mentioned in the preceding clause in the original treaty; but their names are omitted in the MS.   [d] 19th Jan.

Richarde Wytyngdon, ⎰ Robert Whytyngham ⎱ A° viij°.
Mayre of London   ⎱ John Butteler   ⎰

Ande in that yere, the xx day of May, the yere of oure Lorde
M¹ cccc xx, the kyng come unto Troys, in Chaunpeyne, and there
he was worthely ressayvyde of alle the lordys spyrytualle and tem
poralle þat were there whithe the Kynge of Fraunce. And on
the morne the Kyng and Quene of Fraunce, and Dame Katerynne,
and the Duke of Burgayne, mette to gedyr in Synt Petrys
chyrche in Troys; whiche metyng was in the body of the chyrche.
Ande thenne they went upe to the hyghe auter, and there were
the artyculys of the pes redde, and the othys made on aythyr
partye. And thenne was the kyng and Dame Katerynne swryde
to-gedyr. And on the morne aftyr was Trenyte Sonday, that was
the iij day of June, the yere of oure Lorde M¹ cccc xx, in the
chyrche of Troys, the kyng spowsyd Dame Kateryne, Kyng Charlys
doughter of Fraunce; and thenne he was made Regent of Fraunce,
and the convencyons of the whiche acordyd folowynge here aftyr,
that ys for to saye :—

Harry, by the grace of God, Kyng of Inglond, heyre and Regent
of Fraunce, and Lorde of Yrlonde, to perpetualle mynde to alle
Crystyn pepylle, ande to alle that ben undyr owre obeysaunce, we
notefy and declare that thoughe[a] here before dyvers tretes have
ben be twyne the moste excellente Prynce Charlis, owre fadyr of
Fraunce, and hys progenytours, for the pes to ben hadde be twyne
ij realmys of Fraunce and of Inglonde, the whiche here by forne
have borne no[b] frwte, we, consyderynge the grette harmys that have
ben, not oonly by twyne ij realmys for the grette devysyon þat hathe
ben be-twyne hem, but to alle hooly Chyrche, we have take a
trete whythe oure sayde fadyr and us, that for as moche as be the

---

[a] *thoughe.* thoroughe, MS.

[b] *borne no.* These words are taken from J., and are a true rendering of the text
of the original treaty (see Rymer, ix. 895). Our MS. reads, "have ben frwte,"
following perhaps some other translation in which the word "without" has been
omitted. Vit. reads, still more absurdly, "have ben Irendes."

bonde of matrymonye, i-made for the goode of the pes be-twyne us and oure moste dyre modyr Isabelle hys wyffe, the same Charlis and Isabelle ben made fadyr and modyr, and there fore take hem as for owre fadyr and modyr, we shalle have and worschippe as hyt syttythe and semyþe so worthy a prynce and a pryncesse too ben i-worschippyde, pryncypally before alle othyr temporalle personys of the worlde.

Alle so we shalle nought dystroble, nor dyssesyn, nor lette oure sayde fadyr, but that he holde and procede [a] as longe as he levythe, and holdythe, ande he possedythe at thys tyme, the crowne and dygnyte of the ryalte of Fraunce, and rentys and profytys of the same, to the sustenaunce of hys estate and chargys of the realmo of Fraunce, and owr modir al so holdyng as long as she levythe the estate and dygnyte of the quene, aftyr the maner of the same realme, whythe convenable and convenyante parte of the sayde rentys and profytys.

Alle so that the fore sayde Kateryne shalle take and have dwer in oure realme of Inglond, as [quenes of England] [b] here a-forne were wonte to have and take, that ys for to saye, to the summa of xl M[l] scwtys yerely, of the whyche [c] ij shalle be worthe a nobylle Englysche. Alle so the mauers, weyis, and menys that we may, whythe owte transgressyon or offensys ofte [d] i-made by us for to kepe the lawys, customys, usagys, and ryghtys of owre said realme [e] of Inglonde, [we] [f] shalle done owre labur and pursewe that the sayde Katerynne, alsone as hyt may be done and be made sure, for to take and for to have in owre sayde realme of Inglonde fro tyme of oure dethe, the sayde xl M[l] scutys yerly, of the whyche twyne shalle alle way be worthe [g] a nobylle of Englysche mony.

[a] *procede.* A transcriber's error for "possede," *i.e.* possess.

[b] Omitted in MS.; supplied from J.

[c] *of the whiche* repeated, MS.

[d] *ofte.* We should certainly read, "of the oath;" but the words do not occur even in J.

[e] *of owre sayde realme* repeated in MS.   [f] Omitted in MS.

[g] *worthe.* with, MS.; corrected from J.

Alleso yf hyt happe the sayde Kateryn to ovyr levyn us, she shalle take and have in the realme of Praunce, immediatly fro the tyme of oure dethe, dower to the som of xx M^l frankys, [of]^a and up the londys, placys, and lordeschippys that helde and badde Dame Blaunche, sum tyme wyf of Phylyppe, befnelle^b to oure sayde fadyr.

Also that a-non aftyr the dethe of oure sayde fadyr, and fro thens forwarde, the crowne of the realme of Fraunce, with alle the ryghtes and the aportenaunce, shalle remayne and a byde to us and ben of us and of oure ayrys for evyrmore. Ande for as moche as oure sayde fadyr ys holdyn with dyvers sekenys in syche maner as he may nought entende in hys owne person for to dyspose the nedys of the fore sayde realme of Fraunce: therefore, durynge the lyffe of oure sayde fadyr, the facultes and the excresisse of the governaunce and disposyscyon of the goode publique and comyn profyte of the sayde realme of Fraunce, [withe]^c counselle of nobylle and wyse men of the same realme of Fraunce, shalle be and a·byde to us soo that fro hens forwarde we may governe the same realme of Fraunce be us, [and]^d also by othyr that whythe yn the consayle of the sayde nobylle, that we lyste or lykyn for to depute; the whyche faculteys and excressisse of governaunce, thys beyng towarde us, we shalle labur and purpose us spedefully, diligently, and trewly to that that be and ought to be to the worschyppys of God and of oure sayde fadyr and modyr, ande also to the comyn goode of the same realme, with the conselle of the worthy, grete, and nobylle of the same realme for to be defendyd, pesyde, and governyde after the ^{e} ryght and equyte wylle.

Also that we to oure power shalle do that the corte of the

---

^{a} Supplied from J.

^{b} *befnelle.* Should be *besaile, i. e.* great-grandfather, or *proavus.* The readings in J. and V. are equally corrupt.

^{c} Supplied from J.

^{d} *and.* Omitted both in our MS. and in J. and V., all which begin a new sentence or paragraph with the word "also."

^{e} *the.* that, J.

parlyment of Fraunce be kepte and observyd in hys auctoryte and superioryte, and in alle that ys dewe there to, in alle maner of placys that nowe or in tyme to comyn ys or shalle be subjecte to oure sayde fadyr.

Also we to oure power shalle defende and kepyn every chone and alle the perys, noblys, cytteys, and townys, comynalteys, and synguler personys nowe or in any tyme to comyng subjectys to oure fadyr and to us, in owre [a] ryghtys, customys, pryvelegys, fredams, and franches longynge dewe unto us, in alle maner of placys nowe or in tyme comyng subjectys to oure fadyr and to us. Also that we delygently and trewly shalle travayle unto oure power and to that justyse be admynystryde and done in the same realme of Fraunce, and aftyr the lawys, customys, and ryghtys of the same realme of Fraunce, whytheowtyn personalle exepsyon, and that we shalle ke[pe] and holdynne the subjectys of the same realme in tranquyllyte and pes, and to owre poner we shalle defendyn hem [b] ayens alle maner of violens and oppressyon.

Also to oure poner we shalle purpose and do that able [c] personys and profytable be takyn yn to offys as welle of justys of the Parlyment, as of baylyagys, senescallis, provestys, and othyr offycys longyng to the governaunce of demaynes [d] and of othyr officis in the sayde realme of Fraunce for the goode, ryght, and pesyble [rule] [e] in the same realme, and for admynystracyon that shalle be commyttyd unto hem, and that they be syche personys that aftyr the lawys and ryghtys of the same realme, and for the utilyte and profyte of oure sayde fadyr, and at [f] the fore sayde realme, ought to be take and depudyd unto the same offysys.

Also that we to oure poner, and as sone as hytt may compen-

---

[a] *owre.* J. reads more correctly "here," *i. e.* their.
[b] *hem.* hym, MS.; hem, J.
[c] *able.* alle maner, MS.; corrected from J.
[d] *demaynes.* demaytys, MS.; corrected from J.
       Omitted in our MS. and in J. and V.
[f] *at.* So in MS., though the word should certainly be "of." Yet J. reads "that" and V. "atte."

dyusly be done, we shalle travayle [for to] [a] put in obedyens of oure
sayde fadyr alle maner of citteys, townys, castellys, placys, cuntreys,
and personys whythe yn the realme of Praunce ennobedient and
rebellys to oure sayde fadyr, holdyng with the party that ben callyd
Dolfyn or Armanak.

Also that we may the more comodyusly, seurly, and frely exersisse
and fulle fylle thes thynges afore sayde, hit ys also accordyd that
worthy grete nobylles and astates of the same realme of Fraunce,
as welle spyrytualle as temporalle, and also cytteys, notablys, and
comynalteys, cytezyns, and burgeys of townys of the realme of
Fraunce, that be obesyaunt at thys tyme to oure sayde fadyr,
shalle make thes othys that folowyn:—

Fyrste, to us, beryng the faculte and exersisse of disposission and
governaunce of the sayde comyn profyte, and to oure hyestes and
commaundementys that [b] shalle mekely and obedyently [obeie] [c]
and entende in alle maner of thyng consernynge the excersise of
governaunce of the same realme.

Also that the worthy grete noblys and astatys of the sayde realme
of Fraunce, as welle spyrytualle as temporalle, and also citteys and
townys, and notabylle comynalteys, and cyttesyns and burgeys of
the sayde realme, in alle maner of thyngys, welle and trewly shalle
kepe and to oure poner shalle do kepe of alle as moche as to them
longythe or to any of hem, alle the thyngys that bene a-poyntynde
or accordyde by twyxt oure sayde fadyr and modyr and us with
the counselle of hem whome [d] we lyste to calle to.

Also that contynually fro the dethe, and aftyr the dethe, of oure
sayde fady[r] Charlys, they shalle be oure trowe lyge men and owre
ayrys, and they shalle ressayve and admyt us for hyr lyge and hyr
soverayne lorde and verry Kyng of Fraunce, and for suche us [e]
obeye with owte opposicyon, contradicyon, or deficulte; and, but hit
bene to owre fadyr duryng hys lyf, nevyr aftyr thys day they shalle

---

[a] Omitted in MS.; supplied from J.   [b] *that.* thei, J.
[c] Supplied from J.
[d] *whome.* whenne, MS.; corrected from J.   [e] *us.* ns, MS

obeye to man as Kynge or Regaunte of Fraunce, but to us and to owre ayrys.

Also that they shalle not bene in conselle, helpe, or assente that we lese lyffe or lym, or ben takyn with any takyng, that we suffer harme or dyvysyon in persone, astate, worschippe, or goodys, but yf they knowe any suche thyng for to bene done, caste, or imagyd agayne us, they shalle let hit to hyr power, ande they do us to wyte ther of as hastely as they may, by hem selfe, or by message, or by letters.

Also that alle maner of conquestys that sballe be made be us of Fraunce up on the same inobedyentes* owte of the duche of Normandy shalle be done to the profytys of oure sayde fadyr; and that to owre power we shalle do alle the maner of landys and lordschippys that ben in the placys so to be conqueryd longyng to personys obeynge to oure sayde fadyr, whyche sballe swere for to kepe thys present accorde, and shalle be restoryd to the same personys to wham they longe to.

Also that alle maner of personys of Holy Chyrche benefysyd in the duchye of Normandy, or in any othyr place in the realme of Fraunce, subjectys to us, [which] b ben obedyent to owre sayde fadyr, and faveryng the party of the Duke of Burgayne, to the whyche shalle swere to kepe thys present a corde shalle rejoyse pesabylly hyr benefysys of Hooly Chyrche in the duchye of Normandye, or in any othyr placys nexte above sayde.

Also lyke wyse al maner of personys of Hooly Chyrche obedyente unto us and benefysyd in the realme of Fraunce, in placys subjette to owre fadyr, [the which] c shalle swere for too kepe thys present acorde, shalle rejoyse pesabylly hyr benefysys of Hooly Chyrche in placys nexte a-bove sayde.

Also that alle maner chyrchys, unyversyteys, and studyys generalle, also collegys of studyers, and othyr collegys of Holy Chyrche, beyng in placys nowe or in time to come subjecte to

---

* *inobedientes.* in obedyens, MS.; corrected from J.
b Omitted in MS.   c Supplied from J

owre sayde fadyr, or in the duchye of Normandye or othyr placys
of the realme of Fraunce subjecte to us, shalle ressayve hyr ryghtys,
hyr possessyons, rentys, prerogatyvys, liberteys, and fraunchessys
longyng or dewe to hem in any maner wyse in the sayde realme of
Fraunce, [savyng the right of the crowne of Fraunce]ᵃ and of
aytherᵇ othyr person.

Also by Goddys helpe, whenne hit happythe us to come to the
crowne of Fraunce, the duchye of Normandy, and also othyr placys
conqueryd by us in the realme of Fraunce, shalle bowe undyr the
commaundement, obeysaunce, and monarchye of the crowne of
Fraunce.

Also that we shalle enforce us and done for oure power that
recompence be made by oure sayde fadyr, with owt dymycyonᶜ of
the crowne of Fraunce, to personys obeynge to hym and faverynge
to the party, that ys to say, to þᵉ Duke of Burgayne, to whom
longythe landys, lordeschippys, rentys, and othyr possessyons in the
same Duchye of Normandye or othyr placys in the realme of
Fraunce conqueryd by us [hidertoward given by us],ᵈ in placys and
londys gotyn or to be gotyn and ovyrcome in the nameᵉ of oure
sayde fadyr up on rebellys and inobedyente to hym; and yf hyt so
be that lyke maner recompence be nought made to the sayde personys
by the lyfe of owre sayde fadyr, we shalle make that recompe in
suche maner, placys, and goodys, whanne hit happythe us, by
Goddys helpe, to come to the crowne of Fraunce. And yf hyt
so happe that the londys, lordeschippys, rentys, possessyons, that
longythe to suche maner personys in the same duchye and placys
[that]ᶠ ben nought genyfeᵍ by us, the same personys shalle be
restoryde to hem with owte any delay. Also that duryng the
lyfe of oure sayde fadyr, in alle placys nowe or in tyme comyng
subjectys to hym, lettyrs of comyn justyse, and also grauntys of

─────────────

ᵃ Omitted in MS.; supplied from J.
ᵇ *ayther.* every, MS.
ᵈ Supplied from J.
ᶠ This word is superfluous.

ᶜ Should be *diminution.*
ᵉ *name.* same, MS.
ᵍ given.

offys, gyftys, pardonys, or remyssyons, shalle be wrete and procede undyr the name ande the sealle of oure sayde fadyr. And for as moche as sum synguler cas may be-falle that may nought be lorne sene by mannys wytte, in the whyche hit myght be necessary and honustefulle that we doo wrytte oure letters in suche maner cas, yf any happe, for the goode surete of oure sayde fadyr, and for the governaunce that longythe unto us, [as]ª hyt ys be-fore sayde, and for to eschewe perellys that other^b wyse myght falle in [places]^c subjecte to oure sayde fadyr, to wrytte oure letters, by the whyche we shalle commaunde, carge, and defende aftyr the nature and qualyte of the nedys in oure fadyrs be halfe, ande of owrys as Regente of Fraunce.

And also durynge oure fadyrs lyfe we shalle nought nempne nor wrytte us Kyng of Praunce, but utterly we shalle abstayne us fro that name as longe as oure fadyr lyvythe.

Also that oure sayde fadyr duryng hys lyfe shalle nempne, calle, and wrytte us yn Frenche on thys maner: *Nostre treschere fytz, Henry, Roy d'Englyterre heyter de Fraunce;* and in Latyn in thys wyse: *Precarissimus filius noster Henricus Rex Anglie et heres Francie.*

Also we shalle nowe put in possessyons^d or exaccyons, or do put, to the subjectys of owre fadyr, with owte cause resonable and necessary, non^e othyr wyse thanne for comyn goode of the sayde realme of Fraunce, and aftyr teseyng^f and axkyng of the lawys ande customys, resonabylle and aprovyde, of the same realme.

Also that we shalle travayle for owre power, to the effecte and to the avyse and a-sent of three^g estatys of eythyr othyr^h realmys of Fraunce and of Inglonde, al maner obstaculys done a-way in thys

---

ª Omitted in MS.
^b *other.* any, MS.; corrected from J.
^c Omitted in MS. and in J.
^d So in MS., meaning, "We shall not put impositions."
^e *non.* Should be "nor."
^f *teseyng.* the seiyng, J. The Latin is *dictamen.*
^g *three.* thys, MS.   ^h *othyr.* of the, J.

party, that bene [a] ordaynyde and provyde, that frome [b] the tyme that
we or any of owre eyrys come to the oronne of Fraunce, bothe
crounys, that ys to say, of Praunce and of Inglonde, perpetually to
bene togedyr in one and in the same person, that ys to say, fro oure
fadyrs lyfe,[c] and fro thens terme of oure lyfe; and fro thens
forwarde, yn the personys of oure ayrys that shalle bene, one aftyr
a nothyr.   And that bothe realmys shalle be governyd, fro that
we or any of oure ayrys comyn to the same, nought severally [d]
undyr dyvers kyngys in any tyme, but undyr one and that same
[person] [e] whiche the tyme shalle be kynge of bothe realmys and
soverayne lorde as hyt ys above fore sayde; kepyng, nevyrtheles, in
alle maner of eythyr [f] thyngys and lawys, nought makyng subjecte
in any maner of wyse one of the same realmys on to the othyr, or
puttyng [g] or submyttyng the ryght, lawys or usagys of [oon of the
seid realmes to the rightes, lawes, custumes, and usages of] [h] that
othyr of the same.

Also that same [i] forwarde perpetually shalle be stylle yn reste;
and in alle maner of wyse shall cese alle maner of dyssencyons,
hatys, and rancoure, envyes, and warrys, bytwyne the same realmys
of Fraunce and of Inglond and pepylle of the same realmys, drawing
to a-corde of the same pes.   And there shalle be fro hens forthe
and evyrmore and shalle folowe pes and tranquyllyte and goode
acorde and comyn affeccyon and stabylle frendeschyppe be-twyne
the same realmys and hyr subjectys be-fore sayde; and the same
realmys shalle helpe hem selfe with hyr consellys, helpys, and
comyn assentys ayenste alle maner of men that enforce hem for to

[a] *that bene, i. e.*, that it may be.
[b] *frome.* for, MS.; corrected from J.
[c] The reading here is very corrupt, and ought to be as in J. "oure, from thens,
terme of oure liffe; and from thens forward," &c.
[d] *severally.* soverenly, MS.; corrected from J.
[e] Supplied from J.   [f] *eythyr.* other, J.
[g] *puttyng.* partyng, MS.; corrected from J.
[h] Omitted in MS.; supplied from J.
[i] *same.* So in MS.

done or for to be ymagenyd wrongys, harmys, dyssesys, or grevaunce to hem or aythyr of hem to othyr, and they shalle be conversaunt, and marchauntyse to-gedyr frely and sewrely, payng the custome and devoyrys dewe and customyde.

And also that alle tho confyderyd [a] ande aleyde to oure sayde fadyr and the realme of Fraunce be-fore sayde, and also oure confyderatys of the realme of Inglonde be-fore sayde, the whyche in viij monythys fro [b] the tyme of thys accorde of pes notefyed to hem we [c] wylle declare by oure letters to hem that wylle [c] drawe unto thys accorde, and that wylle be comprehendyd undyr thys tretys and accorde of thys pes, ys, [d] savynge, nethertheles othyr of the same crownys, and alle so alle maner accyons, ryghtys, and remedyes that longyn to oure sayde fadyr and hys subjectys, and to us and to oure subjectis a-gayne suche maner alyes and confyderatys.

Also that nayther oure fadyr, neythyr oure brothyr the Duke of Burgayne, shalle be-gyn to make whythe Charlys cheryng hym selfe for the Dolfyn of Venys [e] any trety or pes accorde, but of counsellys and assent [of] alle and [f] eche of us thre, or of othyr [g] astatys of aythyr of the same realmys.

Also that we [with the] [h] assent of oure brothyr of Burgayne and othyr of the nobylle a-perys of the realme of Fraunce, the whyche there to owyn to be callyd, shalle ordayne for hyr governaunce of the persone of oure sayde fadyr, sykerly, lyvyngly, and honestely, aftyr the askynge of hys ryalle astate and dygnyte, by the maner that shalle be to the worschyppe of God, and of owre

[a] *confyderyd.* consyderyd, MS.

[b] *fro.* for, MS.

[c] *we wylle declare by oure letters to hem that wylle.* The text here is peculiarly corrupt, but we forbear to alter it. The true reading is in J.: "woll declare by here (*i.e.* their) lettres that thei wol."

[d] *ys.* This word is superfluous, but the following words, which appear in J., have been omitted: "bene comprehendid undre the bondes, suerties, and accorde of this peas."

[e] Viennes.   [f] *and,* in MS.

[g] *othyr.* the thre, J., which is the right reading.

[h] Omitted in MS.

CAMD. SOC.   T

fadyr, and of oure realme of Fraunce.   And alle maner of personys
that shalle be a boute owre sayde fadyr to done hym personalle
servyse, nought only in offyse, but in alle othyr servyse, as welle
[to] ᵃ nobyllys as [to] ᵃ othyr, shalle ben suche as hathe bene borne
in the same realme of Praunce, or yn place that ben lanyage of
Praunce, good, wyse, trewe, and able ᵇ to the fore sayde servyse.

And owre sayde fadyr shalle dwelle in notabylle placys of hys
obedyens, and no where ellys.

Where-fore we charge and commaunde owre sayde legys and
subjectys, and othyr beyng undyr oure obedyens, that they kepyn
and do kepyn in alle that longythe to hem thys accorde and pes,
aftyr the forme and maner as hyt ys accordyd; and they attempte
in no maner wyse thyng that may be peegydyse or contrarye to the
same accorde and pes, be payne of lyfe, and alle that [thei] ᶜ may
forfete agayne us.

And thenne, aftyr the feste and solempnyte was done of that
maryage, the kyng conqueryd many townys and castellys in
Normandy.   And thenne the kynge layde sege to Myleu sur-Sen;
and duryng the sege the mayre and the sherevys of London were
chosyn.   And at that syge laye the Kynge of Praunce, the Kynge
of Inglonde, and the Kynge of Scottys, and the Quene of Fraunce,
and the Quene of Inglonde, with hyr mayny, &c.

Wylliam Cambryge, ⎰ John Butlere   ⎱ Aᵒ ixᵒ.
Mayre of London   ⎰ John Wellys   ⎱

Ande that same yere, on Candylmasday yn the mornynge, the
kyng com in to Inglonde and the queue with hym and they londyd
at Dovyr; ande the xiiij day of Fevery the kyng com to London,
and the xxj day of the same monythe was crownyde at Westemyster;
and the solempnyte was done in chyrche of Syut Petyr, and she
was brought fulle worthely towarde þᵉ palys into the grete halle, &c.

Nowe of the statys and of the coronacyon of Quene Kateryn and

ᵃ *to.* This word is superfluous in both these places.
ᵇ *able.* alle, MS.; corrected from J.   ᶜ [*thei*]. Supplied from J.

of othyr manyr of servyse. Fyiste the quene sette in hyr astate, and the Archebyschope of Cantyrbury and the Byschoppe of Wynchester sate on the ryght syde of the quene, and they were servyd nexte unto the quene every cours coveryde as the queue; and on the lyfte syde was the Kyng of Schottys sette in hys a-state uppon the lyfte syde of the queue, that was servyd alle wey nexte the queue 'and the byschoppys a-fore sayde; the Duchyes of Yorke and the' Countas of Huntyngdone satte in the same syde, and the Duke of Gloucester was ovyr seer, the Erle of Marche knelyng on the hye deys on the ryght syde of the quene and held a cepture in hys hond of the quenys, and the Erle Marchelle knelyng on the lyfte syde at the dyes and helde anothyr cepture of the quenys; and the Countasse of Keutt was syttyng at hyr ryght fote of the quene undyr the tabylle, and the Counteys Marchalle sate on the lyfte syde of the queue undyr the tabylle; Syr Rycharde Nevyle kervyr before the queue, the Erle of Sowthefolke ᵃ cuppe berer, Syr John Stywarde sewer unto the queue, the Lord Clyfforde panter in the stede of the Erle of Warwyke, the Lorde Wylleby butler in stede of the Erle of Arundelle, the Lorde Gray Ryffyn naperer, the Lorde of Andely amyner ᵇ in stede of the Erle of Cambryge, the Duke of Bedforde Constabylle of Inglond, the Erle of Warwyke Stywarde of Inglond in stede of the Duke of Clarence, the Erle of Worceter Marchalle of Inglonde in the stede of the Erle Marchelle, &c.

The maner of syttyng of the astatys ᶜ yn the halle at Wystemyster.

Fyrste, the baronys of v Portys be-ganne the tabylle in the halle on the ryght honde of the queue, and by nethe hem at the same tabylle the bowgerys of the chauncery; and the mayre of London and hys aldyrman be-ganne the borde on the lyfte syde of the queue in the halle with othyr worthy comyners of the same cytte,

---

ᵃ J. says, "Therles brother of Suffolk, cup berer."

ᵇ *amyner.* J. reads "avener."

ᶜ at the other tables, J.

and othyr men benethe hem at the same tabylle.   The byschoppys
beganne the tabylle in the myddys of the halle on the ryght honde
nexte the v Portys, the Byschoppe of London withyn the tabylle,
the Byschoppe of Dereham nexte hym whythe yn the tabylle, and
the Byschoppe of Bathe and the Byschoppe of Exceter be-fore
hem; the Byschoppe of Norwyche, and the Byschoppe of Saulysbury,
the Byschoppe of Syn Davys, and the Byschoppe of Bangar, the
Byschoppe of Lyncolle, the Byschoppe of Carlylle, and the Abbott
of Waltham with hem.   And thenne aftyr them sate the justyse,
and worthy knyghtys and squeyers.   And thenne the ladys be-ganne
the tabylle in myddys of the halle on the lyfte honde of the quene,
nexte the mayre of London.   The Countasse of Stafforde,[a] sum
tyme doughter of the Duke of Gloucester; the Countesse of Marche[b]
hyr doughter; the Countasse of Arundelle; the Countesse of Westemerlonde; the Countasse of Northehormerlond; the Countasse of
Oxforde; the Lady Nevyle,[c] sum tyme the lordys wyffe Nevyle that
was sone to the Erle of Westemerlonde, and doughter to the Erle
of Somersette; Dame Margarete[d] the dukys doughter of Northefolke and suster to the Erle Marchalle; the yonger doughter[e] to the
Erle of Somersett; the Lady Ros; the Lady Clyfforde, suster to
Harry the Erle of Northehumberlond; the Lady Bergeveny; the Lady
Talbat; the Lady Wylby; the Lady Mawley; the wyffe of Rycharde

---

[a] Anne, daughter of Thomas of Woodstock Duke of Gloucester, who married, first,
Thomas Earl of Stafford, and afterwards his brother Edmund, who succeeded him
in the title.

[b] Anne, daughter of Edmund Earl of Stafford, second husband of the lady
mentioned in the preceding note. She married, as her first husband, Edmund
Mortimer, Earl of March.

[c] Elizabeth, fifth daughter of Thomas Holland, Earl of Kent, was the wife of
John Lord Nevill, son of Ralph Nevill, first Earl of Westmoreland. Her husband
died in 1423, during his father's life.

[d] Margaret Mowbray, daughter of Thomas first Duke of Norfolk (who was
banished by Richard IL), and sister of John Earl of Nottingham and Earl Marshal,
who was not restored to the dukedom of Norfolk till 1424.

[e] Margaret, daughter of John de Beaufort, Earl of Somerset, the son of John of
Gaunt. She married Thomas Courtenay, Earl of Devonshire.

Nevyle, doughter to the Erle of Salusbury,[a] and noo moo ladys of state. And thenne forthe with jentylle wemmen thys tabylle was occupyde and a quarter of the byschoppe ys tabylle ther to. Thes lordys sewyng were asygnyd for to do servyse ryallys before the quene; the Erle of Northehumberlond and the Erle of Westemore-lond, the Lorde Fehewe, the Lorde Furnevale, the Lorde Gray of Wylton, the Lorde Ferrys of Groby, the Lorde of Ponyngys, the Lorde Haryngton, the Lorde Darsy, and the Lorde Della ware, &c.

The servyse of the fyrste cours.

Braune with mustarde, elys in burneus, furmenty with bakyn, pyke, lampray powderyd whythe elys, pouderyde trought, codde-lyng, plays with merlyng fryde, grette crabbys, lesche lumbarde, a bake mete in paste, tartys, and a sotyltc i-callyd pellycane, etc.

The secunde cours in the halle.

Jely, blandesoure, bremme, congur, solys with myllott, chevyn, barbylle, roche, samon fresche, halybutte, gurnarde rostyd, roget[b] boylyde, smelte fryde, lopstere, cranys, lesche damaske, lampray in paste, flampayne. A sotelte, a panter & a mayde before hym, &c.

The servyse of iij cours in the halle.

Datys in composte, creyme motley, and poudrid welkys, porpys rostyd, meneuse fryde, crevys of douce,[c] datys, pranys, rede schry[m]ppys, grette elys and lamprays rostyd, a lesche callyd whythe leysche, a bake mete in paste with iiij angelys. A sotelte, a tygyr and Syntt Gorge ledyng hyt.[d]

---

[a] Alice, sole daughter of Thomas de Montacute, Earl of Salisbury. She was married to Richard Nevill, third son of Ralph first Earl of Westmoreland, and after her father's death her husband was created Earl of Salisbury.

[b] *roget.* roches, J.   [c] *of douce.* de ewe douce, J.

[d] The description of this coronation and banquet, especially the latter, is more full in J., but as that account has already been printed by Nicolas in the "Chronicle of London," pp. 162-5, I have refrained from noting the omissions in footnotes.

Hen. V.
A.D. 1421.

And uppon Ester eve, that was the xxij day of Marche, and the raygne of the kynge þe ix, the Duke of Clarans with many othyr lordys were slayne in Fraunce and many lordys takyn presoners.[a] And the same yere the kyng helde a Parlymentt at Westemyster aftyr Estyr in monythe of May, in the whyche Parlyment was axyde no talege, wherefore the Byschoppe of Wynchester lentte the kynge xx M^l pounde. And in thys Parlymentt was ordaynyde, by cause that golde was gretely a payryde by clyppyng and waschynge, that no man shulde aftyr Crystysmas nexte aftyr put forthe no enpayryd golde in no paymente uppon payne of furfeture there of; where fore every man for the moste party ordaynyd hym balans. And the same yere, a non aftyr Wytson tyde, the kyng saylyd in to Fraunce a-yenne and the Duke of Bedforde was made Lewtenaunte of Inglonde. Ande the same yere came the Duchyes of Holonde in to Inglond.

Roberte Chycheley,	Ric. Goslyne	Anno xº.
Mayre of London	Wylliam Weston	

Ande that same yere the Duke of Bedforde held a Parlyment at Wystemyster, and that be gan the iij day of Decembir; in the whyche Parlyment was grauntyd a quyndesyn and a dyme to the kynge, that tyme beyng at the sege of Mewys in Brye, in Fraunce, and the halfe quyndesym and dyme to be payde antt Candelmasse nexte folowynge, and that the kyng shuld ressayve soche payment as went that tyme: that ys to say, yf a nobylle were worth v s. and viij d. the kyng shulde take hyt for a fulle nobylle of vj s. & viij d.; and yf the nobylle soo appayryde were better thenne v s. viij d., the kyng too paye the ovyr plus of v s. viij d. Also that yere was grette scarsyte of whyte mony that men myght unnethe have any golde changyd, thoughe hit were nevyr soo good and of fulle whyghte. Also that yere, on Syn Nicholas day in Decembyr, the yere of oure Lorde M^{l}cccc and xxj, Harry, the fyrste begotyn sone of Kyng Harry the v, was borne in the castelle of Wyndesore; to whom was god fadyrs at the fonte

---

[a] At the battle of Beaugé.

Harry Byschoppe of Wynchester, John Duke of Bedforde, and the Duchyes of Holond, Jacomyne, was the godmodyr; and at the confirmacyon the Archebyschoppe of Cantyrbury, Harry Chycheley, was godfadyr. Also the same yere, in the monythe of May, the yere of oure Lorde M¹ cccc xxij, and of the raygne of the kynge the x, the cytte in Mewys in Bry, whyche long tyme hadde be besegyd [was yolden]ª in the maner as folowythe aftyr:—

Thys ys the plesynge and the wylle of the Kyng of Fraunce, and of the Kyng of Inglond, hys beuefys,ᵇ heyre, and regant of the realme of Fraunce, that the market place of Mewys in Bry, and they that benne with ynne, be yoldyn and delyveryd in the maner as sewythe aftyr:

Fyrste, alle tho that be with ynne the fore sayde markett, of what a-state that they bene, shalle yoldyn uppe the sayde markett place of Mewys in Bry and hyr bodys prisonerys to the sayde kyngys of Inglond and of Fraunce with yn the x day of thys presentt monythe of May, the yere of oure Lorde a-bove sayde M¹ cccc xxij.

Also that the sayde kyngys, at þᵉ reveren of God and eschewyng of Crystyn mannys blode, shall ressayve [hem]ᶜ as hit folowythe after, that ys to wetyn, Syr Lewys Gaste, Guycharde of Cisse, Mayster Robert Guesene, Phylyppe Gamcelys,ᵈ Peron de Lupe, John Damoy,ᵉ le Bastard de Varru, Denys de Varru, Maystyr John de Romys Termagyn,ᶠ Barnarde Domerville,ᵍ and John de la Motte;ʰ one that blewe and sownyd an horne duryng the sege, that men say ys namyd Grasse; and alle the gunners the consentaunte and compabyle of the dethe of the Duke of Burgayne that was; they that othyr tyme have made othe of the fynalle pes; they that

---

ª Omitted in MS.; supplied from J. These articles are also printed in Rymer, x. 212.

ᵇ *i. e.* beau fils.   ᶜ *hem.* Supplied from J. and Rymer.

ᵈ *Gamcelys.* de Gamoches, J. and Rymer.

ᵉ *Damoy.* Dannoy, Rymer and J.

ᶠ *Romys Termagyn.* Roumos Treemayn, Rymer; Roumes Tremagyn, J.

ᵍ *Domerville.* de Merville, Rymer; Tromervil, J.

ʰ *Motte.* Mette, MS.

Hen. V.
A.D. 1422.

have townys, or strenghtys, or governaunce by othyr for hem; the Englysche, Yrysche, Schottys, and alle oþer that have bene obedyens of the kynge or the regaunte, yf any there bene yn the sayde markett place dwellyng;—that all[a] they shalle a-byde and dwelle to the wylle of the forsayde kyngys. Also the sayde kyngys shall ressayve alle the othyr in the sayde markett place beyng, in to hyr goode grace and mercy for to dwelle presoners, hyr lyvys savyde.

Also for as moche as hyt towchyd the sayde kyngys, Syr Lewys Gaste, the bastarde of Barru, Denys[b] de Barru, and Mayster John de Raynys,[c] they shalle be putt to hyr dome, and justise shalle be done and mynystryde to hem.

Also as touchynge the forsayde Guycharde de Cysse, Peryn de Luppe, Mayster Robert de Groysyne, Phylyppe of Chancellerys,[d] and John Damoy, the forsayd kyngys declaryn that they shalle dwelle and abyde to hyr wylle as be fore sayde, unto the tyme that the townys of strengythe that by hem, or be any of hem, or othyr on hyr be-halfe, or by oþer that any thynge shulde be or may be don for hem, be holdyn, be[e] yoldyn and delyveryd to the sayde kyngys, or to hyr comyssoures and deputes, and aftyr hyr ordynaunce, the whyche thynge they shalle done with alle hyr dylygence possyble, with owte fraude or malyngne; aftyr the whyche yeldynge uppe and delyveraunce the sayde kyngys shalle holdyn or do be holdyn the above sayde Guycharde, Peryn, Mayster Robertt, Philippe, and John Dawney in surete of her lyvys, so that they or any of hem shalle nought be dewly founde coupabyle of the dethe of Duke of Burgayne. And as towche the othyr exceptyde, they shalle a-byde the wylle of the fore sayde kyngys, as hyt ys contaynyd in the secunde artycule.

Also the Erle of Brienne[f] sballe [be][g] quytte a yenne the fore sayde Peron of alle that in whyche he ys bounde or holdyn for

---

cause of hys ransom or othyr wyse, and the sayde Peron shalle playnly quyte hym in takyng hys letters or quytaunce to the sayde erle, and he shalle yelde to hym alle the letters that he hathe of hym or of any othyr uppon that.

Also the [fore] [a] sayde, beyng in the foresayde markett of Mewys in Bry, hangynge the sayde tyme, and that a none, shalle putt or shalle done to putt by inventary alle the cornys, wynys, and othyr vytayle beynge in the sayde markett, and aftyr the placys where they shalle bene, for to benne takynne and delyveryd to the comyssours and deputes of the sayde kyngys. And in lyke wyse shalle benne in hors beyng in the sayde markett.

Also they shalle putt or done putt in any certayne place with yn the sayde markett alle the abyllymentys of werre that benne there ynne, as welle pouders, gounnys, and arblastys, schott, or othyr artylers, with owtyn any fraccyon, brekyng, wastyng, or a-payryng.

[b] Also the a-boven sayde of the sayde markett shalle puttyn or do puttyn alle hyr harneys of werre in a certayne place.

Also the same wyse they shalle putt or do putt in certayne place alle the jewellys and reliquys, bokys, ornamentys, and othyr goodys mevabil, beyng in the sayde markett, longyng unto the chyrchys, abbayys, mynstyrs, pryours, or hospytalys what soo evyr they bene, levyng to hem to be restoryde in hyr placys of othyr [c] chyrchys of the sayde markett, and whythe owte fraude or malynge.

Also [d] they shalle putt or do putt in a place or two alle the golde, sylvyr, vesselle, jewellys of golde and sylvyr, bokys, robys, lynnyn clothe, and also wollyn clothe of alle maner, beyng in the sayde markett, and that longythe to othyr thanne the sayde chyrchys, abbeys, mynysters, pryorys, hospytallys, and that with owte fraude or malyng.

Also, for to fullefylle that they have sayde, they shalle brekynne and undo and make oppyn alle that bene hydde or [withdrawen in the thinges and goodes aboveseid, or any of hem, where that thei

---

[a] Omitted in MS.
[c] *other.* the, Rymer and J.
CAMD. SOC.

[b] This article is not in Rymer.
[d] *Also.* Alle, MS.

ben hidde or]^a dystryde^b in the same markett, with owtynne with
drawyng or to hylyn anythyng what hyt so be; and that may not
be done nor executyde with yn the fore sayde day, they shalle
declarynne and denounsyn with owte fraude, faynyng, or malynge,
unto the comyssourys and deputes of the sayde kyngys, uppon payne
that þey [that]^c shalle done the contrarye, and the consentauntes,^d
and the coupabyle^e there-of, shalle lese the grace of the fore sayde
kyngys and the effecte of thys presentt apoyntmentt.

Also uppon the sayde payne the r above sayde beyng yn sayde
markett shalle be holdyn [and]^g to take and delyvyr, shewyn and
declare, with owte fraude or malynge, to the comyssourys or deputes
of the sayde kyngys [al the goodes and thinges]^a above sayde,
with owtyn any thynge to hem bylyn or withdrawyn or i-borne
away or othyr, for hem or any of hem.

Also they a-bove sayde, beyng in the sayde markett place of
Mewys in Bry, shalle delyvery playnely and shalle yeldyn quyte
alle the presoners that they have and with holdyn of our subjectys
and obeysaunce, and othyr of the sayde servys of the sayde kyngys,
as welle alle that benne in the sayde markett as in othyr places
where that they bene; ande with that they shalle playnly quyte
alle othyr subjectys [obeisaunces]^a and othyr of the sayde servyse
of the above sayde kyngys þat to hem have made any be-beste or
faythe or othe.

Also, hangynge the tyme above sayde, they of the sayde markett
sballe nought ressayvyn nor sufferne to entre, any preson^h what so
evyr he be, in to the sayde markett; nor they sballe not suffer any
maner of person to passyn or go owte there of for to bere owte any
of the sayde goodys beyng there ynne, with owte lyscence of the
sayde kyngys; nor they shalle not purchesse, nor suffer to be pur-

^a Omitted in MS.; supplied from J.
^b dystryde. discovrind, Rymer; distournid, J.
^c Supplied from J.
^d consentauntes. consentmentys, MS.; corrected from J.
^e coupabyle. compabyle, MS.   ^f the. of, MS.
^g This word is superfluous.   ^h preson. So in MS.

Hen. V.
A.D. 1422.

chessyd, any thyng that may be predyjusse[a] of the sayde kyngys, nor non othyr of hyr subjectys, or ellys for to inpechyn the fulle-fyllyng of thys presentt apoyntment, uppon payne to losse by hem, or hem that shalle done the contrarye, and byr consentamentys and compabylys there of the grace of the marcy of the sayde kyngys.

Also uppon the payne and othe alle tho fore sayde beynge in the sayde markett, ande eche of hem, shalle holde and kepe and fulle-fylle alle the poyntementys and artyculys a-bove sayde and eche of hem, with owte hem or any of hem for to brekyn ne[b] any wyse to done there a-gayne.

Also that thei shul make[c] othe and thei shul take[c] hyr letters selyd with hyr selys for the surete to bene holdynne by twyne the kyngys a-bove sayde, and of othe[r] of hem, in to the nombyr of a C personnys, as welle of captaynys as of othyr notabylle personnys, beyng in the sayde markette, and they thatt have non sealys and canne wrytte [thei shul signe the lettres][d] with hyr owne hondys [and][d] they shalle passyn byfore the kyngys tabyllyon of Mewys in Bry. And the same weyse they that have non sealys, nor canne nott wryte, shalle also passe by the kyngys-tabyllyon to benne regysterde.

Also ande fro[e] the day of thys present poyntementt shalle be done and fullefyllyde, and into that day encludydde, at the whyche day they shalle be holdyn to take and delyvery the sayde markett, as hyt ys sayde, in alle maner alle wey dede of werre shalle sessyn on owre party and of othyr.

Also the a-bove sayde of the same markett a noon shalle take and delyvery to the comyssours and deputes of the sayde kyngys, Syr Lowys Gaste, Roberte de Guesseny, Phylyppe Gamochys, John

---

[a] *predyjusse.* So in MS.   [b] *ne.* in, MS.
[c] *thei shul make—thei shul take.* These words are from J. Our MS. reads absurdly, "cherchefulle makyng"—"cherchefulle takynge."
[d] Supplied from J.
[e] *fro* for, MS.; corrected from J.

Damoy, le Bastarde de Barrowe,[a] Denys de Barowe,[a] Mayster John de Raynys, and othyr of the nombyr of xxiiij personys, wherof[b] the comyssours of on party and of an othyr be accordyd.

The whiche artyculys a-bove sayde and[c] declaryd were concludyd, apoyntyd, and accordyde by the Duke of Exceter, the Erle of Warwyke ande of Bryenne, and Syr Watyr of Hungerforde, comyssours and deputes of the sayde kyngys be-halfe in the one partye, and Peron de Luppe, John Damoy, Mayster Phylyppe Malete,[d] and Wylliam Frosche,[e] for hem selfe and for alle þe othyr of the sayde markette, of the othyr party, the secunde day of the monythe of May, the yere of oure Lorde M¹ cccc xxij. And soo the x day of the same monythe the sayde markett of Mewys in Bry and alle the towne was yoldyn in maner and forme as hyt ys a-bove sayde.

The same yere the xiij day of Auguste a newe wedyrcoke was sette at Powlys stypylle in London.

Also the same yere, the laste day of Auguste, the yere of oure Lorde M¹ cccc xxij, the good and nobylle Kyng, Harry the v aftyr the Conqueste of Inglonde, floure of chevalrye of Crystyn men, endyd hys lyffe in Fraunce, at Boys in Vincent, be syde Parys, the x yere of hys raygne, to whom God graunte mercy. Amen.

Ande that same yere, the xx day of Auguste, deyde the Byschoppe of London, Clyfforde, and thenne was made byschoppe Mayster John Kempe, whos bonys, the viij day of Novembyr next folowyng, worthely at Westmynyster were interyde.

Here foloweythe namys of the townys and castellys, abbeys, pylys, and pylettys, in Normandy, that oure fulle excellent lorde the Kyng Harry the v. wanne and conqueryde in Normandy and in Fraunce, to hym and to hys ayrys, in maner and forme as hit ys bove sayde.

---

[a] *Barrowe.* Warra, in Rymer; Verruo, J.

[b] *wherof.* whos of, MS.; corrected from J.

[c] *and.* "have," MS.; corrected from J. and Rymer.

[d] Some names are here omitted, for which see Rymer, xii., 214.

[e] *Frosche.* Fosse, J. and Rym.

Fyrste the towne of Hareflewe and the castelle of the same, the castelle of Toke, the castelle and towne of Cane, the towne and the castelle of Argentyne, the towne and the castelle of Pallex, the towne and the castelle of Mewys in Bry, the towne and the cytte and the castelle of Rone, and many moo, the nombyr of an c townys and castellys, abbeys, and strong-holdys.

Hen. V.
A.D. 1422

Here benne the namys of Mayrys and Sherevys in the tyme of Kynge Harry the vj, the fyrste begotyn sone of Kyng Harry the v., the whyche yere of hys raygne be ganne the fyrste daye of Septembyr, the yere of oure Lorde Mı cccc xxij, and the age of the Kyng Harry the vj nought fully xij monythys whenne he beganne hys raygne.

Hen. VI.
A.D. 1422-?

| Wylliam Walderne, | Wylliam Estefyllede | A° j°. |
| Mayre of London | Robert Tedyrsale | |

Ande that same yere, the xxj day of October, in the mornynge by twyne vij and viij of the belle, Kyng Carlys of Fraunce dyde, whos body ys worthely enteryde at Syn Denys.

Also the same yere the kyngys Parlyment was holde at Weste-myster, and that be-ganne the ix day of November, in the whyche Parlyment was ordaynyde the governaunce of the kynge, howe he shulde be governyd in hys tendyr age.

Also in that Parlyment was grauntyd unto the kyng v. noblys of every sacke wolle duryng the terme of the* yere. Also the same yere, the secunde b day of Marche, was Syr Wylliam Tayloure, preste, brende in Smethefylde for heresye. And the for sayde secunde b day of Marche wasse made the trety of the delyveraunce of Pounte Mylanke, that was take and longe tyme holdyn by the party callyde the Armonackys, and delyveryd as hyt in maner aftyr folowyþe:—

* *the.* So in MS.; J. reads "during iij. yere," and V. "duryng the terme of v. yere after." The subsidy was really granted only for two years. See Rolls of Parliament, iv. 173.

b J. reads "first" in both these places; which agrees best with what follows.

Here folowythe the appoyntment and yeldyng uppe and delyveraunce of the stronge holde of the brygge of Pount Mylancke,
by twyne the Erle of Sawlysbury, Syr John Fastolfe, Stywarde of
Howsholde, Syr Perys of Founteneye, Lorde of Raynys, Stywarde
of the Howsholde of the Regannt of Fraunce, Duke of Bedforde,
Syr John de Pullyngley, Lord of the Mote de Tylly, knyghtys,
and Rycharde Woodevyle Lorde of Preaus, Nycholas Burdete,
Chyffe Butteler of Normandy, Perys Baret Lorde of Cirone, squyeıs,
comyssourys, and deputes therto of the be-halfe of my lorde the
Regannt of Praunce on the one party, and Syr John Gravylle
Lorde of Mountayne, and Syr Lewes Marchelle, Syr Adam of
Stonys,[a] John de Chaunler, John of Myrayle, Roger of Versy, and
othyr mo othyr dyvers[b] of the party of hem that nowe presentt
occupyen the sayde Pounte.

Fyrste the above said beynge in the sayde Pounte [or fortresse
of Melank, shul yelden the same Pount][c] and strengythe to the
hondys of my sayde lorde the Regaunt of Praunce, or of the[d]
commyssourys or deputes, so areryd, strengythe[e] and abylyde of
gonnys, poudrys, arowblastys, schotte, harneys, and othyr ahyly-
mentys of werre, as hyt ys at thys tyme, with owte fraude,
desepsyon, and malynge, and with owte to done to the same
abylymentys of werre and othyr thyngys defensabylle for the sayde
strenghthe any waste or any brekyng, nor non inpayrement of
vytayle or of any othyr thynge for mannys body, the whyche
strenghþe and brygge they shalle yeldyn and delyveryde as hyt
ys sayde on the morowe, the secunde day of thys presentt monythe
of Marche, at the hour of terce, &c.

Also hit ys accordyd and poyntyde that alle they nowe beynge
at thys tyme in the same Poyute or strengythe of Melancke, of what

[a] *Stonys.* Strones, J.
[b] *and othyr mo othyr dyvers.* and John of Marle, ordeyned, J.
[c] Omitted in MS.; supplied from J.
[d] *the.* his, J.
[e] *areryd, strengythe.* arraied and strengthid, J.

Hen. VI.
A.D. 1423.

a-state or condyscyon that he be, they shalle yeldyn hym and putt
hem in alle thynge to the wylle of my sayde lorde þe Regannt, of
multe [a] and grete humylyte and obeysaunce that they may or shalle,
by cause of whyche humylyte and obeysaunce the sayde comyssourys and deputys of my sayde lorde the Regannt [have promysid
that hym self my lord the Regent],[b] of hys hye grace, in usyng of
marcy and in honowr and reverens of God and thys hooly tyme of
Lentt that nowe ys, shalle ressayve hym to grace and lete hem
have hyr lyvys: excepte tho that certayne tyme have benne in
obeysauns of the kynge that was of Inglonde, heyre and Regannt
of Praunce, to whom God pardon, they thatt have made the othe
of the fynalle pes of the realmys of Fraunce and of Inglonde,
and they that have bene consentaunte of the dethe of Duke of
Burgayne that was laste dede; and also Englysche men, Walysche
men, and Yrysche men, and Schottys, yf anny there be there yn;
ande excepte with John Duras, or callyd ellys Scarbrey,[c] Ferrande
of Bone beaute,[d] Olyver de Lawny,[e] and the gonners, and tho
that were fyrste in the buschementt that fyrste enteryd the Pounte,
the whyche alle sballe be leven sympylly to the wylle of my lorde
the Regannt.

Also hyt ys a poyntyd, yf any gentylman, or any othyr of the
bove sayde, nought exceptyde, wylle yelde hym and putt hym in
to the obeysauns of the kyng our soverayne lorde the Kyng of
Fraunce and of Inglonde, and of my sayde lorde the Regannt, and
make the othe in suche cas and [f] customyd, serve the kyng and my
sayde lorde the Regannt, as hyr verry lege men, and to werre a
gayne the partyes callyd Armenackys as they dyde a gayne the
kyngys and oure sayde lorde the Regaunt,[g] hym sylfe shalle ressayve

[a] So in MS.; J. reads, " in the most great."
[b] Omitted in MS.; supplied from J.
[c] or callyd ellys Scarbrey. on callid Stararay, J.
[d] Bone beaute. Barnabroyt, J.
[e] Lawny. Lannoy, J.   [f] So in MS.
[g] J. reads, " and my lord the Regent aforeseid, hymself my seid lord the Regent
of his grace shall receyve hem," &c

hem of hys grace withowte anny [of][a] fynaunce makynge or ramsom,
provyded alle way to done and fullefylle [b] they shalle delyvery
caucion [c] and goode suffycyaunt pleggys.

Also thys tyme alle tho that benne in the same strenghthe or brygge
of Mylanke, that have or holdyn, or that othyr holdyn in hyr be-halfe,
any towne, place, or strengythe, dysobeysauns to oure lorde the Kyng
and my sayde lorde the Regaunt, delyvyr and yelde hem up unto
my sayde lorde or to hys deputys. And with that they shalle doo
alle hyr myght and trewe devyr an gayne hyr parentes and frendys,
yf any there bene, that holde any suche strengythe or towne dysobeysauns, that they shulle yeldyin hem up to my sayde lorde, &c.
Ande unto the tyme that they have done ande i-fullefyllyde the
thyngys above sayde, they shalle dwelle in the wylle of my lorde the
Regaunt, the whiche thyng above sayde and done and fullefylle
dewly, he shalle ressayve hem as hyt ys above sayde.

Also yf any be in the same sayde brygge or strengythe of
Melancke, havyn and holdyn, in what [place] [d] that they bene, any
presoners, be they Fravnysche, Englysche, Burgonys, or othyr, of
the oboysauns or servyse of owre lorde the Kyng and of my lorde
the Regaunt, they shalle yoldyn hem and delyvery hem frely and
quytly, with owte takyng of the sayde personys or of hyr pleggys
any fynaunce or ramsomys.

Also hyt ys apoyntyde that they that bene in the strengytheys of
Ponnte Melanke, withynne the day of the morne at the howre of
terce, shalle putt or do putt, in a certayne place or two of the
sayde strengythe, alle hyr harnys of werre, with owte any thynge
brokyn or a-payryng. Also they shalle do putt in anothyr certayn
place alle the golde and sylvyr, and sylvyr vesselle and jewellys,
with othyr goodys beyng in the foresayde strengythe, with owtyn
any thynge to holdyn or hydyn, in what place or maner that hyt

---

[a] This word is superfluous.
[b] *to done and fullefylle.* that that done and fulfillid, J.
[c] *caucion.* nunsyon, MS.; corrected from J.
Omitted in MS.

be, they sballe delyvery hem to the comyssourys of oure lorde the
Regaunt, uppon payne to lese the benefycys of thys present poynte- ment and the grace of my sayde lorde the Regannt.

Also they sballe put in the sayde strengythe in oo place or ij alle the hors beyng there yn, and alle hyr harneys, for to be delyveryd on the state and plyghte that they benne nowe at thys tyme, whythe alle othyr thyngys a-bove sayde, unto the comissurys and deputes of my sayde lorde the Regaunte, uppon the payne above sayde.

Also uppon the same payne ys tretyd and appoyntyde that durynge the sayde trete they shalle nought lette or suffer any maner person to partyn owte of the sayde strengthe of Melanke, nor noo person to entyr, with owte leve and lyssens of my sayde lorde the Regaunt; and uppon the same payne they shalle denounsyn, seale,[a] and delyvery to hym or to hys comyssurys the for sayde[b] persoonys except, where-of they have any knowynge.

And to that ende that the thinges[c] above sayde ben holly fulle- fyllyde fyrmely and worthely, the above sayde comyssourys and deputys, in þat one party and of that othyr, of thys present ap- poyntement, have sette hyr sealys, in the fyrste day of Marche, the yere of oure Lorde M¹ cccc xxij.

And in the monythe of Apprylle was made the allyaunce by twyne the Regaunt of Fraunce, the Duke of Bedforde, the Duke of Burgayne, and the Duke of Bretayne, in maner and forme aftyr folowynge :—[d]

To alle tho that thys present letters shalle see or hyre, Robert le Jone, lorde of the Foreste, caunseler of oure lorde the kynge, and hys bayly of Amyas, sendythe gretynge. We do you to wete that thys day before us have bene brought, coveryd,[e] and dylygently

---

[a] *seale.* So in MS.; J. reads "take."

[b] *the for sayde.* for the sayde, MS.; corrected according to J.

[c] *thinges.* kyngys, MS.; corrected from J.

[d] For the text of this treaty in the original French, see Rymer, x. 280.

[e] *covered.* So in MS.; J. reads "have bene, brought, seen and redde," which agrees with the text in Rymer.

beholdyn, a letter yevyng of ryght excellent pryncys my Lorde
Regaunt of Praunce, Duke of Bedforde, my Lorde Duke of
Burgayne, and my lorde the Duke of Bretayne, [have] ᵃ selyde with
hyr manuelle sygnettys, and enselyd with dowbylle queue of hyr
sealys in redde wex, sygnyde and inselyde also whyþe emanuelle
sygnys of Mayster John Rynelle, secretary of oure lorde the kynge,
Mayster Quyntyne Menarde, secretary of my lorde the Duke of
Burgayne, and Mayster John Browne,ᵇ secretary of my lorde the
Duke of Bretayne, hoole and saufe in sealys and in wrytyngc,
as by the specefyynge of the same letters hyt ys shewyd, of whyche
letters the tenoure folowythe:

    John Regannt of Praunce, Duke of Bedford, &c., Phylyppe
Duke of Burgayne, &c., the Duke of Bretayne, &c.   To alle thot
þat thys prcsentt letters shall see we sende gretyng.   [We] ᶜ do you
to wctyn that for the consyderacyon of the grette frendeschyppys
and nygheyng of lynagys that nowe ar by twyne us, and also mevynge
the maryagys concludyd, acordyd, and conservyde by-twyxte us,
John Regannt of Fraunce and Duke of Bedford and othyr ᵈ dyre
welle belovyde suster a ᵈ cosyn Anne of Burgayne, on that one party,
and of dyre and welle belovyd brothyr Arture Duke ᵉ of Turreyne,
Erle of Monforte and of Ivery, and of oure dyre and welbelovyd
sustyr and cosyn Margarete of Burgayne, on that othyr party, ande
for the goode governaylle of oure lorde the kynge and of realmys of
Fraunce and Inglond, of us and of oure lordeschyppys, landys, contreys, and subjcctys, we and every one of us sweryn, behotynne, and
promysyn to benne and dwellyng, as longe as we shalle lyve, in
goode and verry love, fraternyte and unyon, that one whythe that
othyr, that welle shalle love and cherysche and holdyn to·gedyr as
brctherynne ar kynnys men, or parentes and goode frendys, we

ᵃ This word is superfluous.
ᵇ Rymer gives his name Jehan le Brius.
ᶜ Omitted in MS.; supplied from J.
ᵈ *othyr—a.* So in MS.
    Arture Duke. Arture of the Duke, MS.

shalle kepe and defende the honowre þat one of that othyr as welle prevely as a-pertely, with-owte any fraude and dyssymylacyon in any wyse; we shalle do wetyn one of that othyr of alle that we shalle knowyn and undyr-stonde that may turne and be to profyte or damage, honour or dyshonoure, or one of that othyr, and of oure lordeschippys, landys, and contreys, and subjectys; and yf any persone telle or make any wronge reporte to us or to any of us one of that othyr, we shalle geve there to noo credens nor faythe, but we shalle whytheholdyn smartely agayne us, and eche of us in ryght any suche that have made that wrongfully reporte, and by goode love and verry charyte a-none we shalle do to knowe of hym of whom suche reporte was made, and thereyn for to done that shalle long to be done be resone.

Also, yf we or any of us have to done or nede for oure worschyppe or oure contrayes, londys, [and]* lordschyppys to kepe or to defende a-gayne any that wolde grevyn or damagynne us or any of us, we and eche of us shalle be holdynne to helpyn and servynne hym amonge us that so shalle have nede, whenne we be there to requyryd, with summys of v c men of armys or of folke of schotte,[b] whettyr that may a-vayle or plese or lykyng to hem that so shalle have nede. And he that shalle be requyryd shalle be holdyn to sende at hys owne dysposyssyon hys men or forke[c] for the fyrst monythe; and for the surplus of the tyme that the saudyers shalle serve, the requyrant shalle ben holdyn to sendyn hem at hys propyr dysposycyon. And yf any of us wylle have grete[d] power, he that shalle be requyryd shalle be holdyn to helpe at the costys and dyspens of the requyrant as farforthe as he goodely shalle, as he may, hys contrayes [and]* lordeschippis resonabely a-fore warnyde.

Also whythe alle oure[e] myghte, and by[f] alle the beste maner

* Omitted in MS.; supplied from J.
b *folke of schotte.* "gens de trait " in the original French.
c *forke.* So in MS.   d *grete.* gretter, J.
e *oure.* othyr, MS.; corrected from J.
f *by.* se; corrected from J.

that we canne or may devyse for [a] relevynge of the pore pepylle of the realme that bathe sufferd and sufferythe hyt [b] so moche myschief; and for that we shalle spedyn us to doo away the warre of the realme, and so sette hyt in pes and reste and tranquyllyte, to that ende that God there-yn be servyde and worschippyd, and that marchaundyse there may have the cours: Alle thys thyngys we and eche of us promyse and hotyn to fullefylle and trewly kepe as longe as we shalle lyve, by the maner above sayde, whythe any wyse for any contrarynys shalle not offende,[c] undyr the oblygacyon of alle oure goodys mevabylle and unmevabylle nowe beynge presente and tho that bene to come.

In wytnes here of we have done sette oure selys to thys present lettyrs, and we have sygnyd hem whythe oure owne honde, and undyr wryte oure propyr namys. Gevyn at Amyens the xvij day of Aprylle, and the yere of oure Lorde M[l] cccc xxiij. Also sygnyd by my foresayde Lorde the Regaunte of Fraunce, Syr John Duke of Bedforde, and by my Lorde Duke of Burgayne, by my Lorde Duke of Bretayne. And uppon the foldyng of the same letters ys wryttyn: " Par [d] mone Senowre le Regaunt de le realme de Fraunce, Deuke de Bedeford, John Rynylle. [Par Monsieur le Duc de Burgoigne, Q. de Menart.][e] Par [d] mone Senowrys Duke de Bretayne, J. le Breune. In wytnysse whereof to thys present letters we have sette to oure sealys of the baylyage of Amyes. Gevyn at Amyes, the xviij day of the monythe of Aprylle, and the yere of oure Lorde M[l] cccc xxiij.

Also the same yere Newgate was be gon to be made a Newgate by the executourys of that famos marchant and merser, Rycharde Whytyngdone.

---

[a] *for.* or, MS.; corrected from J.

[b] *i. e.* yet.

[c] *whythe any wyse . . . . offende.* J. reads, more intelligibly, and according to the original, " withouten ever to done the contrarie in any maner."

[d] *Par.* Pur, MS., in both these places; corrected by J. and Rymer.

[e] Omitted in MS.; supplied from Rymer.

Wylliam Crowmere,	Nicholas Jamys	A° ij°.
Mayre of London	Thomas Wansforde	

Ande that same yere there was a Parlyment at Westemyster, and that be-ganne the xxj day of October; and in that yere, the xxj day of Feveryr, was Syr Thomas [a] Mortymere drawe, hangyd, and quarteryde, and hys hede smete of at Tyborne, and hys body was buryd at Syn Johnys at Clerkyn-welle and hys herte at Fryer Menowrys be syde Newgate. And that yere was the batylle in Verney, in Perche, the xxvij day of Auguste, by my lorde the Regaunte of Fraunce, John Duke of Bedforde, with othyr lordys with hym of Englysche lordys; and in that batayle was slayne the Erle Dugelas, the Erle of Bogham, the Erle of Marre, and alle the Scottys that durste a-byde in the fylde were slayne and take. And there was take on the Fraynysche syde the Duke of Launsun and the Erle of Almarre, and many mo othyr knyghtes an squyers were takyn and slayne, the nombyr of v m¹ Scottys and Armonackys, &c.

And that same yere, in the monythe of Feverer, the Stywarde of [b] the Kyngys of Scottys, whas name was Jamys, weddyd the Erlys doughter of Somersett at Syut Mary Overes.

John Mychelle,	Symon Seman	A° iij°.
Mayre of London	John Bythewater	

Ande that yere there was a Parlyment att Westemyster; and that Parlyment beganne the laste day of Aprylle. And at that Parlyment the Erle Marchalle was made Duke of Northefolke; and in that Parlyment was moche altercacyon by-twyne þe lordys and the l comyns for tonage and poundage. And at that Parlyment was l grauntyd that alle maner of alyentys shulde be put to hoste as Englysche men benne in othyr londys, and ovyr that condyscyon was the touage grauntyd; the whyche condyscyon was brokyn in the same yere by the Byschoppe of Wynchester, as the moste pepylle sayde, he beyng Chaunseler the same tyme, and there-fore there was moche hevynesse and trowbylle in thys londe. And that

[a] *Syr Thomas.* The name should be Sir John.
[b] So in MS.

yere, the xiij day of Feverer at nyght, were caste many byllys in the cytte and in the subbarbys a-gayne the Flemyngys, and sum were set in the byschoppe ys gate of Wynchester, and in othyr bischoppys gatys.   And in the morowe the Byschoppe of Wyn-chester sent Richarde Woodevyle, squyer, to kepe the Towre of London with men of armys as thoughe hyt hadde bene in the londe of warre, and so induryd tylle the feste of Symon and Jude nexte aftyr folowynge.   And that yere there were many worthy men of London apechyde of treson by a false boy Peloure by excytacyon of the Byschoppe of Wynchester, as many men noysyde and sayde; yf were trewe or no I remytte me to Gode.   And of many moo othyr townys, as Cauntyrbury, Exceter, and Brystowe, Covyntre, Yorke, Chester, &c.

Ande that yere the Duke of Gloucester with hys wyffe wentte into Ennowde; and she was Duches of Holand.   And there he lefte hyr byhynd hym.

Ande the same yere the Byschoppe of Wynchester sende to Wyndesore for certayne men of the kyngys howsholde, and lefte the kyng but with a fewe men, and for alle the prentys * of Courte, unto Westemyster; and there they come in there beste a-raye; and thenne he sende for the Mayre of London and hys aldermen.   And there he restyde many worthy men of the cytte.   And that yere dyde the Erle of Marche in Irlonde, the xviij day of Janyver, in the castelle of Trynne.

And that yere come the kyngys sone of Portyng-gale in to Englonde; and on Mychelle-mas evyn he com to London, and was loggyd in the byschoppe ys place of London.

Ande in that yere there was a Perlyment at Westemyster, and that Parlyment be-ganne the laste daye of Aprylle.   And that Par-lyment badde an evylle faryng ende, to shamefully for to be namy[d] of any welavysyd man.

---

* There appears to be an omission here in the MS. We ought doubtless to read, "and for all the prentices *of the Inns* of Court." In V. the corresponding passage is, "and he sent to the Innes of Court for to come to hym."

John Covyntre,   { Wylliam Myldrede } A° iiij°.
Mayre of London   { John Brockeley

And that same yere that the mayre rode to Westmyster on the
same daye for to take hys othe, that ys, was the xxix daye of Septembyr,[a] whenne that he come home to hys mete with hys aldyrmen
and with hys goode comyners, or that they badde fully ete, the
Duke of Glouceter sende for the mayre and hys aldyrmen that they
shulde come spoke with hym; and whenne they come he cargyd the
mayre that he shulde[b] kepe welle the cytte that nyght and make
goode wache; and so there was, alle that nyghte, for my Lorde
of Glouceter and the Byschoppe of Wynchester were not goode
frendys as in that tyme. And on the morowe certayne men kepte
the gatys of the brygge of London by the commaundement of the
Lorde of Gloucter and of the mayre. And by-twyne ix and x of
the belle þer come certayne men of the Byschoppys of Wynchester
and drewe the chaynys of the stulpys at the brygge ende in Southe-
worke ys syde, the whiche were bothe knyghtys and squyers, with
a grete mayny of archerys, and they enbaytaylyd them, and made
defens of wyndowys and pypys as hyt hadde bene in the londe of
warre, as thowe they wolde have fought agayne the kyngys pepylle
and brekyng of the pes. And thenne the pepylle of the cytte hyrde
there of, and they in haste schytte in ther shoppys and come downe
to the gatys of the brygge in kepyng of the cytte ande savacyon of
the cytte a-gayns the kyngys enmys, for alle the shoppys in London
were schytte in one howr. And thenne come my Lorde of Cauntyrbury ande the Prynce of Portynggale, and tretyd by twyne my
Lorde of Glouceter and the Byschoppe of Wynchester, for they rode
viij tymes by twyne the duke and the byschoppe that day. And
thonkyd be God, thoroughe goode governaunce of the mayre and
hys aldyrmen, alle the pepylle was sessyde and wentte home ayenne
every mann, and none harme done thorough calle the cytte, thonkyd
be God.

[a] October, according to V.
[b] *that he shulde*. Repeated in MS.

Hen. VI.
.D. 1425-6.

Ande the v day of Novembyr aftyr that, the kynge came fro Eltam to London; ande with hym come the Duke of Glouceter and the Prynce of Portynggale, and alle the lordys that were a-boute London that tyme, with the mayre and alle his aldyrmen, and with alle the trewe and goode comyners of the cytte of London; and that was with a gode araye. And the x day of Janyver came the Duke of Bedforde to London, and my lady hys wyffe with hym, and they come to the Byschoppe of Wynchester; and the mayre and alle the cytte fette hym and mette whythe hym at Merton, and broughte hym to Westemyster. And in the kyngys palys he was loggyd, and my lady hys wyffe and the Byschoppe of Wynchester in the abbay faste by hym. And the mayre with the cytte gaf my lorde of Bedforde a payre of basonnys of sylvyr over gylte, and M^l marke in them to hys welcome. And yet they hadde but lytylle thanke.

Ande the xxj day of Feverer be ganne the counsel at Synt Albonys, but there hyt was enjornyd unto Northehampton. And the xxv day of Marche nexte aftyr be-ganne the Parlyment at Layceter, and that induryd unto the fyrste day of June, and every man was warnyd and i-cryde thoroughe the towne that they shulde leve hyr wepyn yn hyr ynnys, that ys to saye, hyr swerdys and bokelers, bowys and arowys. And thenne the pepylle toke grete battys in hyr neckys and so they wentte. The nexte day they were chargyde that they shulde leve hyr battys at hyr ynnys, and thenne they toke grete stonys yn hyr bosomys and hyr slyvys, and so they wennte to the Parlyment with hyr lordys. Ande thys Parlyment sum men callyd the Parlyment of Battys. And at thys Parlyment was the kyng made knyght, and xxxv moo whythe hym of lordys and lordys sonys. Fryste my Lorde of Yorke, the Erle of Oxynforde, and hys brother, the sone and the eyre of the Duke of Northefolke, the sone and the ayre of the Erle of Urmounde, the sone of the Lorde Hungerford, and Syr John Chaynye, Chyffe Justysse of the Kyngys Bcnche, Syr Wylliam Babyngton, Chyffe Justys of the Comyn Place, and Syr John June, the Chyffe Baron of the Kyngys Chekyr, and many mo, to the nombyr above sayde. And the fyrste day of Juylle be-ganne the counselle at London at Westemyster, ande duryd fully iij wekys.

Ande the same yere, the xxviij day of Novembyr, deyde the Countasse of Huntyngdon at the Colde Herborowe, in London, and she ys buryd at the Fryer Prechowrys at Ludgate.

Ande same yere, the vj daye of Marche, Arthure of Bretayne with othyr lordys, the nombyr of x. m^l. knyghtys and squyers, made a saute to the towne of Synt Jakys de Bouerne. Ande there were slayne of hem a m^l and v c of men of armys, of the whiche were viij c legge harnys with hyr cote armourys one of hem.[a] And he toke alle hyr ordynauns of gonnys and alle hyr vytayle, with alle the othyr stoffe that was at the sege, that is to saye, xiiij gonnys, with the powdrys, and iij c pypys of wyne, and ij c pypys of brede and floure, and a m^l.[b] panyers with fyggys and raysonys, and herynge, and othyr stuffe of pavys and tentys, &c.

John Raynewelle, the goode Mayre of the cytte of London	Robert Arnolde John Hygham	A° v°.

Ande that yere John Duke of Bedforde and Regaunte of Fraunce wennte in to Fraunce agayne, and the Byschoppe of Wynchester whythe hym, and they londyd at Calys. And ther the Byschoppe of Wynchester was made Cardynalle upon oure Lady Daye in Lentyn, in Saynt Mary chyrche. Ande there was grete solempnyte, for there come two legatys and broughte hys bullys and hys hatte from the Pope,[c] and the Regaunt set on hys hatte ond hys bedde.

Ande that same yere a theffe that was i-callyd Wille Wawe was hangyd at Tyborne. And that yere was smytte owte many buttys of Romnaye of Lumbardys makyng in dyvers placys of the Cytte, for they were corrupte and also they very pyson, &c.

Ande that same yere, the xiiij day of Juylle, cam the Erle of Saulysbury in to London owte of Fraunce. And that yere there

---

[a] *one of hem.* upon hem, V.   [b] *m^l.* ij^{ml}, V.

[c] *Pope.* This word is crossed through.

was a Parlyment at Westemyster, and that beganne a Synt Ed-
wardys day in Lent.   And that yere the towre on the draught
brygge of London was be-gonne.   And the Mayre layde the fyrste
stone, and mo othyr aldyrmen with hym.

| John Gedney, | Robert Otle | Anno vj°. |
| Mayre of London | Harry Frowyke | |

Ande that yere the Erle of Warwyke com home in to Inglonde
owte of Fraunce, and he was made governer of the kynge.

Ande that yere the Pope [a] sende into Inglond, and in to alle
Crystyn londys, a pardon ayenste the erytekys the whyche were in
the londe of Hungery, yn the cytte of Prage; the whyche pardon
was that me[n] shulde every Sonday in the begynnyng of every
monythe shulde goo in processyon, whythe vij Psalmys and the
Letany, and they shulde have a c dayes of pardon unto the same processyon.   The kyng and the queue, and alle othyr lordys spyrytualle
& temporalle, wentt on processyon thoroughe London the ij day
of June.   And that same day the Erle of Saulysbury toke hys
jornaye towarde Fraunce the secunde tyme; and he schyppyd at
Sondewyche, and he londyd in Normandy, and wente forthe unto
Orlyaunce, and there he layde sege unto the towne as hyt ys a-bove
sayde.

Ande that same yere, the fyrste of September, the Cardynalle
and Byschoppe of Wynchester came yn to Ingelonde, and soo to
London; and he was ressayvyd there worthely and ryally of the
mayre and of alle hys bretheryn, for they roode and fette hym yn
to the cytte of London, ande the spyrytualle party whythe processyon.   And þat yere hyt was a wete somer for hyt raynyd for
the moste party from oure Lady Day in Lentyn unto the feste of
Mychelmas nexte folowynge.   And that yere there was a grete
morayne of bestys, and pryncypally of schyppe, for the more party of
alle Inglonde, for sheppe deyde ynne every contray of Ingelonde.

| Harry Barton, | Thomas Dufhous | Anno vij°. |
| Mayre of London | John Abbotte | |

* *Pope.*   This word crossed through, and "bishope" written over in a later hand.

Hen. VI.
A.D. 1428-9.

Ande that same yere, the xxx day of October, there was a grette fyre at Baynardeys Castelle, the whyche fyre dyde moche harme.

And the viij day of Novembyr the Duke of Northefolke wolde have rowyde thoroughe the brygge of London, and hys barge was reutte agayne the arche of the sayde brygge, and there were drownyde many men, the nombyr of xxx personys and moo of gentylmen and goode yemen.

Ande the same yere, the xxx day of October, the Erle of Saulysbury was hurte at the sege of Orlyaunce beforesayde, and the secunde day of Novembyr he dyde. Ande the fyrste Sonday of Advente he was enteryde at Poulys by the Cardynalle of Wynchester and ij Arche-byschoppys, one of Cantyrbury and that othyr of Yorke, that tyme beynge in London.

And the secunde daye of Advente there were ij heretykys objuryd atte Poulys Crosse, and the iij herytyke commyttyde to preson, for he was convycte. And that same yere the bonys of Mayster John Wykclyffe were take uppe and brentte at Lutterworthe in Layceter schyre there that he was buryde. And thys was done by the commaundement of þe pope and alle hys clargye. And the xij evyn aftyr was i-broughte unto London, and badde hys masse at Poulys, and hys bonys buryde at Birsham.

Ande the same yere, the xij day of Feverer, Syr John Fastolfe, Syr Thomas Ramston, and Syr John Salveyne, toke and slowe[a] the nombyr of viij schore Schottys of cote armyvorys, and toke iiij C Dolfynnys mayne that were towarde Orlyaunce for to have brokyn the sege, &c.

And that same yere the Duke of Burbone[b] was sworne Englysche in the kyngys manyr of Eltam besyde Grenewyche. And the xxj day of Feverer Syr Rycharde Nevyle was made Erle of Saulysbury. And that same yere there was a stronge thefe that was namyd Bolton was drawe, hanggyd, and i-quarteryde. And that same

---

[a] This is the action commonly spoken of as "the battle of Herrings."

[b] John Duke of Bourbon, who had been a prisoner in England since the battle of Agincourt.

yere there was a ryche wedowe i-slayne at Whyte Chapylle; and
the same theffe that kylde hyr fledde to Syn Gorgys yn Sowtheworke; and the Fryday nexte folowynge he for-swore the londe;
and he was a-sygnyd the same way that he slowe the woman, and
there wemmen mette with hym and slowe hym in the waye by
twyne the Whyte Chapylle and Algate.

Ande the same yere, the v day of June, there was a fryer i-slayne
in the Towre of London, and the person of the same Towre with
hym also. And that yere hyt was a dyre yere of corne and
pryncypally of whete and of alle maner of vytayle, for a buschelle
of whete was worthe xx d. And that same yere, in the monythe of
May, was the sege of Orlyaunce i-broke with the Pusylle, Bastarde of
Burbon, and othyr Armynackys. And there was slayne the Lorde
Molaynys, and Glasdale, squyer, and many moo worthy men. And
the x day of June the Erle of Sowthefolke brothyr, and the Lorde of
Ponyngys sone hys ayre, were slayne at a jornaye be-syde Orlyaunce,
and the Lorde Talbot, and the Lorde Schalys, and Syr Thomas
Ramston were takyn, and the erlys brother of Sowthefolke was
slayne, and many mo othyr, &c.

Ande the xxij day of June the Cardynalle of Wynchester toke
hys jornay, and was purposyd into the londe of Beame; but he
cam not there, but bode stylle yn Praunce whythe the Regaunte
that tyme. And on Synte Petrys day aftyr Syr John Radeclyffe
wentte unto Fraunce unto the Regaunte with a nothyr mayny.
And the same yere, the xxij day of Septembyr, be-gan the Parlyment at Weïtemyster, and hyt duryde unto the xxiij day of
Feverer nexte folowynge; in the whyche Parlyment was grauntyd
that John Raynewelle shulde ᵃ be mayre of the stapylle of Callys iij
yere folowynge.

Wylliam Estefylde,　⎰ Wylliam Russe　⎱ Aº viijº
Mayre of London　⎱ Raulyn Holande　⎰

Ande that yere, the vj day of Novembyr, the yere of ouro Lorde
a Mˡ.cccc.xxix and the Sonday letter or Dominical letter B, Kyng

ᵃ *shulde* repeated in MS.

Harry the vj was crownyd at Westemyster on Syn Lenardys day. Hen. VI.
A.D. 1429.
And at the coronacyon was made xxxij knyghtys of the Bathe;
and on the morne aftyr the Pryncys sone of Portynggale was made
knyghte in the Whyte Halle at Westemyster.

Nowe of the solempnyte of the coronacyon. Alle the prelatys
wente on processyon beryng eche of hem a certayne relyke; and
the Pryor of Westemyster bare a rodde callyde *Virga regia*, ande
the Abbot of Westemyster bare the kyngys ceptoure. And my
Lorde of Warwyke bare the kynge to chyrche in a clothe of
scharlet furryd, evyn as the newe knyghtys of the Bathe wente
whythe furryde hoodys with menyver. And thenne he was led
up in to the hyghe schaffold, whyche schaffolde was coveryd alle
with saye by twyne the hyghe auter and the quere. And there the
kyng was sette in hys sete in the myddys of the schaffold there,
beholdynge the pepylle alle a-boute saddely and wysely. Thenne
the Arche-byschoppe of Cantyrbury made a proclamacyon at the iiij
quarterys of schaffolde, sayynge in thys wyse: " Syrys, here comythe
Harry, Kyng Harry the v ys sone, humylyche to God and Hooly
Chyrche, askynge the crowne of thy[s] realme by ryght and dyscent
of herytage. Yf ye holde you welle plesyd with alle and wylle be
plesyd with hym, say you nowe, ye! and holde uppe youre hondys."
And thenne alle the pepylle cryde with oo voyce, "Ye! yel" Thenne
the kynge went unto the hyghe auter, and humely layde hym downe
prostrate, hys bedde to the auter warde, longe tyme lyyng stylle.
Thenne the arche-byscoppys and byschuppys stode rounde a-boute
hym, and radde exercysyons ovyr hym, and many antemys i-song
by note. And thenne the arche-byschoppes wente to hym and
strypte hym owte of hys clothys in to hys schyrte. And there was
yn hys schyrte a thynge lyke grene taffata, whyche was i-lasyd at
iiij placys of hym. Thenne was he layde a downe a yenne, and
helyd hym with hys owne clothys yn the same maner a-fore sayde.
And thenne the Byschoppe of Chester[a] and of Rouchester[b] songe

---

[a] Bishop of Chester, *i. e.* of Coventry and Lichfield. His name was William
Heyworth.   [b] John Langdon.

a letany ovyr hym.   And the Arche-byschoppe of Cantyrbury
radde many colettys ovyr hym.   Thenne the arche-byschoppys
toke hym uppe a gayne and unlasyd hym, and a-noyntyd hym.
Fyrste hys bryste and hys ij tetys, and the myddys of hys backe,
and hys bedde, alle a-crosse hys ij schylderys, hys ij elbowys,
hys pamys of hys hondys; and thenne they layde a certayne
softe thynge as cotton to alle the placys a-noyntyd; and on hys
bedde they putt on a whyte coyffe of sylke.   And so he wentte
viij dayes; and at the viij dayes the byschoppys dyde wasche hit
a-waye with whyte wyne i-warmyd leuke warme.   And the knyghtys
of the Garter helde a clothe of a-state ovyr hym alle the whyle of
his waschynge.   To the fyrste processe, aftyr the oyntynge he layde
hym doune prostrate a-gayne.   Thenne the arche-byschoppys raddyn
solempne colettys with a solempne prefas.   And thenne they toke
hym up a-gayne and putte a-pon hym a goune of scharlette whythe
a pane of ermyn, and Synt Edwarde ys sporys, and toke hym hys
cepter in hys honde, and the kyngys yerde i-callyd *Virga regia* in
hys othyr honde, sayyng there-with, *Reges eos in virga ferrea,*[a] *&c.,*
he syttyng thenne in a chayre by fore the hyghe auter.   And
thenne alle the byschoppys scseden with a swerde, they alle syttynge
there hondys thereon, ande alle they saynge thes wordys thys to
hym, *Accingere*[b] *gladio tuo super femur tuum, potentissime.*[c]   And at
every tyme the kyng answeryd and sayde, *Observabo.*   Thenne toke
they the swerde a gayne fro hym, and layde the swerde on the hyghe
auter.   Thenne bought the kyng hys swerde a gayne of Holy Chyrche
for an c s. in signe and in tokyn that the vertu and power sholde
come fyrste fro Hooly Chyrche.   Thenne sette they on hys bedde Synt
Edwarde ys crowne.   Thenne rose he owte of hys chayre and layde
hym downe prostrate a gayne.   And there the byschoppys sayde
ovyr hym many hooly colettys.   And thenne they toke hym up and
dyspoylyd hym of hys gere a-yen, and thenne a-rayde hym as a
byschoppe that sholde synge a masse, with a dalmadyke lyke unto

---

[a] *ferrea.* feria, MS. Psalm ii. 9.   [b] *Accingere.* Accinge, MS.
[c] Psalm xliv. 4 (xlv. 3).

a tunycule with a stole a bowte hys necke, not crossyd, and a pon hys fete a payre of sandellys as a byschoppe, and a cope and glovys lyke a byschoppe; and thenne sette a yen on hys bedde Synt Edwarde ys crowne, and layde hym a-pon the schaffolde and sette hym a sete of hys astate, and ij byschoppys stondyng on every syde of hym, helpyng hym to bere the crowne, for hyt was ovyr hevy for hym, for he was of a tendyr age. And then they be-ganne the masse, and the Arche-byschoppe of Cauntyrbury songe the masse. And a nothyr byschop radde the pystylle. And the Byschoppe of Worsethyr radde the gospelle at the auter. And at the offretory come the kynge downe and made the oblacyon of brede and wyne, there whythe offerynge a pounde weyght of golde, the whiche contaynyd xvj marke of nobbelys. And thenne wente he uppe agayne in to the schaffolde and satte there in hys sete tylle the iij Angus Dei, and thenne he come downe agayne and layde hym downe prostrate, sayng there hys *Confyteor*,* and alle the prelatys sayde *Misereator*.* And thenne he sate uppe, knelynge with humylyte and grete devocyon, ressayvyng the iij parte of the holy sacrament apon the paten of the chalys of the Arche-byschoppe handys. Thenne there come the Byschoppe of London with the grete solempne chalys of Syut Edwarde and servyd hym whythe wyne; the whyche chalis by Synt Edwarde ys dayes was praysyd at xxx.M^l marke; and the Cardenalle of Wynchester and a nothyr byschoppe helde to hym the towelle of sylke; and so he knelyd stylle tylle mas was i-doo. Thenne rosse he up a-gayne an yede a-fore the schryne, and there was he dyspoylyde of alle the orna-mentys that he weryde, lyke the ornamentys of a byschoppe, as hyt was sayde by-fore; and thenne he was a-rayde lyke a kynge in a ryche clothe of golde, with a crowne sette on hys bedde, whyche crowne Kynge Rycharde badde made for hym selfe. And so the kynge was ladde thoroughe the palys yn to the halle, and alle the newe knyghtys be-fore hym in hyr a-raye of scharlette; and thenne all the othyr lordys comynge aftyr hym; thenne come the othyr

* Sic

Ien. VI.
.D. 1429.

lordys comynge aftyr hem. Thenne come the chaunceler with hys crosse bare heddyd; and aftyr hym come the cardenelle with hys crosse in hys abyte lyke a chanon yn a garment of rede chamelett, furryd whythe whyte menyver. And thenne folowyde the Kynge, and he was ladde by-twyne the Byschoppe of Dyrham and the Byschoppe of Bathe; and my goode Lorde of Warwyke bare uppe his trayne. And byfore hym rode my Lorde of Saulysbury— *dardh* as Constabylle of Ingelonde in my Lorde of Bedforde hys stede, and thenne my Lorde of Glouceter as Stywarde of Inglonde. And aftyr hym rode the Duke of Northefolke as Marchalle of Ingelonde. And before the kynge iiij lordys bare iiij swerdys, ij in there schaberdys and ij nakyde. And one wa[s] poynteles of the iiij swerdys above sayde. And as they [were]ᵃ syttyng at mete the kynge kepte hys astate. Ande on the ryght honde sate the Cardynalle whythe a lower astate; and on the lyfte syde sate the chaunceler and a byschoppe of Fraunce, and noo moo at that tabylle. And on the ryght honde of the halle at that borde kepte the baronys of the —Fyffe portys, and soo forthe, clerkes of the Chaunsery; and on the lefte honde sate the Mayre of London and hys aldyrmen, and othyr worthy comynerys of the cytte of London. Ande in the myddys of the halle sate the byschoppys, and justysys, and worthy knyghtys, and squyers, and soo fyllyde bothe the myddylle tabyllys of the halle. And at the ryght honde of the halle, uppon a schaffolde, stode the kyngys of harowdys alle the mete tyme in hyr cote armorys and hyr crownys in hyr heddys. Ande at the fyrste course they come downe and wente by fore the kyngys champyon, Syr Phylyppe Dymmoke, that rode in the halle i-armyde elene as Syn Jorge. And he proclaymyd in the iiij quarterys of the halle that the kynge was ryghtefulle ayre to the crowne of Ingelonde, and what maner man þat wolde nay hyt, he was redy for to defende hyt as hys knyghte and hys champyon. Ande by that offyce he holdythe hys londys, &c.

ᵃ Omitted in MS.

The fyrste course that was i-servyd yn to the halle before the Hen. VI.
A.D. 1429.
kynge.

The fyrste that come yn was a berys bedde, enarmyde in a castelle ryalle. Furmenty with venson. Vyant ryalle gylte. Grosse chare. Swanne. Capyn stewyde. Hayryn. Grete pyke. Rede lesche whythe a whyte lyon crownyde there yn. Custarde ryalle with a lybarde of golde sette there ynne holdyng a flowredelys. Frytoure like a son, a floure de lysse there yn. Ande a sotelte, Synt Edwarde and Syut Lewys armyd in hyr cotys of armys, bryngyng thys yong kyng, Harry the vj, in fygure y-armyde by twyne hem two, in hys cote of armys, whythe thys reson :

"Loo here ben ij kyngys ryght profytabylle and ryght goode,
Holy Syut Edwarde and Synt Lowys.
Also the branche borne of hyr blode,
Lyvynge a monge Crystyn moste soverayne of pryse,
Enherytoure to the flowredelysse.
God graunte he may thoroughe grace of Cryste Jesu
The vj^te Harry to raygne, and be as wyse,
And hym resemble in kynghode and vertu."   Amen.

The secunde coursse unto the kynge syttynge in the halle.

Viaunde blanke. Gely * wrytyn and notyd, *Te Deum laudamus.* Pygge in doory. Crane. Byttore. Cony. Chykynnys endoryd. Parteryche. Pecoke. Grete breme; leche whythe an antloppe crownyde there yn, and schynynge as golde. Flampayne pouderyde with lybardys and flowredelyssys of golde. Frytoure. Custarde. A lybarde ys bedde whyþe ij esterygys fetherys. And a sotellete,— The Emperoure and Kynge Harry the v^te in mantellys of garterys, bryngyng yn Kyng Harry the vj^te yn the same sute, whythe thys reson imperyalle :

"Ayens myscreaunt[s] the Emperoure Segysmounde
Hathe shewyde hys myghte which is ^b imperyalle

---

* *Gely*. Goly, MS.   ^b *which is*. with hys, MS

Sythe Harry soo nobylle and worthy knyghte[a]
In Crystys cause yn actys mercyalle.
Cheryschynge the Chyrche, the Lollers hadde a valle
To geve ensampylle to kynges that shulde shewe hyr ryght.
And to thys branche in specyalle
Whylys he dothe raygne to plese God, and drede hys myght
    eternalle."[b]   Amen.

The thyrde course of thys ryalle feste in to the halle.

Quynsys in composte. Blaundsore. Veneson rostyde. Egretys.
Curlewys rostyde. Wodekocke. Ploverys. Quaylys. Snytys.
Grete bryddys. Larkys. Grete crabbys. Lesche i-made as vyolet
colourys. Bakemetes. Chekynnys, i-pouderyde with losyngys, gylte
whythe the flourys of borage. Frytoure cryspe. A sotelte,— Owre
Lady syttynge, and hyr Chylde in hyr lappe, holdyng in every
honde a crowne, Syn Gorge knelyng on that one syde and Synt
Denys in that othyr syde, and they ij presentyng the kynge to
owre Lady whythe thys reson:
"O blessyd lady, Crystys modyr dyre,
    And Syn Gorge callyd hyr owne knyght;
Hooly Syn Denys, O martyr, moste entere,
    To the here vj[te] Harry we present to the in youre syghte.
Shechythe[c] youre grace on hym,
Thys tendyr and whythe vertu hym avaunce,[d]
Borne by dyscent and tytylle of ryght
Justely to raygne in Ingelonde and yn Fraunce."

[a] *Sythe Harry—knyghte.* Sithen Henry the vth so noble a knyght was foundo, J.
[b] These verses are not written in lines, and were evidently transcribed from
another copy which was not written in lines either. The copyist has consequently
made some mistakes. Among other things he seems to have thought that " myghte "
and " knyghte " were rhymes in the poem.
[c] So in MS. Fabyan reads " Shedyth; " J. reads " Shewith of grace on hym your
hevenly light."
[d] The reading both in Fabyan and in J. is, " His tender youth with virtue doth
avaunce."

Ande that yere there was a Parlyment at Westemyster, and that be gan the xxij day of Septembyr and hyt duryd unto the xxiij day of Feverer nexte folowynge. And in that Parlyment was grauntyde ij fyftenys to brynge thys yonge kynge in to Fraunce.

And that same yere, the xx day of Janyver, there was an erytyke, one Rycharde Hundenne, wolpacker, brent at Toure Hylle. And the xxiiij day of the same monythe there was a batylle in Smethefylde by twyne two men of Fevyrsham, that on John Upton, pellaunte, and that othyr John Downe, fendaunte. And on Syn Mathewys daye, in Feverer, the kynge toke hys leve of the cytte of London, and he rode thoroughe London unto Eltham towarde Fraunce. And that yere the kynge helde hys Ester at Cauntylbury. And in Syn Gorgys day in the mornyng the kyng schippyd in the mornyng, and he londyd at Calys the same daye at x of the belle be fore none whythe hys lordys. And the xxiij day of the monythe of May the Pusylle was takyn be fore Compayne by the Duke of Burgayne. And the xxx day of May the Arche byschoppe of Burdowys [a] dyde in the wyntyr in London, and he ys buryd at Whythe Freers in Flete Strete. And in the monythe of Auguste, the iij day, deyde the Contasse of Urmonde be syde Schene, and the viij day of the same monythe she was broughte to London and ys buryde at Syn Thomas of Aerys. And that yere there come enbassytourys oute of Spayne and also oute of Portynggale for to trete whythe oure kynge.

| Nicholas Wotton, Mayre of London | Watyr Chyrchesey Robert Large | A° ix°. |

Ande that same yere, the xiij day of Janyver, be-gan the Parlyment at Westemyster. And the xix daye of the same monythe come the bouys of the Lord Bowcer to London and they ben buryde at Westemyster. Ande the same yere com enbassystourys from the Kyng of Scottys unto the Parlyment for to trete of pes bytwyne Ingelonde and Schotlonde. Also the same yere, the secund day of Marche, there was an erytyke i-brente in Smethe-

[a] David de Montferrand.

fylde whas name was Mayster Thomas Bagle. And the xx day of
the same monythe endyd the Parlyment above sayde. And that
yere in Lentyn deyde Pope ª Martyn. And at Estyr aftyrwarde
—the Erle of Perche of Mortenne, the Lorde of Fewater, ande the
Lorde of Audeley, wente in to Fraunce with a new retenewe to
the kyng; in the secunde day of May wente the Cardynalle of
Wynchester in to Fraunce, the Byschoppe of Northewyche and
the Lorde Cromewelle whythe a nothyr mayny; and the ij day
of June aftyr went the Erle of Salysbury in to Fraunce whythe a
fulle fayre mayny.

Ande that yere there was on namyd hym selfe Jacke Sharpe that
wolde have made a rysynge in the cytte of London, for he wolde
have take owte the temperalteys of Hooly Chyrche; but the xix day
of May he was take at Oxforde and v moo of secte, and whythe yn
fewe dayes he was drawyd, hangyde, and quarteryde, and hys hede
sete on London Brygge, and hys quarterys i-sent to dyvers townys
of Ingelonde, as to Oxforde, Abyngdon, and to moo othyr. And
sum of his ᵇ felowys were takyn at Covyntre, and there they were
drawe, hangyd, and quarteryd; and a woman was be-heddyd at
the galons. Ande the xxiij day of May the Pusylle was brent at
—Rone, and that was a pon Corpus Crysty evyn. And the xxiij day
of Julyy there was one Russelle i-drawe, hanggyd, and quarteryde,
and hys bedde was sette on Londyn Brygge, and hys quarterys in
dyvers placys in London; for he wolde have made newe lordys,
dukys, erlys, and baronys, aftyr hys entente & hys oppynyon, &c.

Ande the same yere, in the monythe of Juylle, the xvij day, the
posterne be-syde the Towre sanke downe into the erthe vij fote
and more. And the same yere, the xj day of Auguste, the Erle
of Warwyke, the Erle of Stafforde, slowe and toke a grete nombyr
of pepylle be-syde Bevys; and ther was take on Potyn and a
scheparde that was namyd le Bergere, and he namyd hym sylfe
hooly and a saynte, for the Fraynysche men badde a be-leve on

---

ª Crossed out, and "byschope" written in a later hand.
ᵇ "his" inserted in a later hand.

hym that yf he hadde layde hys honde on a castelle walle that
hyt shulde have fallyn downe by the power of hys holynys.

| John Wellys, | John Adyrley | Anno x°. |
| Mayre of London | Stevyn Browne | |

Ande that yere the kyng passyde the see in to Fraunce, and
wente unto Parysse; and he come thedyr the thyrde day of Decembyr. And the xiij day of the same monythe he was crownyde at
Parysse; for there he was worthely and ryally ressayvyd as they
cowthe devyse whythe alle the statys of the towne. And there he
hylde hys feste raylly to alle maner of nacyons that were in that
contre, that yf hyt plesyde hem thedyr for to come. And in Syn
Johnys day in the Crystysmasse weke the kynge remevyd towarde
Roone, and on the xij evyn he come unto Calys. Ande the xxix
day of Janyver he londyd at Dovyr. And yn Syn Volantynys day
he come unto London; and he was worthely fette in to the cytte
whythe the mayre and hys aldyrmen whythe alle the worthy
comyns of the cytte and every crafte in hyr devys.

And whenne the kynge come to Londyn Brygge there was made
a towre, and there yn stondynge a gyaunte welle arayde and welle
be-sene, whythe a swerde holdynge uppe on hye, sayynge thys reson
in Latyn, *Inimicos ejus induam confusione.* And on every syde
of hym stode an antiloppe, that one holdynge the armys of
Ingelond and that othyr the armys of Praunce. Ande at the
drawe brygge there was a nothyr ryalle toure, there yn stondynge
iij empryssys ryally arayde, whythe crownys on hyr heddys, the
whyche namys folowyn here: fyrste, Nature; the secunde, Grace;
the thyrde, Fortune, presentyng hym whythe gyftys of grace. The
fyrste gaffe hym Scyence an Cunnynge, and the secunde gaffe hym
Prosperyte and Ryches. And on the ryght syde of the emperyssys
stode vij fayre maydyns clothyde alle in whyte, i-powderyde
whythe sonnys of golde, presentynge the kyng whythe vij gyftys
of the Holy Goste in the lykenys of vij whyte dovys by fygure
owtwarde, whythe thys resonys: *Impleat te Dominus spiritu* sapiencie*

* *spiritu.* spiritus, MS.

Hen. VI.
A.D. 1432.

et intellectus, spiritu consilij et fortitudinis, sciencie et pietatys, spiritu timorys Domini.   And on the lyfte syde of thes emperysse stode vij othyr fayre maydyns in whythe, powderyde whythe sterrys of golde, presentyng the kyng whythe vij gyftys of worschyppe.   The fyrste was a crowne of glorye, the seconde with a cepter of clennysse, the iij whythe a swyrde of ryght and vyctorye, the iiij whythe a mantelle of prudence, the v whythe a schylde of faythe, the vj an helme of helme, the vij a gyrdylle of love and of parfyte pes.   And thys maydens song an hevynly songe unto the kynge of praysynge and of hys vyctorye and welle comynge home.   And whenne he come unto Cornehylle, there yn the vij scyence, and every scyence schewynge hys propyr comyng wondyrly i-wroughte.

And whenne he come to the Condyte of Cornhylle there was a tabernacule, and there yn syttynge a kynge whythe a ryalle aparayle. And on the ryght syde sate the lady of Mercy, ande on the lyfte syde sate the lady of Troughthe, and the lady of Clennysse hem inbrasyng with Reson.   And by-fore the kyng stode ij jugys of grete worthynys, whythe viij sergauntys of lawe ther presente for the comyn profyte representynge of dome and of ryghtuysnysse, with thys scryptura,

"Honowre of kyngys in every mannys syght
Of comyn custome lovythe equyte and ryghte."

And so the kyng rode forthe an esy passe tylle he come unto the Grete Condyte, ande there was made a ryalle syghte lyke unto Paradys, whythe alle maner of frontys of delys.   And there were vyrgynnys there, drawyng waterys and wynys of joye, and of plesaunce and comforte, the whyche ranne to every mannys comforte and helthe.   Thes maydyns were namyd: Mercy, Grace, and Fytte. And in thys Paradys stode ij olde men lyke hevynly folke, the whyche were Ennocke and Ely, saluynge the kynge whythe wordys of grace and vertu.

And soo rode he forthe unto the Crosse in Cheppe.   There stode a ryalle castelle of jasper grene, and there yn ij grene treys stondyng uppe ryght, shewyng the ryght tytyllys of the Kyng of

Inglond and of Fraunce, convaying fro Synt Edwarde and Synt Hen. VI.
Lowys be kyngys unto the tyme of Kyng Harry the vj^{te}, every A.D. 1432.
kynge stondynge whythe hys cote armowre, sum lyberdys and sum
flouredelysse; and on that othyr syde was made the Jesse ^a of owre
Lorde ascendyng uppewarde from Davyd unto Jesu. And so rode
he forthe unto the Lytylle Condyte. And there was a ryalle
mageste of the Trynyte, fulle of angelys syngyng hevynly songys,
blessynge ande halowynge the kyngys whythe thes resonys in
Latyn wrytyn: *Angelis suis* ^b *mandavit de* ^c *te ut custodiant te, etc.*
Longitudinem dierum replebo in eum ^d *et ostendam illi salutare meum.* ^e
And thenne wente he forthe unto Poulys, and there he was res-
sayvyd whythe many byschoppys and prelatys whythe dene and
the quere, and whythe devoute songe, as hyt longythe to a kynge.
Ande so he offerryd there and thankyd God of hys goode speede
and of hys welfare. And thenne he rode to Westemyster, and there
he restyd hym; and on the nexte day folowynge the mayre and
the aldyrmen ^f whythe a certayne comeners that were worthy men,
and they presentyde the kynge whythe an hampyr of sylvyr and
gylte, whythe a M^{l li} there yn of nobellys, &c.

Ande the xij day of May be-ganne the Parlement at Westemyster, and that duryd unto the xvj day of Juylle nexte followynge.

And that same yere on Syn Kateryn ys eve was the Lorde
Fewater drownyd, and moche pepylle whythe hym. And moche
harme done in the see of loste of schyppys that were lade whythe
wyne fro Bordowys by the grete tempasse in the see.

---

^a *Jesse.* Perhaps the writer meant "Geste," a history; but more probably he has
left out some words. Fabyan speaks here of "the sprynge of Jesse, wherin was
shewyd the genelogy of our blessed Lady."

^b *Angelis suis.* Angelus suus, MS.

^c *de.* This word is crossed through as if it were positively inaccurate, and the
sentence read "Angelus suus mandavit te."

^d *Longitudinem—in eum.* So in MS.

^e *meum.* eum, MS.; see Ps. xc. (xci.) 11, 16.

^f *aldyrmen.* aldyrman, MS.

John Parnys,　　　 { John Olney 　　　 } Anno xj°.
Mayre of London　 { John Padysley

Ande that same yere be ganne the generalle consayle at Basyle of alle Crystyn londys; and thedyr come the Parganers, that ys to saye they of Parge;[a] and Mayster Perrys, clerke, of Ingelonde, a regeaunte [b] and a herytyke, come from Oxforde thedyr whym [c] as an herytyke; and there were many artyculys and poyntys of the faythe determyte ande spokyn. And soo they partyde, and wente agayn unto Prage whythe owte any lettynge; and the cause was for they of Prage badde worthy clerkys of oure faythe in plegge for hem of Prage for to goo save and come save, and ellys they hadde gon to the fyre, as moste men supposyd.

Ande that same yere, a-non aftyr Ester, was the conselle of Ingelonde holdyn at Calys by the counselle of Ingelonde, for there was the Duke of Bedeforde, Regaunte of Fraunce, and the Duke of Glouceter, with many moo lordys of the Counselle; and there were cartayne personys done unto dethe, that ys to wete, iij sowdyers were banyschyde the towne of Caleys. And the same yere deyde the Duchyes of Bedforde in Fraunce, the wyffe of the Regyaunte, whos terment was solempny holde at Syn Poulys in London. And the same yere the Duke of Bedforde, and Regyant of Praunce, weddyde the dukys doughter of Syn Fowle the xxij day at Tyruyn.[d] And that same yere the kynge hylde hys Parlyment at Wystemystyr, that be ganne the viij day of Juylle; and soo forthe hyt induryd unto Lammas, and thenne hyt was enjornyde unto Syntte Edwarde ys day nexte folowynge; unto the whyche Parlyment came the Regaunt of Fraunce. Ande he come unto London on Syn Johnys evyn the Baptyste, and was worthely ressayvyde of the Mayre of London whythe alle hys aldyrmen and worthy comyners of the cytte. And the same yere the Erle of Hontyngdone wente into Fraunce whythe a fayre mayny for to kepe the contreye, and

　[a] The heretics of Prague in Bohemia.
　[b] The writer means, apparently, a renegade, as Fabyan calls him.
　[c] *whym.* The writer probably meant to have written "with them."
　[d] Therouenne.

he dyde many fayre jornayes. And that same yere a-non aftyr the xij day, the xxix day of Janyver was the Lorde Fehewe ys brothyr [a] was stallyd Byschoppe of London. Hen. VI. A.D. 1433-5.

Ande that same yere apperyde stella comata, othyr wyse namyde a blasynge starre, yn the sowthe weste, etc.

John Brocle, Mayre of London { Thomas Chalton John Lynge } A° xij°.

Ande that same yere, the ix day of November, was the terement of the Erle of Syn Fowle worthely i-holde at the chyrche of Syn Poulys in London.

Ande the x daye of Marche the Lorde Talbot wente in too Fraunce whythe a goodely meyne. Ande that yere at the Counselle of Basyle deyde the Byschoppe of Rochester. [b] And that same yere was slayne the Erle of Arundelle in France.

Robert Otley, Mayre of London { Thomas Barnewelle Symon Eyre } A° xiij°.

Ande that yere was the Counselle of Aras of alle Crystyn nacyons for to trete of pes by twyne thes ij realmys, Ingelonde and Fraunce, there beynge iij cardynallys; the Cardynalle of Wynchester for the realme of Ingelonde, and hys name was Syr Harry Bewforde, the Kyng of Ingelonde ys onkylle; the Cardynalle of Syn Crosse, and the Cardynalle of Ciprys. And there was the Duke of Burgayne and many moo othyr lordys of that party. Ande of Ingelonde the Erle of Huntyngdone, whythe many othyr spyrytualle and temporalle of oure partye. But was not to noo profyte, for the Fraynysche parte was not alle trewe in hyr comyng.

Ande that same yere, the xiiij day of Septembyr, deyde the Duke of Bedforde, Regaunte of alle Fraunce, in the castelle of Rone, bytwyne ij and iij in the mornynge; and hys body ys buryde in Nostre Dame Chyrche of Roone. And of hys soule ande alle Crystyn soulys God have marcy, Amen.

[a] Robert FitzHugh, LL.D. He was appointed bishop in 1431, and consecrated on the 16th September in that year.
[b] John Langdon.

Ande that same yere there was a grete wyntyr and a oolde froste, that duryd fro Syn Kateryns day to Synt Valentynys day next sewynge, soo that noo schippe myght passe; wherefore the vyntage come by londe ynne cartys unto London fro the Downys, thoroughe Kent and ovyr Scheters Hylle, for men provesyde be-fore þat the vyntage of Gascon and Gyan shulde come ovyr Scheters Hylle, and men made but a mocke ther of.

And that yere the kyng hylde a Parlyment at Westemyster, that duryd fro Mychellemasse unto the Feste of Crystysmas next folowynge.

Harry Frowyke,   { Thomas Catworthe } A° xiiij°.
Mayre of London   { Robert Clopton   }

Ande that same yere, aboute Crystysmas, the Fraynysche parte gate a yenne Arflewe* and many moo othyr townys. And that same yere the Fraynysche party in the monythe of Aprylle wanne a-gayne Parys. And that same yere the Mayre of London sende, by the goode a-vyse and consent of craftys, sent sowdyers to Calys, for hyt was sayde that the Duke of Burgone lay sege unto Calis. And soo he dyd sone aftyr, as ye shalle hyre here after. And at the Parlyment be-fore hyt was ordaynyde that the Duke of Yorke shulde in to Fraunce with certayne lordys with hym in stede of the Regaunt. And whythe hym went the Erle of Salysbury. Ande the Erle of Mortayne wente to Calys sone aftyr Estyr. And the xiiij day aftyr he made a roode in to Flaunders, and he slowe and toke xv. c. of Flemmyngys, and many bestys; the nombyr ys more thenne I canne certaynely reherse. And a-non aftyr the Duke of Burgone layde hys sege unto Calys whythe a stronge ordynaunce and a myghty, with xl M¹ men and moo. And they made grete bulworkys, and grete bastylys, and stronge fortyfycacyon. And on Mary Magdelene ys day the kyng hylde hys counselle at Cauntyrbury, whythe a grete party of hys lordys.

Ande xij day of Juylle the Erle of Mortayne, the Lorde Camyse, whythe othyr moo knyghtes and squyers went owte whythe a

* Harfleur.

Hen. VI.
A.D. 1436-7.

goodely mayny unto the Bastyle, and wanne hyt manfully, and sette hyt a fyre; and in that same Bastyle was v. c. men of armys, of the whyche v. c. schapyd not a way the nombyr of xij men, as letters made mencyon that were sente into Ingelonde. Ande a-non the Duke of Burgone with alle hys oste fledde cowardely; and he lefte the moste parte of hys stoffe and ordynance be hynde, for he hadde haste in hys fleynge; for there were lefte many grete gonnys, and many of othyr ordynaunce, whythe moche vytayle of flesche, flowre, wyne, bere, and a grete nomber of barellys whythe botyr, &c.

Ande the xxvj day of Juylle the Duke of Glouceter whythe alle the substaunce of the lordys of Ingelonde schyppyde at Sondewyche with xl. M¹. men of alle the contreys of Ingelonde, for every towne, cytte, or borowe fonde certayne men whythe dyvers lyvereys of the bagys of the towne, and soo dyd abbeys and pryorys in the same wyse of alle Ingelonde. And the same day they londyd at Calys,— and there they hylde hyr consaile the Fryday, Satyrday, and Sonday. And on the Monday he toke hys jornaye in-to Flaunders warde; ande he rode thoroughe Pycardye and dyd moche harme yn the contre of Flaunders, for he brent Poperyng and Belle, ij goode townys, and many moo othyr vylagys in Flaunders and in Pycardye; and soo he come home a-yenne to Calys whythe owte any lettynge of any person, thonkyd be God.

Ande that same yere the Erle of Northehomerlonde made a viage in-to Scotlonde, and there he made a nobylle jornay.

John Mychell,	Thomas Morestede	
Mayre of London	Wylliam Gregory	A° xv°.

Ande that same yere Queue Kateryn dyde at Bredmonsey the iij day of Janyver. And that same yere on of the gatys of Londyn Bryge and one of the g[r]ettyste arche of the same bryge, fylle a downe in to Temys wondyrfully; thonkyd be God, noo man, woman, nor chylde i-hurte nor perchyde. And that yere the kynge or-daynyde the Parlyment to be holde at Caumbryge, but aftyr warde by goode counselle hyt was tornyde and holde att Westemyster; the whyche Parlyment be gunne the xxj day of Janyver. And to that

Parlyment come the Byschoppe of Tyrwynne ande the counselle of the Erle of Armanacke.

Ande the ix day of Feverer Quene Kateryn aforesayde was broughte to Powlys yn London, and there sche hadde a solempne deryge ande a masse on the morne. And thenne she was badde unto Westemyster. And the iij day aftyr she was worthely enteryde and buryde in Oure Lady chapylle at Westemyster in the Abby; of whos soule God have mercy.

Ande the same yere the Kynge of Schottys was trayturly slayne in hys owne londe, of a false squyr and the squyer ys sone, of the same londe, that was namyd Robert Grame. The whyche squyer and hys sone were take anon aftyr, and there they were playnely put to dethe, as welle worthy was, to be traye any kynge or prynce.

And the same yere dyde Queue Jane [a] at Averyng at the Bowre, in Esex, in the monythe of Juylle, and she ys buryde at Cauntyrbury whythe hyr hosbonde, Kynge Harry the iiij[the]. Ande the same yere the kyng put downe the Mayre of Norwyche, and certayne aldyrmen were devydyd unto othyr certayne placys, sum to Lynne and sum to Cauntyrbury. And John Wellys, Aldyrman of London, was made Wardon of Northewyche.

Ande the same yere the Erle of Warwyke went into Fraunce the xxix day of Auguste; he schippyd at Portysmouthe, and the Duke of Yorke come home into Ingelonde owte of Fraunce.

| Wylliam Estefylde, Mayre of London | Wylliam Chap..nan Wylliam Halys | A° xvj°. |

Ande that same yere deyde the Emperowre of Rome,[b] and hys termentte was solempnly holde at Syn Poulys at the cytte of London the iij day of May, there beynge the kynge and hys lordys. And the same yere on Estyr day there was on John Gardyner take at Synt Mary at the Axe in London, for he was an herytyke; for whenne shulde have benne housclyd he wypyd hys mouthe whithe a foule clothe and layde the oste there yn; and so he was takyn by

[a] Joan of Navarre, widow of King Henry IV.   Sigismund.

Hen. VI.
A.D. 1438-9.

the person of the chyrche, and the xiiij day of May he was i-brent in Smethefylde.

Ande the same yere the Erle of Mortayne was made Erle of Dorsette, and he was sentte unto Anjoye and Mayne.

And the same yere there was a grete conselle at Calys, there beynge in oure party the Cardynalle Arche-byschoppe of Yorke and many moo spirytualle and temporalle lordys. And on that othyr party the Duchyes of Burgone and many moo lordys, bothe spyrytualle and temporalle.

Ande the same yere the iiij day of June certayne men of Kentte were a-reste at Maydestone for ryeynge, and v. of hem were drawe, hanggyde, and quarteryde, and be-heddyde, and hyr heddys were sette on Londyn Brygge; and sum of hyr heddys at Cauntyrbury and in othyr certayne townys in Kente a boute in the schyre, for to cause men to be ware. And that yere was grete dyrthe of corne, for a buschelle of whete was worthe ij s vj d. And that yere was grete pestylaunce, and namely in the northe contrayc. And the same yere deyde the Countasse of Stafforde, and the Clerke of the Rollys, Mayster Jon Franke; and he was holde one of the rycchyste men that deyde many dayes be-fore

| Stevyn Browne, | { Hewe Duke | } A° xvij° |
| Mayre of London | { Nychol Yoo | |

Ande the same yere duryde the dyrthe of corne and of alle maner of grayne thoroughe Ingelonde. And the laste day of Aprylle deyde the Erle of Warwyke at Roone. Ande the same yere the Cardynalle Archebyschoppe of Yorke,[a] the Byschoppe of Northe-wyche,[b] the Byschoppe of Syn Davys[c] and many othyr docters, and the Duke of Northefolke, the Erle of Stafford, the Lorde Bowcer, and the Lorde Hungerforde, with a grete mayny, wente unto Calys; and they hadde the Duke of Orlyaunce with hem for to trete of pes by twyne Ingelonde and Fraunce. And there mette with hem the grete lordys of Fraunce, that ys to wyte, of spyrytualle and temporalle, the Archebyschoppe of Raynys,[d] whythe many moo

---

[a] John Kemp, afterwards Archbishop of Canterbury.

[b] Thomas Brown.   [c] Thomas Rodeburn.   [d] Rheims.

othyr byschoppys, the Erle of Wendon,[a] the Bastarde of Orlyaunce, and many othyr lordys of Fraunce; and thedyr come the Byschoppe of Spayne and of Colayne, and many moo othyr dyvers contreys that com fro the Counselle of Basylle.

Ande the same yere in the same tretys the Fraynsche party wanne Mewys in Bry ayenne, in the whyche was Captayne Syr Wylliam Chambyrlayne. And the same yere the Erle of Huntyngdone wente unto Gyenne whythe a grete navy. And the same yere went Syr [Richard][b] Woodevyle in to Normandy and Syr Wylliam Peytowe, and many moo othyr, whythe a fayre mayne. And that same yere, a-pon Wytsondaye, the kyng made knyghtys at Kenyngton, that ys to wete, the soue and hayre of the Lorde of Huntyngdon, and the soue ande the ayre of the Erle of Aroundelle, Lewys John, and Wylliam Estefylde, marchaunt of London. And the mayre ordaynyd that yere that comyn wemmen shulde were raye hoodys, and bawdys to the pelory. And thys was cryde the v day of Auguste the same yere, and so hyt was done at dyvers tymys. And the same yere, att the generalle counseylle, the Emperoure of Costantyne the Nobylle[c] and hys soue, whythe alle the clergy of Gryke, obeyd hym unto the Chyrche of Rome of certayne artyculys of the faythe; and they hylde more thanne v. c. yere, and alle the realme of Ermonye[d] that haddyn ben owte ix. c. yere, fro the beleve not on the Hooly Goste, nor on the sacrament, nor noo Pyrgatorye, nor noo suffragys of Hooly Chyrche, as prayers and almysdedys. And there were of Rome viij cardynallys and moo thanne v. c. myters, whythe owte docters. And thus was proclaymyd at Powlys Crosse the xxviij day of August above sayde, etc.

Robert Large,   { Robert Marchalle } A° xviij°.
Mayre of London   { Phylyppe Malpas }

Ande that yere was the Parlyment concludyd, and ordaynyd that Lumbardys sholde goo to hoste. And that same yere alyens were putte to hyr fynaunce to pay a certayne a yere to the kynge. Also in the same yere there were ij traytours hangyde on a payre of

---

[a] Vendôme.   [b] Omitted in MS.
[c] Constantinople. John Palæologus, Emperor.   [d] Armenia.

galowys that were made in Temys for the same purpose, be syde Syn Kateryns.

And that same yere there was a preste i-callyd Syr Rycharde Wyche and hys servand brent atte the Tourehylle, for the whyche there was moche trobil a-monge the pepylle, in soo moche that alle the wardys in London were assygnyd to wake there day and nyght that the pepylle myght nought have hyr ylle purpose as at that tyme.

John Patesle,   { John Sutton   } Anno xix°.
Mayre of London   { Wylliam Wetynhale }

Ande in that same yere the Duke of Orlyaunce made hys othe at Westemyster and there uppon ressayvyde the blessyd sacrament on Cryspyn and Cryspynyan ys day. And the Fryday aftyr Allehalowyn day he went towarde Fraunce, and whythe hym he badde Syr John Corneuale, knyght, and many othyr knyghtys and squyers. Ande that same yere werre the barrys in Smethefylde newe made, for Syr Rycharde Woodevyle, knyght, was chalengyd of a knyght of Spayne for to donne certayne poyntys of armys in the felde.

Ande the xvj day of May the Duke of Yorke, the Erle of Oxynforde, the Erle of Ewe, the Erle of Ormounde, and Syr Richard Woodevyle, whythe many othyr knyghtys and squyers, toke the way towarde Praunce, and they schippyd at Portysmouthe.

And the same yere the Crosse in Chepe was take a downe and a newe sette uppe there þat the olde Crosse stode. And in the same yere there were take certayne traytourys, the whyche purposyd to slee oure lege lorde the kyng by crafte of egremauncey,* and there instrumentys were opynly shewyde to alle men at the Crosse in Powlys chyrche yerde a-pon a schaffolde i-made there-for. Att the whyche tyme was present one of the same traytours, whiche was callyd Roger Bulbroke, a clerke of Oxforde, and for that same tresoun my Lady of Glouceter toke sayntwerye at Westemyster; and the xj day of Auguste thenne next folowynge she toke þe way

* Necromancy.

to the castelle of Lesnes. And on Syn Symon and Jude ys eve was the wycche be syde Westemyster brent in Smethefylde, and on the day of Symon and Jude the person of Syn Stevynnys in Walbroke, whyche that was one of the same fore sayde traytours, deyde in the Toure for sorowe.

Robert Clopton,   { Wylliam Combys } A° xx°.
Mayre of London   { Rycharde Ryche   }

Ande in that same yere the Lady of Glouceter for the same treson she was juggyde by the spyrytualle lawe to iij sondyr or dyvers placys, that ys to wete, on Mondaye, the xiij daye of Novembyr, to Powlys; and on the Wanysday i-sygnyd unto Crychyrche; and on the Fryday nexte folowyng to Synt Mychellys in Cornehylle. And on the Satyrday next folowyng was Roger Bulbroke hanggyde. and drawe, and quarteryde at Tyburne.

Ande the xxx day of Janyver was certayne poyntys of armys done in Smethefylde by twyne a knyght of Catelan and a Engelysche squyer, i-callyde Syr John Ascheley; of the whiche tyme the sone of the sayde knyght, in presens of alle the pepylle there, was made -knyght opynly by the kyngys owne bondys. And the sayde John Ayschelay also was made knyght att the same tyme.

Ande the xxv day of May my Lorde Talbot toke hys way towarde the see, for to passe yn to Fraunce whythe hys retenowe. Ande in that same yere deyde John Wellys, the nobylle Aldyrman, and sum tyme Mayre of London.

John Hatherley,   { Thomas Bemound } A° xxj°.
Mayre of London   { Rycharde Nordon   }

Ande in that same yere there was a pynner hyngge hym sylfe on a Palme Soudaye. And he was alle nakyd save hys breche; and then he was caryd in a carte owte of the cytte.

And that same yere was a woman of Westemyster brentt at Toure-hylle for kyllynge of hyr hosbond.

Ande that same yere there was founde in a walle in the Gylhalle a certayne sum of mony, and alle in pense, and every peny weyde j d. ob., and sum a goode dele more, and sum more; and hyt was of many dyvers cunys, for sum were made yn London and sum in Cheschyre, and sum in Lancaster, and in many othyr dyvers placys of the londe, but alle was the kyngys owne kune.

And on the same yere, the viij day of Septembyr, there was done a grete vyage yn Fraunce by the Duke of Somesette and his retynowe; and at the same viage were slayne and takyn to the nombyr of iij. M¹. vij. c., whereof were ix lordys and a squyer, whyche that was a grete captayne.

Thomas Catworthe, { John Norman } A° xxij°.
Mayre of London { Nicho' Wyfolde }

Ande in that yere were streppettys* i-dreve a-boute the Cytte of London whythe raye hodys. And in that same yere one on the pelerry, the whyche wrought by a wycckyd spyryte, the whyche was callyd Oberycom, and the maner of hys proces and werkyng was wretyn and hanggyd a bowte hys necke whenne he was in the pellery.

Harry Frowyke, { Sthevyn Foster } A° xxiij°.
Mayre of London { Hewe Wyche }

Ande that same yere the Duke of Sowthefolke and othyr whythe many worthy knyghtys and squyers wentte ovyr the see to fette home the queue.

Ande the same yere was Syn Poulys stypylle fyryd a-pon Candylmas evyn whythe the lyghtenynge. And that same yere, the x day of October, was ordaynyd by the archebyschoppys and bysschoppys, and there uppon proclaymyd oppynly ynne chyrchys, that the day of Synt Edward shulde be kepte hooly day fro that day forthewarde.ᵇ And yn the same yere a schippe y-namyde Grace de Dyen, whyche was chargyd of goode of Sprusse, sche was loste a lytylle whythe yn Temys. And yn the same yere come dyvers enbassytourys of lordys of Fraunce for to trete of the pes. And that same yere was the Erle of Warwyke made Duke of Warwyke. And a pon the fyrste day of Aprylle Queue Margarete

* Strumpets.

ᵇ Probably the Translation of St. Edward the King and Confessor, which was on the 13th October.

londyd at Portysmowthe, and a-pon the x day of the same monythe sche was weddyd at a lytylle velage in Hampschyre i-namyd ——— ᵃ And a gayne hyr comynge to London were ordaynyde many notabylle devysys in the cytte, as at the brygge of London, and in othyr dyvers placys, at Ledynne halle, and in Corne-hylle, and in iiij placys yn Chepe, that ys to say, at the Grete Condyte, and at the Standarde, and at the Crosse, and atte the Lytylle Condyte. And uppon Thorsday, the xxvj day of May, the kyng made xlvj Knyghtys of the Bathe yn the Towre of London. And uppon the morowe, that was the Fryday, lordys of the realme, whythe nobylle and grete and costelowe araye, the Mayre of London and the aldyrmen in scharlet, whythe alle the craftys of London in blewe, wythe dyvers dyvysyngys, every crafte to be knowe from othyr, rydyng agayne Quene Margarete and brought hyr unto the Toure of London, the quene havynge whythe hyr xvij charys with ladys. And a-pon the morowe, the Satyrday, she was brought thoroughe London syttyng in a lytter by twyne ij goode and nobylle stedys i-trappyd with whyte satton, and sche was conveyyde unto Westemyster. And apon the morowe the Sonday was the coronacyon, and ij dayes aftyr there was grette revylle of justys of pes in the sayntewery at Westemyster, &c.

Ande in the monythe of Juylle next folowynge there come owte of Fraunce a grette enbasset of lordys to trete by-twyne ij realmys of Ingelonde and of Fraunce and for dyvers contreys to hem, &c.

Symon Ayre,   { John Derby   } Aᵒ xxiiijᵒ.
Mayre of London { Geffrey Fyldyng

Ande in that same yere was a Parlyment holdyn at Westemyster, and same yere there was on Wylliam Nete, yeman of the Quenys charyetes, drawyn and hanggyd in Horse Downe for sleyng of a damselle callyd Johne Gooche.

Ande that same yere there was a pechyng i-made uppon the

ᵃ Here a blank was left for the name, but has been improperly filled up by the rubricator inserting a mark indicative of a new paragraph.

Erle of Ormounde[a] by the pryour of Kylmayn[b] for certayne poyntys Hen. VI
A.D. 1445-7. of treson, the whyche was takyn in to the kyngys grace, where uppon hyt lykyd oure soverayne lorde to graunte a generalle pardon unto the sayde Erle. But nevyrtheles the sayde pryour appayryde in Smethefylde the iiij day of the monythe of October, as hyt was apoyntyde, fulle clenly harnyssyd, redy whythe alle hys fetys and whythe alle hys wepyns, kepynge the fylde tylle hyghe none.

And that same yere the Prevy Sealle[c] comynge fro enbassetry owte of Fraunce was gretely comberyd with fortune of the see, in soo moche that many of hys men were drownyde. And in that same yere was a nothyre chalenge i-made in Smethefylde by on Arblastre and a-nothyr man of London, but hyt was putte of by trete, and the same Arblastre ranne yn to the contente.

Ande that same yere my Lorde of Glouceter wente yn-to a place i-callyd the Vyse. And that same yere was a gernarde be-gon for pore pepylle of the contraye that myght nought utter hyr graynys; and hyt was made by the coste and goodys of Symon Eyre, Mayre of London.

John Olney,	{ Robert Horne	} Anno xxv°.
Mayre of London	{ Geffray Bolayne	

Ande in that same yere there was an armyrer and hys owne man fought whythe yn the lystys in Smethefylde the laste day of Januer, ande there the mayster was slayne and dyspoylyde owte of hys barnys, and lay stylle in the fylde alle that day and that nyght next folowynge. And thenne afty[r]ward, by the kyngys commaundement, he was d[r]awyn, hanggyde, and be-heddyde, and hys hedde sette on London Brygge, and the body hynggyng a-bove erthe be-syde the towre.

Ande that same yere was a Parlyment be-gon at Byry; and that same yere there was grete wache at Syn Donstonys in the Este, by the sofferens of oure sufferayne lorde the kyng, in every warde of

[a] James Butler, fourth Earl.

[b] Thomas Fitzgerald, grandson of Thomas Earl of Kildare, was at this time Prior of the Knights of St. John at Kilmainham in Ireland.

[c] Adam de Moleyns, Bishop of Chichester.

Hen. VI.
A.D. 1447.

London alle the xvj dayes in Crystysmasse by the commaunde-ment of the kynge. Ande at Schroffe tyde nexte aftyr there was ordaynyd a Parlyment at Synt Edmondys Bury; ande att the comyng of the goode Duke Umfray, sum tyme Duke of Glouceter, uppon the Satyrday anon as he was a lyght of hys hors he was a-restyde of dyvers lordys for treson by commaundement of the –kyng, and men sayde at that tyme. And uppon the Thursse-day next folowynge he dyssesyd ande passyde owte of thys wrecchyde and false trobely worlde. And he ys buryde at Syn Albonys.

Ande uppon Ester nexte folowynge, Harry Byschoppe of Wyn-chester and Cardynalle, and lythe enteryde at Wynchester. And a-non aftyr the dethe of the Duke of Glouceter there were a reste many of the sayde dukys [a] to the nombyr of xxxviij squyers, be-syde alle othyr servantys that nevyr ymagenyd no falsenys of the [b] that they were put a-pon of. And on Fryday the xiiij day of Juylle nexte folowynge by jugement at Westemyster, there by fore v personys were dampnyd to be drawe, hanggyd, and hyr bowellys i-brente by fore hem, and thenne hyr heddys to ben smetyn of, ande thenne to be quarteryde, and every parte to be sende unto dyvers placys by assygnement of the jugys. Whyche personys were thes: Arteys the bastarde of the sayde Duke of Glouceter, Syr Rogger Chambyrlayne knyght, Mylton squyer, Thomas Har-berde squyer, Nedam yeman, whyche were the sayde xiiij day of Juylle i-drawe fro Syn Gorgys thoroughe owte Sowthewerke and on Londyn Brygge, ande so forthe thorowe the cytte of London to the Tyborne, and there alle they were hanggyde, and the ropys smetyn a-sondyr, they beynge alle lyvynge, and thenne, ar any more of any markys of excecusyon were done, the Duke of Sowthefolke brought them alle yn generalle pardon and grace from our lorde and soverayne Kynge Harry the vj[te].

Also that same yere dysscsyde the Duke of Exceter, and he was enteryd at Syn Kateryns.

---

[a] Tho word "servants" appears to be omitted.   [b] *of tho,* i. e. of that.

Stephyn Browne,   { John Cauntelowe } A° xxvij°.ᵃ
Mayre of London   { Wylliam Marowe, }

Ande that same yere the Duke of Yorke, Rycharde Plantagenet, was exsylyde in to Irlonde for hys rebellyon, as thoo a boute the kynge informyde hym, fully ande falsely as hyt was ᵇ aftyr warde i-knowe.

And that same yere was a tretys of trewys takyn whythe the Schottys by Mayster Adam Molaynys for iiij yere, that tyme he beyng enbasytor in to Schotlonde, and aftyr that Prevy Seale, ande thenne i-made Byschoppe of Chychester, and with ynne shorte tyme aftyr put to dethe.

Thomas Chalton,   { Thomas Canyngys } A° xxviij°.
Mayre of London   { John Hewlyn   }

Ande that same yere was the moste pa[r]te of Normandy y-loste, and a Parlymentte was at Westemyster. In the meue whyle was the [city]ᶜ of Roon, Mustarde Vylers, and Herflete i-loste by fore Crystys-masse, and thenne the Parlyment was prolongyd tylle aftyr Syn Hyllary ys day. Ande at that tyme beyng many sowdyers at Portys-mowthe, the whyche haddyn take the kyngys wagys for to pass ovyr the see. And anon aftyr Crystysmasse was sende unto the see syde the Prevye Sealle, whyche was callyd Mayster Adam Molaynys, to have take the monster at the see syde, he beynge that tyme Byschoppe of Chychester. Ande for hys covetysse, as hyt was reportyde,—schippemen put hym to dethe, and sum mys-a-wysyd men of the sowdyers holpyn welle there-to. And thys was done at Portys-mouthe.

Ande aftyr Synt Hyllary ys day the Parlyment was remevyd unto Laycetter; ande yn the meue tyme was Cane yoldyn, ande alle the remenaunt of Normandy, savyng Chyrborowe. And the Duke of Sowthefolke was a-pechyde at that Parlyment, he beynge at London, of verry graunte treson, and of many poyntys; among alle othyr, for that he schulde have solde Normandy, and also for the dethe of that nobylle prynce the Duke of Glouceter, and for many

---

ᵃ The 26th year is omitted.   ᵇ *was* repeated in MS.   ᶜ Omitted in MS.

othyr poyntys of treson, for the whyche he was exylyd owte of
Ingelonde for certayne yerys.　Ande at hys passynge ovyr the see
warde he was mette with by-twyne Dovyr and Calys by dyvers
schyppys, of the whyche was here Admyralle Nycholas of the
Towre; and yn that shyppe soo beyng in the see they smote of hys
bedde of the fore sayde Duke of Sowthefolke, and they caste bothe
–body and hys bedde in to the see.　And aftyr that hyt was takyn
uppe and brought unto the towne of Dovyr, and aftyr from thens
brought unto Wynkylfylde in Sowthefolke, and there hyt ys
i-buryde; whos name was Syr Wylliam Pole.

Ande aftyr that the comyns of Kent a rosse with certayne othyr
schyrys, and they chesse hem a captayne, the whyche captayne
compellyd alle the gentellys to a-rysse whythe hem.　Ande at the
ende of the Parlyment they come whythe a grete myght and a
stronge oste unto the Blacke hethe, be syde Grene wyche, the
number of xlvj M[1]; and there they made a fylde, dykyd and stakyde
welle a-bowt, as hyt ben in the londe of warre, save only they kepte
ordyr among them, for als goode was Jacke Robyn as John at the
Noke, for alle were as hyghe as pygysfete, unto the tyme that they
shulde comyn and speke with suche statys and massyngerys as were
sende unto hem; thenne they put alle hyr pouer unto the man that
namyd hym captayne of alle hyr oste.　And there they a-bode
certayne days too the comyng of the kynge fro the Parlymentte at
Leyceter.　Ande thenne the kyng send unto the captayne dyvers
lordys bothe spyrytualle and temporalle, to wytte and to have
knowleche of that grette assembelynge and gaderyng of that grete
a[n]d mysavysyd feleschyppe.　The captayne of hem sendyng
worde agayne unto the kynge, that hyt was for the wele of hym
oure soverayne lorde, and of alle the realme, and for to dystrye
the traytours beyng a-boute hym, whythe othyr dyvers poyntys
that they wolde see that hyt were in schorte tyme a-mendyde.
Uppon whyche answere that the kyug,[a] thedyr sent by hys lordys,
dyd make a crye in the kyngys name of Engelonde that alle the

* So in MS.

kyngys lege men of Engelonde shulde a-voyde the fylde. And
a-pon the nyght aftyr they were alle voydyd and a-goo.

The morne aftyr, the kynge rode armyd at alle pecys from Syn
John ys be-syde Clerkyn welle thoroughe London; and whythe
hym the moste party of temporalle lordys of thys londe of Enge-
lond in there a beste raye. Aftyr that they were every lorde
whythe hys retenowe, to the nombyr of x M^l personys, redy as they
alle shulde have gon to batayle in to any londe of Crystyn-dome,
whythe bendys a-bove hyr harnys that every lorde schulde be
knowe from othyr. And yn the fowarde, as they wolde have
folowyde the captayne, was slayn Syr Umfray Stafforde and
Wylliam Stafford, squyer, one the mannylste man of alle thys
realme of Engelonde, whythe many moo othyr of meue personys at
Sevenocke, in Keutt, in hyr oute ragyng fro hyr oste of our
soverayne lordys the kyng, Harry the vj^{te}. And the kyng loggyd
that nyght at Grenewyche, and soue aftyr every lorde whythe hys
retynewe rood home in to hyr contraye.

Ande aftyr that, uppon the fyrste day of Juylle, the same captayne come agayne, as the Kenttysche men sayde, but hyt was
a-nothyr that namyd hymselfe the captayne, and he come to the
Blacke Hethe. And uppon the morowe he come whythe a grette
hoste yn to Sowtheworke, and at the Whythe Herte he toke his
loggynge. And a-pon the morowe, that was the Fryday, a gayn
evyn, they smote a sondyr the ropys of the draught brygge and
faught sore a manly, and many a man was mortheryde and kylde in
that conflycte, I wot not what [to]^a name hyt for the multytude of
ryffe raffe. And thenne they enteryde in to the cytte of London as
men that badde ben halfe be-syde hyr wytte; and in that furynys they
wente, as they sayde, for the comyn wele of the realme of Ingelonde,
evyn strayght unto a marchaunte ys place i-namyd Phylyppe
Malpas of London. Yf hyt were trewe as they surmysyd aftyr ther
doyng, I remytte me to yuke and pauper—*Deus scit et ego non.*
But welle I wote that every ylle begynnynge moste comynly hathe

^{a} Omitted in MS.

an ylle endyng, and every goode begynnyng hathe the wery goode
endyng.   *Proverbium :—Felix principium finem facit esse beatum.*
And that Phylyppe Malpas was aldyrman, and they spoylyd hym ande
bare a-way moche goode of hys, and in specyalle moche mony, bothe
of sylvyr and golde, the valowe of a notabylle som, and in specyalle
of marchaundys, as of tynne, woode, madyr, and alym, whythe grette
quantyte of wollyn clothe and many ryche jewellys, whythe othyr
notabylle stuffe of fedyr heddys, beddyng, napery, and many a
ryche clothe of arys, to the valewe of a notabylle sum—*nescio, set
Deus omnia scit.*

Ande in the evenynge they went whythe hyr sympylle captayne
to hys loggynge; botte a certayne of hys sympylle and rude mayny
a-bode there alle the nyght, weny[n]ge to them that they hadde wytte
and wysdome for to have gydyde or put in gydyng alle Ingelonde,
alsosone at they hadde gote the cytte of London by a mysse happe
of cuttynge of ij sory cordys that nowe be alteryde, and made ij
-stronge schynys of yryn unto the draught brygge of London.   But
they badde othyr men with hem, as welle of London as of there
owne party.   And by hem of on parte and of that othyr parte they
lefte noo thyng unsoffethe,[a] and they serchyd alle that nyght.

Ande in the morne he come yn a-gayne, that sory and sympylle
and rebellyus captayne whythe hys mayny; that was Satyrday, and
hyt was also a Synt Martyn ys day,[b] the dedycacyon of Synt
Martynys in the Vyntry, the iiij day of Juylle.   And thenne
dyvers questys were i-sompnyd at the Gylhalle; and ther Robert
Horne beynge alderman was a-restyde and brought in to Newegate.
And that same day Wylliam Crowemere, squyer, and Scheryffe
of Kentt, was be-heddyde in the fylde whythe owte Algate at þe
mylys ende be-syde Clopton ys Place.   And a nothyr man that
was namyde John Bayle was be-heddyd at the Whytte Chapylle.
And the same day aftyr-non was be-heddyd in Cheppe a-fore the
Standard, Syr Jamys Fynes, beyng that tyme the Lorde Saye and
Grette Treserer of Ingelonde, the whyche was brought oute of the

---

  [a] Unsought?   [b] The Translation of St. Martin of Tours.

Toure of London unto the Gylde Halle, and there of dyvers tresons
he was exampnyd, of whyche he knowlachyd of the dethe of that
notabylle and famos prynce the Duke of Glouceter. And thenne
they brought hym unto the Standard in Cheppe, and there he
ressayvyd hys jewys and hys dethe. And so forthe alle the iij
heddys that day smetyn of were sette uppon the Brygge of London,
and the ij othyr heddys takyn downe that stode a-pon the London
Brygge by-fore. And at the comyng of the camptayne yn to
Sowtheworke, he lete smyte of the hedde of a strong theff that was
namyd Haywardyn. And uppon the morowe the Sonday at hyghe
mas tyme a lette to be heddyd a man of Hampton, a squyer, the
whyche was namyd Thomas Mayne. And that same evyn Londyn
dyd a rysse and cam owte uppon hem at x [of] * the belle, beyng that
tyme hyr captaynys the goode olde lorde Schalys and Mathewe
Goughe. Ande from that tyme unto the morowe viij of belle they
were ever fyghtynge uppon London Brygge, ande many a man was
slayne and caste in Temys, harnys, body, and alle; and monge the
presse was slayne Mathewe Goughe and John Sutton aldyrman.
And the same nyght, a-non aftyr mydnyght, the Captayne of Kentte
dyde fyre the draught brygge of London; and be-fore that tyme he
breke bothe Kyngys Bynche ande the Marchelsy, and lete owte alle
the presoners that were yn ᵇ them. And uppon the morowe by
tymys came my lorde the Cardynalle of Yorke,ᶜ and my Lorde of
Cauntyrbury,ᵈ and the Byschoppe of Wynchester,ᵉ and they tretyde
by twyne the Lorde Schalys and that captayne, that the sore conflycte and skarmasche was sessyde, aude gaffe the captayne and hys
mayne a generalle chartoure for hym and for alle hys company in
hys name, callyng hym selfe John Mortymere, and thoroughe that
mene they were i-voydyde the moste partye. And the vj day aftyr
that, the Satyr-daye at evyn, the iij heddys were takyn downe of
London Brygge, that ys to say, the Lorde Say ys bedde, Crowmers,

* Omitted in MS. ᵇ yn. ym, MS.
ᶜ John Kemp, afterwards Archbishop of Canterbury.
ᵈ John Stafford. ᵉ William Waynflete.

and the Bayleyes, and the othyr ij heddys sette uppe a-yenne that stode a-pon London Brygge be-fore, and the body whythe hedde were i-burydde at the Gray Fryers at London. And uppon the xij day of Juylle, the yere a-foré sayde, the sayde camp-tayne was cryde and proclaymyd traytoure, by the name of John Cade, in dyvers placys of London, and also in Sowtheworke, whythe many moo, that what man myght or wolde bryng the sayde John Cade to the kyng, qwyke or dede, shulde have of the kynge a thousande marke. Also who som evyr myght brynge or wolde brynge any of hys chyffe counsellourys, or of afynyte, that kepte any state or rewlc or governansse undyr the sayd fals captayne John Cade, he schulde have to hys rewarde of the kynge v. c. marke. And that day was that fals traytoure the Captayne of Kcntte i-take and slayne in the Welde in the countre of Sowsex, and uppon the morowe he was brought in a carre alle nakyd, and at the Herte in Sowetheworke there the carre was made stonde stylle, the wyffe of the howse myght se hym yf hyt were the same man or no that was namyd the Captayne of Kente, for he was loggyd whythe yn hyr howse in hys pevys tyme of hys mys rewylle and rysynge. And thenne he was hadde in to the Kyngys Bynche, and there he lay from Monday at evyn unto the Thursseday nexte folowynge at evyn; and whythe yn the Kynges Benche the sayde captayne was be-heddyde and quarteryde; and the same day i-d[r]awe a-pon a hyrdylle in pccys whythe the hedde by-twyne hys breste from the Kyngys Benche thoroughe owte Sowthewcrke, and thenne ovyr Londyn Brygge, and thenne thoroughe London unto Newegate, and thenne hys hedde was takyn and sette uppon London Brygge.

And the same yere was the Byschoppe of Sawlysbury slayne at Edyngton, a myle owte of the towne, a-pon a hyghe hylle; hyt was the xiiij day of June, and alle hys goode mevabylle was departyde to every man dwcllynge there that any of hys lyflode laye; for bothe oxsyn, sheppe, hors, swyne, carte, plowe, corne, hay, tymbyr, strawe, harnys in castcllys of hys, clothynge for hys owne body, bokys, chalys, and alle that longyd to any manyr of hys, and the very ledde that coveryd the howsys and wodys wer fylde downe in sum placys, but not in every place, but in som, as at Shyrbone in Dorsette schyre. And the men that toke a-pon hem alle thys mys rewle, whenne they undyrstode that hyt was wronge that they badde done bothe to hym, and in specyalle unto the kynge, they a-non wente thoroughe owte alle the towne of Shyr-borne an toke to every man, woman, and chylde that was above xij yere age and iij chore, cveryche of hem badde vj^d; and they madde them to swere to be trewe ande holde to gedyr, by cause yf the kynge wolde have take any execucyon a-pon hyt he moste have take hyt a-pone alle the hoole schyre and contrays there that hys lyflode was. And for cause here of the kynge gaffe a generalle pardon to alle maner men.

Ande that same yere was slayne Tresham, the man of lawe, that was Speker of the Parlymentt, and hys sone was soore woundyde in Northehampton schyre. And by the kynge and hys counselle a Parlyment was ordaynyde to be-gyn on Syn Leonarde ys day nexte folowynge. In the meue tyme many strange and woundyrfulle hylle were sete in dyvers placys, sum at the kyngys owne chambyr doore at Westemyster, in hys palysse, and sum at the halle dore at Westemyster, ande sum at Poulys chyrche dore, and in many othyr dyvers placys of London.

Ande in the ende of the saydc same yere Rycharde, the Duke of Yorke, come to the sayde Parlymentt, for the sayde Duke was before banyschyd for certayne yerys, whythe a notabylle felyschippe of fensabylle men, and the Duke of Northefolke whythe a grete multytude of defensabylle men. And every lorde whythe hyr retynowe welle harnysyd and welle be-sene; and every lorde badde hys bagge a-pon hys harnys, and hyr mayny also, that they myght ben knowe by hyr baggys and levereys.

Nycholas Wyfolde,	Wylliam Deere	
Mayre of London	John Myddelton	A° xxix°

Ande that same yere, the ij day of Decembyr, the Duke of

Somersett was a-tachyde in the Fryer Prechourys at London.   And that day he was robbyde of alle hys goodys, and hys jewyllys were takyn and borne a-way by lordys mayny.   Ande in the morowe they dyspoylyd the placys and longgynges of many dyvers lordys, and they bare away alle the goodys that were with ynne hem, that ys to say, Syr Thomas Stodenham,[a] thenne beynge wardroper, Syr Thomas Hoo the Lorde Hastynge, sum tyme the Chambyrlayne of Normandy.

And the same day was a man of ·the forsayde feleschyppe, the whyche was at the spoylynge and robbynge of the Fryer Pre-chourys, be-heddyde at the Standarde in Cheppe, for to ben an exampylle unto alle othyr; but hyt was nevyr the bettyr, for hyt causyd moche the more herte brennyng a gayne the duke and the lordys by-fore sayde, &c.

And that same day, the aftyr non, the Duke of Yorke roode thoroughe London.   And he made to be cryde in dyvers placys that what[b] maner a man that robbyd or ryfylde any persone schulde have as hastely jewys as the sayde man badde.   And uppon Thursday nexte folowynge the kynge come fro Westemyster, ryddyng thoroughe London; and whythe the Duke of Yorke, and the moste dele in substans of alle the lordys in thys londe, with hyr retenowys of fensabylle men; whyche was a gay and a gloryus syght if hit hadde ben in Fraunce, but not in Ingelonde, for hyt boldyd sum mennys hertys that hyt causyd aftyr many mannys dethe. Wher was or ys the defaute I wotte not, &c.

Ande the same yere, on Candylmas daye, the kynge was at Cauntyrbury, and whythe hym was the Duke of Excetyr, the Duke of Somersette, my Lorde of Schrofuysbury, whythe many moo othyr lordys and many justyces; and there they helde the cessyons iiij dayes, and there were dampnyde many men of the captayne ys men for hyr rysyng, and for hyr talkyng a gayne the kyng, havynge more favyr unto the Duke of Yorke thenne unto the kynge.   And the dampnyde men were drawe, hanggyde, and quarteryde, but

[a] Todenham.   [b] *what* repeated in MS.

they were pardonnyde to be buryde, bothe hyr quarters of hyr bodys and hyr heddys with alle.

Ande at Rochester ix men were be-heddyd at that same tyme, and hyr heddys were sende unto London by the kyngys commaundement, and sette uppon London Brygge alle at one tyme; and xij heddys at a nothyr tyme were brought unto London at* sette uppe undyr the same forme, as hys* was commaundyd by the kyng. Men calle hyt in Kente the harvyste of hedys.

| Will.ᵇ Gregory Skynner, Mayre of London | Warter Phylyppe | Anno xxxᵒ. |

An that yere come a legat from the Pope of Rome with grete pardon, for that pardon was the grettyste pardon that evyr come to Inglonde from the Conqueste unto thys tyme of my yere, beyng Mayre of London, for hyt was plenar indulgens. And at every chathydralle chyrche of Inglonde, and every abbay of name, and pryory, hadde in hyr placys confessorys assygnyd to hyre confessyons, and to a soyle them of hyr synnys *a pena et culpa*. And in every toune and cytte there that thys pardon was pupplyscyde, and confessors i-namyd, were the stacyons assygnyd unto the penytentys to goo on pylgermage to offyr hyr prayers unto God, and noo thyng ellys; and thoo men that were confessyd gaffe mony unto the Pope to mayntayny hys warrys agayne the Turke, that was fulle cruelle unto Crystyn men, and thoroughe thys londe of Ingelonde every man was fayne to do and gyffe aftyr hyr poner. And that yere the Pope put that hethyn hounde and fals tyrant to a grete rebuke, and slayne moe of hys Turkys then Mˡ persons of grete dygnyte of hyr contre, &c.

| Mayster Fyldynge, Mayre of London | Ric. Lee Ric. Alle | Anno xxxjᵒ. |

That yere hyt was competent welle and pessabylle as for any rysynge a-mong oure selfe, for every man was in cheryte, but sum

---

* So in MS.

ᵇ The Christian name "Will." is added by a somewhat later hand. The date "1451" is also added in the margin in a hand decidedly more modern.

what the bertys of the pepyl hyng and sorowyd for that the Duke
of Glouceter was dede, and sum sayde that the Duke of Yorke
hadde grete wronge, but what wronge there was noo man that
darste say, but sum grounyd and sum lowryd and badde dysdayne
of othyr, &c.

| John Norman, | John Walden | Anno xxxij°.[a] |
| Mayre of London | Thomas Coke | |

Ande that yere there was a batayle at Synt Albonys by-twyne
Kyng Harry the VI. and the Duke of Yorke, and thys batayle was
the weke be-fore Whytte Sonday.   And Kyng Harry was in
barnys hys owne propyr person, and was hurte with the shotte of
an arowe in the necke.   And the Duke of Yorke brought hym
unto London as kynge and not as a presener.   The Erle of Wyltschyre bare the kyngys baner that day in the batayle, for he was
at that tyme namyd but Syr Jamys Urmon;[b] and thys sayde Jamys
sette the kyngys baner agayne an howse ende and fought manly
with the helys, for he was a feryd of lesynge of beute, for he was
namyd the fayryd knyght of thys londe.   And with yn a lytyl
whyle aftyr was made the Erle of Wyltschyre.

The chaptaynys of thys fylde undyr the Duke of Yorke was the
Erle of Warwyke, the Erle of Saulysbury.   And in that batayle wer
slayne the Duke of Somersett, the Erle of Northehomerlonde, the
Lorde Clyfforde, with many moo othyr, bothe of gentylle men and
yemen.   And the kynge lete alle thys mater be in a dormon a
grete and a long tyme aftyr, as ye shalle hyre, for hyt was noo
seson to trete of pesse, for sum were welle contente and sum evylle
plesyd, but at the laste the pepylle sayde that the Duke of
Somersett was worthy to suffer that dethe by so moche that he

---

[a] What is recorded under this year, viz. the battle of St. Alban's, really took
place in the thirty-third year of Henry VI., but the mayor and sheriffs of that year
are omitted, and all the remaining years of this reign are wrong numbered, that
which is called the thirty-third year being really the thirty-fourth, and so on.

[b] Sir James Butler, Earl of Wiltshire and Ormond.   The writer is wrong in
saying that he was made Earl of Wiltshire after the battle.   He was created Earl
of Wiltshire in 1449, and succeeded to the earldom of Ormond in 1452.

-brought Kyng Harry at Claryngdon be-syde Saulysbury and there he toke hys grete sekenys.

| Wylliam Marowe, | John Jonge | Anuo xxxiij°.[a] |
| Mayre of London | Holgrave | |

Here was the rysynge and wanton reule of þe mayre and the mercers of London a-gayne the Lombardys. The Lombardys were so yntretyd that they were fayne to voyde the Cytte of London, ande many of them come to Sowthe Hampton and unto Wynchester for to be an habyte there. And they toke grete olde mancyons in Wyncherter for terme of lyffe, and sum but for yerys, and causyd the londe lordys to do grete coste in reparacyons, and when alle was don they come not there, and that causyd grete loste unto the londe lordys.

Also sum of the Lumbardys were take ande put in warde, and the comyn talkynge ande noyse was that they shulde nevyr be delyveryd butt contynue in perpetualle preson.

Also that yere a thyffe, one Thomas Whytchorne, was take in the Neweforeste be-syde Beuley and put yn preson at Wynchester. And when the day of delyverans com he appelyd many trewe men, and by that mene he kepte hys lyffe in preson. And thoo men that he appelyd were take and put yn stronge preson and sufferde many grete paynys, and was that they sholde confesse and a-corde unto hys fals pelyng; and sum were hongyd that badde noo frende shyppe and goode, and thoo that hadde goode gate hyr charters of pardon. And that fals and untrewe peler hadde of the kynge every day j d. *ob.* And thys he contynuyd al moste iij yere, and dystryde many men that were sum tym in hys company. And at the laste he appelyd on that outerly sayde that he was fals in hys appelynge, and sayde that [he][b] wolde preve hyt with hys bondys, and spende hys lyfe and blode a-pone hys fals body. And thys mater was fulle dyscretely take and hyrde of bothe pelerrys parte, and of the defendente ys parte also. And a notabylle man, and the moste petefullyste juge of al thys londe in syttyng a-pon lyffe and dethe,

---

[a] Should be "xxxiv." See page 198, note [a].   [b] Omitted in MS.

Hen. VI.
A.D. 1455-6.

toke thys sympylle man that offeryd to fyght with the peler, ande
fulle curtesly informyd hym of alle the condyscyons of the fyghtyng
and duelle of repreffe that shulde be by-twyne a peler of the kyngys,
fals or trewe, in that one party, and by-twyne the defendent, trewe
or false, in that othyr party. ¯For in cas that the peler prevaylyd
in that fyght he shulde be put in preson ayen, but he shulde fare
more better than he dyd be fore tyme of fyghtynge, and be i-lowe
of the kyng ij d. every [day] ª as longe as hit plesyd the kyng that
he shulde lyf. For in prosses the kynge may by the lawe put hym
to dethe, as for a man sleer, bycause that hys pelyng, fals or trewe,
bathe causyd many mannys dethys, for a very trewe man schulde
with yn xxiiij howrys make opyn to be knowe alle suche fals hyd
thyngys of felony or treson, yf he be nott consentynge unto the
same felowschyppe, undyr payne of dethe; and thys peler ys in
the same cas, wherefore he moste nedys dy by very reson. Thys
ys for the pelers party.

The defendaunte ys party ys, as that nobylle man, Mayster Myhelle
Skyllyng, sayde ande informyde the defender, that he and the peler
moste be clothyd alle in whyte schepys leter, bothe body, hedde,
leggys, fete, face, handys, and alle. Ande that they schulde have
in hyr hondys ij stavys of grene hasche, the barke beynge a-pon,
of iij fote in lenghthe, and at the ende a bat of the same govyn
owte as longe as the more gevythe any gretenys. And in that
othyr ende a horne of yryn, i-made lyke unto a rammys horne, as
scharpe at the smalle ende as hit myght be made. And there
whyþe they schulde make byr foule batayle a-pone the moste sory
and wrecchyd grene that myght be founde a-bowte the towne,
havyng nothyr mete ne drynke whythe, bot both moste be fastynge.¯
And yf hyr frowarde wepyn ben i-broke they moste fyght with hyr
hondys, fystys, naylys, tethe, fete, and leggys; hyt ys to schamfulle
to reherse alle the condyscyons of thys foule conflycte; and yf they
nede any drynke, they moste take hyr owne pysse. And yf the
defendent sle þat pelers, fals or trewe, the defendent shalle be

ª Omitted in MS.

bangyde by-cause of man sleynge, by soo moche that he bathe i-slayne the kyngys prover, for by hys meny the kynge badde mony of suche as were appelyd, and that mony þat rosse of hyr stuffe or goodys þat they hadde was put to þe kynge almys, and hys amener dystrybutyd hit unto the pore pepylle. But the kyng may by hys grace pardon the defendent yf he wylle, ys[a] the defendent be welle namyd and of competent governaunce in the toune or citte there at hys abydyng ys; but thys fulle seldon sene by cause of the vyle and unmanerly fyghtynge. And by reson they shulde not ben beryd in noo holy sepulture of Crystyn mannys beryng, but caste owte as a man þat wylfully sleythe hym selfe. Nowe remembyr thys foule batayle, whethey ye wylle doo hyt or noo. And bothe partys consentyde to fyght, with alle the condyscyons that long there too. And the fendent desyryd that the juge wolde sende unto Mylbroke there that he dwellyde, to inquere of hys gydynge and of conversacyon. And alle the men in that toune sayde that he was the trewyste laborer in alle that contre, and the moste gentellyste there with, for he was a fyscher and tayler of crafte. And the peler desyryd the same, but he was not a-bydynge in no place passynge a monythe. And in every place there as inquesyscyon was made men sayde, "Hange uppe Thome Whythorne, for he ys to stronge to fyght with Jamys Fyscher the trewe man whythe an yryn rammys horne." And thys causyd the juge to have pytte a-pon the defendent.

The maner of fyughtynge of thes ij poore
wrecchys by-syde Wynchester.

The peler in hys a-rayment ande parelle whythe hys wepyn come owte of the Este syde, and the defendent owte of the Sowthe-Weste syde in hys aparayle, with hys wepyn, fulle sore wepynge, and a payre of hedys in hys hond; and he knelyd downe a-pone the erthe towarde the Este and cryde God marcy and alle the worlde, and prayde every man of forgevenys, and every man there beyng

[a] ys So in MS. for "if."

present prayde for hym.   And the fals peler callyde and sayd "þou fals trayter! why arte þou soo longe in fals bytter be-leve?"   And thenne the defendent rosse upe and hym and sayde, "My quarelle ys as faythefulle and alle soo trewe as my by-lyve, and in that quarelle I wylle fyght," and with the same worde smote at the peler that hys wepyn breke; and thenne the peler smote a stroke to the defendent, but the offycers were redy that he shulde smyte no more, and they toke a-way hys wepyn fro hym.   And thenn they fought to gederys with hyr fystys long tyme and restyd hem, ande fought agayne, and thenn restyd agayne; and thenn they wente togedyr by the neckys. And then they bothe with hyr tethe, that the lethyr of clothyng and flesche was alle to rente in many placys of hyr bodys.   And thenn the fals peler caste that meke innocent downe to the grownde and bote hym by the membrys, that the sely innocent cryde owt.- And by happe more thenne strengythe that innocent recoveryd up on hys kueys and toke that fals peler by the nose with hys tethe and put hys thombe in hys yee, that the peler cryde owte and prayde hym of marcy, for he was fals unto God and unto hym. And thenn þe juge commaundyd hem to cesse and hyr bothe hyr talys; and the peler sayde that he hadde accusyd hym wronge-fully and xviij men, and be-sought God of marcy and of for-gevenys. And thenn he was confessyd ande hanggyd, of whos soule God have marcy.   Amen.

As for the defendent was pardonyd of hys lyfe, leme, and goodys, and went home; and he be-come an hermyte and with schorte tyme dyde.

| Mayster Canyngys, | Raffe Verney | Aº xxxiiijº. [a] |
| Mayre of London | Stewarde | |

That same yere the Lorde Egramounde brake owt of Newcgate with many othyr men.

| Geffray Bolayne, | Reyner | Anno xxxvº. [b] |
| Mayre of London | Edwar | |

[a] Should be "xxxv." See page 198, note [a]
[b] Should be "xxxvj."

Ande thys same yere at Covyntre there was made a pesse by-twyne the Duke of Somersett Harry, and the Erle of Saulysbury, and the Erle of Warwycke, for the dethe of hys fadyr Duke of Somersette, that the Duke of Yorke put to dethe at Synt Albonys. And thys tretys was made at Covyntre, in the holy tymc of Lentyn, by the mene of Kyng Harry the VI. And alle that holy tyme of Lentyn there myght noo mane* man that shulde preche by-fore the kynge, but that he shulde shewe hys sarmon in wrytyng, were he docter or other, in so moche the lordys woldys A B C wolde assygne what he schulde say, as for any thynge that longyd unto the comyn wele, and yf he passyd hyr commaundement he schulde lese hys costys, and goo as he come, withowte mete and drynge. But a becheler of holy dcvynyte come to that cytte, and whenn he come to preche by-fore the kyng, as Maystyr Wylliam Saye, Dene of Poulys and Dene of the kyngys chapylle, hadde desyryd and asygnyd, A B C axyd hys name, and hys name was Mayster Wylliam Ive, at that tyme beyng at Wynchester in Wycham ys college. And A B C sayde that they moste nedys se hys sarmon and hys purposse, that he was a vysyd to say by-fore the kynge the Sonday nexte comynge. And he fulle goodly toke them hys papyr; and they seyng and redynge hys papyr, commaundyd to leve owte and put a way many troughtys. But that same Mayster Wylliam Ivc sayde but lytylle, but whenn he come to pulpyt he sparyd not to sayd the troughthe, and reportyd by-fore the kyng that A B C made the sarmonys that were sayde fore, and not thoo that prechyd, and that causyd that þe men that prechyd hadde but sympylle sarmons, for hyr purposse was alle turnyde upsodowne, and that they badde made love days as Judas made whythe a cosse[b] with Cryste for they cyste ovyr the mane. The grete rewarde that he badde for hys labyr was the rydyng of viij^{xx} myle yn and owte for hys travayle, and alle hys frendys fulle sory for hym. But *qui veritatem dicit caput fractum habebit,* &c. And that same yere alle thes lordys departyd from the Parlyment, but they come nevyr alle to-

* So in MS.   [b] kiss.

gedyr aftyr that tyme to noo Parlyment nor conselle, but yf hyt were in fylde with spere and schylde.

Mayster Skoot,	Raffe Gosselyn	
Mayre of London	Nedham	Anno xxxvj°.[a]

Ande thys yere was done a grete jornaye at the Blowre Hethe by the Erle of Saulysbury ande the Quenys galentys. And that day the kynge made vij knyghtys, fyrste, Syr Robert Molyners, Syr John Daune, Syr Thomas Uttyng, Syr John Brembly, Syr Jon Stanley, Syr John Grysly, and Syr Rychard Hardon; and v of thes knyghtys were slayne fulle manly in the fylde, and many men of yemonry soore hurte, and a fulle nobylle knyght, the Lorde Audeley, and Syr Thomas Hamdon, knyght, was the getynge of the fylde, and Thomas Squyer and Counteroller of the Pryncys house fulle sore hurte. And [the][b] batayle or jornay lastyd alle the aftyr none, fro one of the clocke tylle v aftyr non, and the chasse lastyd unto vij at the belle in the mornynge. And men were maymyd many one in the Quenys party. There were in the Quenys party v M[l]., and in that othyr party v C, a grete wondyr that evyr they myght stonde the grete multytude not ferynge, the kynge beyng with yn x myle and the queue with yn v myle at the castelle of Egyllyssale. But the Erle of Saulysbury badde ben i-take, save only a Fryer Austyn schot gonnys alle that nyght in a parke that was at the backe syde of the fylde, and by thys mene the erle come to Duke of Yorke. And in the morowe they founde nothyr man ne chylde in that parke but the fryer, and he sayde that for fere he a-bode in that parke alle that nyght. But in the mornyng, by-twyne the fylde and Chester, Syr John Dawne ys sone that was at home in hys fadyrs place hadde worde that hys fadyr was slayne; a-non he raysyd hys tenantys and toke by-syde a-lytyl towne i-namyd Torperlay Syr Thomas Nevyle, Syr John Nevyle, and Syr Thomas Haryngdon, and brought hem unto the castelle of Chester, ande there they a-boode tylle the batayle of Northehampton was done, &c.

Also alle that seson the Erle of Warwyke with sowdyers of

[a] Should be "xxxvij." See p. 198, note [a].   [b] Omitted in MS.

Calysse were comynge unto the Duke of Yorke, and he come ovyr-wharte Colsylle be-syde Covyntre, and the Duke of Somerset whythe hys men rode a-longe thoroughe the towne, and yet non of hem mette whythe othyr as hyt happyd, or by lyckely hode they wold have made a newe fraye. Ande the same day Androwe Throllope consayvyd that the Erle of Warwyke was goyng unto the Duke of Yorke and not unto the kynge, and utterly for-soke hym and come unto the kynge and was pardonyd; and that made the duke fulle sore a-frayde when he wyste that sum olde soudyers went from hym unto the kynge, &c.

| Wylham Hewlyn, | Plomer | Anno xxxvij⁰.ᵃ |
| Mayre of London | Sokker | |

Wylham Hewlyn, Mayre of London { Plomer Sokker { Anno **xxxvij°.**ᵃ

Ande thys same yere there was a grete afray at Lodlowe by twyne the kynge and the Duke of Yorke, the Erle of Salusbury, the Erle of Warwyke, the Erle of Marche. The Duke of Yorke lete make a grete depe dyche and fortefyde it with gonnys, cartys, and stakys, but hys party was ovyr weke, for the kyng was mo thenn xxx M¹ of harneysyd men, by-syde nakyd men that were compellyd for to come with the kynge. And thenne the duke fledde fro place to place in Walys, and breke downe the bryggys aftyr hym that the kyngys mayny schulde not come aftyr hym. And he wente unto Irlonde. And there he taryd tylle the jornay was endyd at Northehampton. And heᵇ made newe grotys of a newe kune in Irlonde; in on syde of the grote was a crowne and in that othyr syde a crosse. And there he made many newe statutys, and hys yong sonys were sende by yende the see unto the Duke of Burgayne, and they were fulle welle ande worschypfully ressayvyd.

The Erle of Saulysbury, the Erle of Warwycke, the Erle of Marche, Syr John Wenlocke, alle thes come unto Devynschyre to Syr John Denham, and alle thes by the conveynge of Syr John Denham; and they bought a smalle vessclle in that contray, an they were conveyde unto Garnesey, ande from Garnesaye unto Calys, for fere of dethe that they sayde was ymagenyde by the kyng and

---

ᵃ Should be "xxxviij." See as before.　　　ᵇ *he* repeated in MS.

hys lordys, and of hyr owne housolde mayny for hyr dystruccyon, by
the counselle and consent of King Harry the VI. Thes lurdys
departyd owte of Ingelonde on Synt Edwarde ys evyn, Synt
Edwarde bothe kynge and confessoure, the xij day of October,[a] and
they taryd at Calys xxxvj_wekys. But the Erle of Warwycke
come unto Sondewyche, and there he toke þe Lord Ryvers with
hys ladye, the lady and Duchyes of Bedforde,[b] and brought hem to
Calys, for he was commaundyd to have londyd at C[a]lys by the
kynge, but he was brought there sonner then hym lekyd.

Ande Duke Harry of Somerset was i-commaundyd to goo to
Gyon, and soo he dyd, and fulle manly made sautys to Calys, ande
ranne byfore Calys almoste dayly, and many a men were hurte by
hym and hys men.

Ande thes fore sayde lordys sende letters unto many placys of
Inglonde howe they were a vysyde to reforme the hurtys and mys-
chevys ande grevys that raynyd in thys londe; and that causyd
them moche the more to be lovyde of the comyns of Kente and of
London; and by thys mene the comyns of Kent sende hem worde to
ressayve hem and to go with hem in that a-tente that they wolde
kepe trewe promys, and as for the more parte of thys londe hadde
pytte that they were attaynte and proclaymyd trayters by the
Parlement at was holde at Covyntre.

Also that same yere the Duchyes of Yorke com unto Kyng
Harry and submyttyd hyr unto hys grace, and she prayde for hyr
husbonde that he myght come to hys answere and to be ressayvyd
unto hys grace; and the kynge fulle humbely grauntyde hyr grace,
and to alle hyrs þat wolde come with hyr, and to alle othyr that
wolde com yn with yn viij dayes. And after viij days to done þe
execusyon of the lawe as hit requyryd. And many men, bothe

---

[a] This is really the date of the breaking up of their camp at Ludlow, not of their
leaving England.

[b] Jaquetta, widow of the Regent Bedford. She was the daughter of Peter of
Luxemburg, Count of St. Pol, and soon after her first husband's death married Sir
Richard Woodville, who was created Baron Rivers by Henry VI. in 1448, and Earl
Rivers by Edward IV. (who was his son-in law) in 1466.

knyghtys and squyers, come whythe Syr Water Deverose, in hyr schyrtys and halters in hyr hondys, fallynge by-fore the kynge, and alle hadde grace and marcy bothe of lyffe and lym.

The mysrewle of the kyngys galentys at Ludlowe, whenn they badde drokyn i-nowe of wyne that was in tavernys and in othyr placys, thcy fulle ungoodely smote owtc the heddys of the pypys and hoggys hedys of wyne, that men wente wete-sehode in wyne, and thenn they robbyd the towne, and bare a-waye beddynge, clothe, and othyr stuffe, and defoulyd many wymmen.

The Duchyes of Yorke was take to the Duke Bokyngham and to hys lady, for they two ben susters, and there she was tylle the fylde was done at Northehampton, and she was kept fulle strayte and many a grete rebuke.

Alle soo thes for sayde lordys come agayne unto Sondewyche the xxj day of June nexte folowyng. And the comyns of Kente and there welle-wyllers brought hem to Lundon, and so forthe to Northehampton. And there they mete with the kynge and foughte manly with the kyngys lordys and mayny, but there was moche favyr in that fylde unto the Erle of Warwycke. And there they toke the kynge, and made newe offycers of the londe, as tho chaunceler and tresyrar and othyr, but they occupyde not fo[r]the-with, but a-bode a seson of the comyng of Duke of York owte of Irlonde. And in that fylde was slayne the Duke of Bokyngham, stondyng stylle at hys tente, the Erle of Schrovysbury, the Lord Bemond, and the Lord Egremond, with many othyr men. Ande many men were drownyd by syde the fylde in the revyr at a mylle. And that goode knyght Syr Wylliam Lucy that dwellyd be-syde Northehampton hyrde the gonne schotte, and come unto the fylde to have holpyn þe kynge, but the fylde was done or that he come; an one of the Staffordys was ware of hys comynge, and lovyd that knyght ys wyffe and hatyd hym, and a-non causyd hys dethe.

Richarde Lee,	John Lambard	
Mayre of London	John Flemmyng	Anno xxxviij°.[a]

* Should be " xxxix." See page 198, note [a].

Ande thys same yere the Duke of Yorke come owte of Yrlonde, and londyd at the Redde Clyffe in Loncaschyre, and hys lyvery was whyte and brewe in hyr clothyng, and i-brawderyd a-bove with fetyrlockys.   And thys he come forthe towarde London; ande þen hys lady the duchyes met with hym in a chare i-coveryd with blewe felewette, and iiij pore coursserys ther-yn.   And so he come to Habyngdon, and there he sende for trompeters and claryners to bryng hym to London, and there he gave them baners with the hole armys of Inglonde with owte any dyversyte, and commaundyd hys swerde to ben borne uppe ryghte be-fore hym; and soo he rode forthe unto Lundon tylle he come to Westemyster to Kyng Harrys palys, ande there he claymyde the crowne of Inglonde.   Ande he kepte Kynge Harry there by fors and strengythe, tylle at the laste the kynge for fere of dethe grauntyd hym þe crowne, for a man that hathe by lytylle wytte wylle sone be a feryd of dethe, and yet I truste and bee-leve there was no man that wolde doo hym bodely harme.   But the lordys entretyd that Kyng Harry shuld rejoyse the crowne durynge hys lyffe, and aftyr hys lyffe that the crowne sholde returne unto the dukys ys [a] hayrys as hyt requyrythe by that tytylle, and here uppon they were swore to ben faythefulle and trewe unto Kyng Harry.   And alle so that hyt shulde [be] [b] graunte treson to them that spake any evyr [c] by the Duke of Yorke or hys wyffe, or any of hys chyldryn.   And alle the lordys grauntyd there to, and soo hyt was proclaymyd in London and in many placys of Inglond.   And that the for-sayde duke sbulde have owte of the crow[n]e yerely to hys expence, for hym and hys hayrys durynge Kyng Harrys lyffe, x M[l] marke in mony.   Thys a-cordement was made the laste day of October.

And that same nyght the kynge remevyde unto London a-gayne hys wylle, to the byschoppe ys palys of London, and the Duke of Yorke com unto hym that same nyght by the torchelyght and toke a-pon hym as kyng, and sayde in many placys that thys ys owrys by very ryght.   Ande thenn the quene hyrynge thys she voydyde

_____

* So in MS.   ᵇ Omitted in MS.   ᶜ evil.

unto Walys, but she was met with be-syde the Castelle of Malepas, and a servand of hyr owne that she hadde made bothe yeman and gentylman, and aftyr a-poyntyd for to be in offysce with hyr soue the prynce, spoylyde hyr and robbyde hyr, and put hyr soo in dowt of hyr lyffe and sonys lyffe also.   And thenn she com to the Castelle of Hardelowe in Walys, and she hadde many grete gyftys and gretely comfortyd, for she badde nede there of, for she hadde a fulle esy many a-boute hyr, the nombyr of iiij personnys.   And moste comynly she rode by-hynde a yonge poore gentylle-man of xiiij yere age, hys name was Jon Combe, i-borne at Amysbery in Wyltschyre.   And there hens she remevyd fulle prevely unto the Lorde Jesper, Lorde and Erle of Penbroke, for she durste not a byde in noo place that [was] * opyn but in pryvatt.   The cause was that conterfete tokyns were sende unto hyr as thoughe that they badde come from hyr moste dradde lorde the Kyng Harry the VI.; but hyt was not of hys sendyng, nothyr of [his] * doynge, but forgyd thyngys, for they that brought the tokyns were of the kyngys howse, and sum of þe pryncys howse, and sum of hyr owne howse, and bade hyr beware of the tokyns, that she gave nou credans there too; for at the kyngys departynge fro Covyntre towarde the fylde of Northehampton, he kyste hyr and blessyd the prynce, and commaundyd hyr that she shulde not com unto hym tylle that [he] * sende a specyalle tokyn unto hyr that no man kuewe but the kynge and she.   For the lordys wolde fayne badde hyr unto Lundon, for they kuewe welle that alle the workyngys that were done growe by hyr, for she was more wyttyer then the kynge, and that apperythe by hys dedys, &c.

Then the Quene havynge knowelechynge of thys praty whyle sche sende unto the Duke of Somersett, at that tyme beynge in Dorset schyre at the Castelle of Corffe, and for the Erle of Devy-schyre, and for Elysaundyr Hody, and prayde hem to com to hyr as hastely as they myght, with hyr tenantys as stronge in hyr harnys as men of warre, for the Lorde Rosse, the Lorde Clyfforde, the

* Omitted in MS.

Baron of Grestocke, the Lorde Nevyle, the Lorde Latymer, were
waytyng a-pon the Duke of Excete[r] to mete with hyr at Hulle.
And thys mater was not taryd but fulle prevely i-wrought; and
she sende letters unto alle hyr chyffe offycers that they wold doo
the same, and that they shulde warne alle þo servantys that lovyd
hyr or purposyd to kepe and rejoyse hyr offysce, to wayte a-pon
hyr at Hulle by that day as hit a-poyntyd by hyr.   Alle thes pepylle
were gaderyd and conveyde so prevely that they wer hole in nombyr
of xv M¹ or any man wolde be-leve hyt; in so moche yf any man
sayde, or tolde, or talkyd of suche gaderyng, he shulde be sehende,
and sum were in grete donger, for the comyn pepylle sayde by
thoo that tolde þᵉ, troughthe, " Ye talke ryght ye wolde hit were,"
and gave noo credens of hyr sayynge.   But the laste the lordys purposyd to knowe the troughþe.   And the ix day of December nexte
folowyng the Duke of Yorke, the Erle of Salysbury, the Erle
Rotlond (he was the Duke of Yorke ys secunde sone, one the beste
dysposyd lorde in thys londe), and Syr Thomas Haryngdon, whythe
many mo knyghtys and quyers and grete pepylle with hem, and
soo departyd owte of London towarde Yorke, &c.

Ande the same yere, the xxx day of December, the Duke of
Exceter, the Duke of Somersett, the Erle of Northehomberlond,
the Lorde Roos, the Lorde Nevyle, the Lorde Clyfforde, with many
mo lordys, knyghtys, squyers, and gentyllys, and the commyns of
the Quenys party, met with the Duke of Yorke at Wakefylde, and
there they made a grete jorney a-pon the Lorde and Duke of Yorke,
and toke hym and the Erle of Saulysbury, the Erle of Rutlond, and
the Lorde Haryngdon, and Syr Thomas Nevyle, and Syr Thomas
Haryngdon, and many mo knyghtys were take a slayne by syde
alle the comyns.   But thys good Duke of Yorke with hys lordys
a-fore sayde loste hyr heddys; God have marcy on there soulys, for
they loste in that jorneys the nombyr of xxv c men.   And in the
Quenys party were slay but ii c men, &c.

As for the sege of the Towre, hyt ys com* and opyn i-knowe, I

* Apparently the writer intended to say " commonly."

passe ovyr. But sone aftyr the ende of the sege the Lorde Schalys, that notabylle warryoure, was slayne at Synt Mary Overeyes with water men, and laye there dyspoyly nakyd as a worme. But the lordys were fulle sory of hys dethe.

Alle so Edwarde Erle of Marche, the Duke of Yorke ys sone and heyre, badde a gre jornaye at Mortymer ys Crosse in Walys the secunde day of Februar nexte soo folowynge, and there he put to flyght the Erle of Penbroke, the Erle of Wylteschyre. And there he toke and slowe of knyghtys and squyers, and of the,* to the nomber of iij M¹., &c.

Ande in that jornay was Owyn Tetyr i-take and brought unto Herforde este,ᵇ an he was be heddyde at the market place, and hys hedde sette a-pone the hygheyste gryce of the market crosse, and a madde woman kembyd hys here and wysche a way the blode of hys face, and she gate candellys and sette a-boute hym brennynge, moo then a c. Thys Owyne Tytyr was fadyr unto the Erle of Penbroke, and badde weddyd Quene Kateryn, Kyng Harry the VI. ys modyr, wenyng and trustyng all eway that he shulde not be hedyd tylle he sawe the axe and the blocke, and whenn that he was in hys dobelet he trustyd on pardon and grace tylle the coler of hys redde vellvet dobbelet was ryppyd of. Then he sayde, " That hede shalle ly on the stocke that was woute to ly on Queue Kateryns lappe," and put hys herte and mynde holy unto God, and fulle mekely toke hys dethe.

Alle soo the same day that the Erle of Marche shulde take hys jornaye towarde Mortymer ys Crosse fro Herforde este,ᵇ he mousterd hys many with owte the towne wallys in a mersche that ys callyd Wyg mersche. And ovyr hym men say ᶜ iij sonnys schynyng.

Ande the xvij day nexte folowynge Kyng Harry roode to Syut Albonys, and the Duke of Northefolke with hym, the Erle of Warwycke, the Erle of Arundelle, the Lorde Bouser, the Lorde Bonvyle, with many grete lordys, knyghtys, and squyers, and commyns of an c M¹ men. And there they hadde a grete batayle

---

ᵃ So in MS.   ᵇ Haverfordwest.   ᶜ saw.

whythe the Queue, for she come ever on fro the jornaye of Wacke-
fylde tylle sche come to Synt Albonys, with alle the lordys a fore
sayde; and hyr mayny and every lorde ys men bare hyr lordys
leverey, that every man myghte knowe hys owne feleschippe by
hys lyverey.   And be-syde alle that, every man and lorde bare
the Pryncys levery, that was a bende of crymesyn and blacke with
esteryge ys fetherys.   The substance that gate that fylde were
howseholde men and feyd men   I wene there were not v M¹ men
that fought in the Quenys party, for þᵉ moste parte of Northeryn
men fledde a-way, and sum were take and spoylyd owte of hyr
harnysse by the way as they fledde.   And sum of them robbyd
evyr as they yede, a petyffulle thynge hit ys to hyre hit.   But the
day before that batayle there was a jornay at Dunstapyl; but the
kyngys mayny lackyd good gydyng, for sum were but newe men
of warre, for the chevyste captayne was a boucher of the same
towne; and there were the kyngys mayny ovyr throughe only by
the Northeryn men.   And sone aftyr the bocher, for schame of hys
sympylle gydynge and loste of the men, the nombyr of viij c, for
very sorowe as hyt ys sayde, hynge hym selfe; and sum men sayde
that hyt was for loste of hys goode, but dede he ys—God knowythe
the trought.

And in the myddys of the batayle Kynge Harry wente unto hys
Quene and for-soke alle hys lordys, ande truste better to hyr party
thenne unto hys owne lordys.   And ₜₕₑnn thoroughe grete labur
the Duke of Northefolke and the Erle of Warwycke a schapyd
a-waye; the Byschoppe of Exceter, that tyme Chaunceler of Ingelond,
and brother unto the Erle of Warwycke, the Lorde Bouser, whythe
many othyr knyghtys, squyers, and comyns fledde, and many men
slayne in bothe partys.   And the Lorde Bonevyle was be-heddyd,
the comyn sayynge that hys longago causyd hym to dye.   The
Prynce was jugge ys owne sylfe.   Ande ther was slayne that manly
knyght Syr Thomas Keryel.   The nomber of ded men was xxxv c an
moo þat were slayne.   The lordys in Kyng Harrys party pycchyd
a fylde and fortefyd hyt lulle stronge, and lyke unwyse men brake

Hen. VI.
A.D. 1461.

hyr raye and fyld and toke a-nothyr, and or that they were alle
sette a buskyd to batayle, the Quenys parte was at hond whythe
hem in towne of Synt Albonys, and then alle Þyng was to seke and
owte of ordyr, for hyr pryckyers come not home to bryng no
tydyng howe ny that the Queue was, save one come and sayd that
she was ix myle of. And ar the goners and borgeners couthe
levylle hyr gonnys they were besely fyghtyng, and many a gyune
of wer was ordaynyd that stode in lytylle a-vayle or nought; for
the burgeners hadde suche instrumentys that wolde schute bothe
pellettys of ledde and arowys of an elle of lenghthe with vj fetherys,
iij in myddys and iij at the othyr ende, with a grete myghty bedde
of yryn at the othyr ende, and wylde fyre with alle. Alle thes iij
thyngys they myght schute welle and esely at onys, but in tyme of
nede they couthe not schut not one of thes, but the fyre turnyd
backe a-pon them that wold schute thys iij thyngys. Also they
badde nettys made of grete cordys of iiij fethem of lengthe and of
iiij fote brode, lyke unto an haye, and at every ij knott there was
an nayl stondyng uppe ryght, that there couthe no man passe ovyr
hyt by lyckely hode but he shulde be hurte. Alle so they badde
pavysse bore as a dore i made with a staffe foldynge uppe and
downe to sette the pavys where the lykyd, and loupys with
schyttyng wyndowys to schute owte at, they stondyng by hynde þᵉ
pavys, and the pavys as fulle of iijᵈ nayle aftyr ordyr as they myght
stonde. And whenn hyr schotte was spende and done they caste
the pavysse by-fore hem, thenn there myght noo man come unto
them ovyr the pavysse for the naylys that stode up-ryghte, but yf
he wolde myschyffe hym sylfe. Alle so they badde a thynge made
lyke unto a latysse fulle of naylys as the net was, but hit wolde be
mevyd as a man wolde; a man myght brysc hyt to-gedyr that the
lengythe wolde be more then ij yerdys long, and yf he wolde he
myght hale hyt a brode, thenn hit wolde be iiij square. And that
servyd to lye at gappys there at horsemen wolde entyr yn, and
many a caltrappe. And as the substaunce of men of worschyppe
that wylle not glose nor cory favyl for no parcyallyte, they cowthe

not undyrstond that alle thys ordenaunce dyd any goode or harme but yf hyt were a mong us in owre parte with Kyng Harry. There fore hyt ys moche lefte, and men take hem to mallys of ledde, bowys, swyrdys, gleyvys, and axys. As for speremen they ben good to ryde be-fore the foote men and ete and drynke uppe hyr vetayle, and many moo suche prety thyngys they doo, holde me excusyd thoughe I say the beste, for in the fote men ys alle the tryste.

Ande at the nyght aftyr the batayle the kynge blessyd hys sone the Prynce, and Doctor Morton brought forthe a boke that was fulle of orysons, and there the boke was oppenyd, and blessyd that yong chylde *cum pinguedine terre et cum rore celi*, and made hym knyght. And the yong knyght weryd a payre of bregant yerys i-coveryd with purpylle velvyt i-bete with golde-smythe ys worke. And the Prynce made many knyghtys. The fryste that he made was Androwe Trolloppe, for he was hurte and myght not goo for a calletrappe in hys fote; and he sayde, " My lorde, I have not deservyd hit for I slowe but xv men, for I stode stylle in oo place and they come unto me, but they bode stylle with me." And then come Whytyngam, Tresham, and many moo othyr, and were made knyghtys that same tyme.

Ande the Kynge and the Queue toke hyr jornay unto Yorke wardys, for they demyde that the Northeryn men wolde have ben to crenelle in robbyng yf they badde come to London. But by the a-vyse of Docter Morton they sende certayne knyghtys and men unto London and to Westemyster, but they myght not be sufferde to entery in to the towne. Ande sum of hyr mayny were slayne for hyr cursyd longege. Ande the mayre ordaynyd bothe brede and vytayle to be sende unto the quene, and a certayne sum of money with alle. But whenn men of London and comyns wyste that the cartysse shulde goo to the Quene, they toke the cartys and departyde þe brede and vytayle a-monge the comyns. And on John Byschoppe was a grete doer of thys mater, for he was chyffe coke to the knyght Syr John Wenlocke. But as for the mony,

I wot not howe hit was departyd; I trowe the pursse stale the mony.

Then come tydyngys of the comynge of þe* Erle of Marche unto London; thenn alle the cytte were fayne, and thonkyd God, and sayde that

He that had Londyn for sake
Wolde no more to hem take,

and saydo, "Lette us walke in a newe wyne yerde, and lette us make us a gay gardon in the monythe of Marche with thys fayre whyte ros and herbe, the Erle of Marche." And the Erle of Warwycke mette with the Erle of Marche by-syde Oxforde, x myle owte of hit, at a towne of hys owne i-namyd Burford a-pon the-Wolde; for the Erle of Marche come fro Walys, and was fulle sore a-ferde of the loste of the ij fyldys that were loste by-fore, Wakefylde that one, and Synt Albonys that othyr, and he sorowde sore for hys fadyr the Duke of Yorke, and for hys good brother the Erle of Rutlond, and for alle othyr lordys and comyns, &c.

There the Erle of Warwycke informyd hym of the gydynge and dysposyscyon of Kyng Harry, and of the Quene, and of the love and favyr that the comyns hadde unto hym, and by ryght to occupy the crowne of Inglonde, and soo hys hert was sum what made gladde and comfortyd. But he was sory that he was soo pore, for he badde no mony, but the substance of hys mayny come at hyr owne coste.

Alle soo the xxvj day of Februer nexte folowyng Edwarde Erle of Marche com to London owt of Walys and the Erle of Warwycke with hym, and xl M¹ men with hem bothe, and they enteryd unto the cytte of London, and there he toke uppon hym the crowne of Inglond by the avysse of the lordys spyrytual and temporalle, and by the elexyon of the comyns. And so he be-gan hys rayne the iiij day of Marche, in the yere of oure Lorde God M¹ cccc lxj, the Sondy letter D as for that yere.

* *the* repeated in MS.

Thys ys the fyrste of hys rayne of Kynge Edwarde the iiij[the].

Nowe gon messyngers by twyne contraye and contraye, and harowdys were fulle schante, for they ne wyste what was beste to done, but sufferens and fayr speche dyd them moche ese.   And bothe þe newe kynge and the olde were fulle besyd to make hyr party stronge, &c.

The xiij day of Marche the kynge, owre newe Kynge Edwarde, toke hys jornaye unto the Northe, and the Duke of Northefolke with hym.   The Erle of Warwycke and the Lorde Fauconbrygge, with many knyghtes, squyers, and comyns, to the nombyr of ii c M¹ men.

And the xxviij day of Marche, that was þe Palme Sunday evyn, the Lorde Fewater was slayne at Ferybryge, and many with ᵃ hym was slayne and drownyd.   And the Erle of Warwycke was hurte yn hys legge with an arowe at the same jornaye.

Ande the xxix day of the same monythe of Marche, that was Palme Sunday, the kyng mette with the lordys of the Northe at Schyrborne.   And there was on Harrys party that was kynge——

Prynce Edwarde, Kyng Harrys son.
The Duke of Exceter.
The Duke of Somersett.
The Erle of Northehumberlond.
The Erle of Devynschyre.
The Lorde Roos.
The Lorde Bemound.
The Lorde Clyfforde.
The Lorde Nevyle.
The Lorde Wellys.
The Lorde Wylby.
The Lorde Harry of Bokyngham.
The Lorde Ryvers.
The Lorde Schalys.

ᵃ *whithe* repented after *with* in MS.

The Lorde Maule.[a]

The Lorde Ferys of Groby.

The Lorde Foschewe.[b]

The Lorde Lovelle.

Syr Thomas Hammys, captayne of alle the fote men.

Syr Androwe Thorlloppe.

Syr Thomas Tressam.

Syr Robert Whytyngham.

Syr John Dawne.

And the yonge Lorde of Schrouysbury, and many moo othyr, bothe lordys, knyghtys, and squyers.

Here ben the namys of the lordys that were slayne in the felde in Kynge Harrys party.

The Erle of Northehumberlond,

The Lorde Clyfforde,

The Lorde Nevyle,

The Lorde Wellys,

The Lorde Maules,[a]

And many moo then I can reherse; but whythe þes and othyr that were slayne in the fylde ys a grete nombyr, by syde xlij knyghtys that were slayne aftyr; the hoole nombyr ys xxxv M¹ of comeners. Jhesu be þou marcyfulle unto hyr soulys. Amen.

And the lordys before wretyn fledde, the substance in to Schotlond with the Kynge Harry and Queue Margarete, and sone the Prynce with hym, fulle of sorowe and hevynys, no wondyr. God knowythe, but every man deme the beste tylle the trought be tryde owte. For many a lady lost hyr beste be lovyd in that batayle.

The Erle of Devynschyre was seke, and myght not voyde a waye, and was take and be heddyd. And the Erle of Wylte schyre was take and brought unto Newe Castell to the Kynge. And there hys

[a] Ralph Bigot, Lord Mauley.—See Paston Letters (new ed.) ii. 6. His name is not given in Nicolas' Peerage, but he was evidently the son or grandson of Sir John Bigot and Constance his wife, sister of Peter Lord Mauley, who died in 1415.

[b] This seems undoubtedly to be the celebrated Sir John Fortescue, though why he is called Lord I cannot tell. See Rolls of Parl. v. 477.

hedde was smete of, and send unto London to be sette uppon London Brygge.   And Docter Morton, the Prynces chaunceler, was take with hym and put in the Towre, but he schapyd a way longe tyme aftyr, and ys by yonde the see with the Quene, &c.

Ande the Kynge taryd in the Northe a grette whyle, a made grete inquerens of the rebellyens a-gayne hys fadyr.   And toke downe hys fadyrs hedde fro the walle of Yorke.   And made alle the contray to ben sworne unt hym and to hys lawys.   And then he returnyd unto Lundon agayne.   And there he made xviij knyghtys and many lordys.   And then he rode to Westemyster. And there he was crounyd the xxviij day of June, and the yere of oure Lorde M^l cccc lxj, blessyd be God of hys grete grace, etc.

| Hewe Wythe, | Gorge Irlond | Anno ij° |
| Mayre of London | John Loke | |

And thys same yere the Erle of Oxforde, the Lord Abbry, the Lorde of Oxforde ys sone, Syr Thomas Todenham knyght, John Mongomery, and William Terelle squyer, were takyn in Esex, and brought unto Lundon to the Towre.   Ande thenne they were ledde to Westemyster to the Kynges palys, and there they were attaynte of hyghe and myghthy treson that they ymagenyd agayne þe Kynge. And thenn they were drawe to the Towre from Westemyster. And at the Towre hylle was made a schaffolde for them, and there hyr heddys were smetyn on, and hyr bodys beryd, as hyt plesyd them to be qwethe hyr bodys.

| Thomas Coke, | Bartholomewe Jamys | Anno iij°. |
| Mayre of London | Wylliam Hampton | |

Thys yere Quene Margarete com owt of Frauns with lij schyppys, with Freynysche men and sum Engelysche men in the schyppys. And they londyd in Northe Humberlonde, hyt was vij dayes be-fore Alle Halwyn tyde.   And there sche toke the castelle of Anwyke and put hyt fulle of Fraynyschemen.   And thenn she retornyd in to Schotlonde by water.   And there rosse suche a tempaste uppon hyr that she for soke hyr schippe, and a schapyd with the bote of þe schyppe.   And the schyppe was drownyd with moche of hyr stuffe and iij grete schippys moo.   And iiij c and vj Fraynysche men

Edw. IV.
·A.D. 1462-

were take in the chyrche of Hooly Ylond. Thenn Kyng Edward
hyrde telle of thys, and made hym redy towarde the Northe with
many lordys, gentellys, and comyns with hym. And there he
layde a sege to Anwyke Castelle, and to the castelle of Bamborowe,
and to Dunsterborowe. Bamborowe and Dunsterborowe was kepte
by Syr Raffe Persy and Syr Harry Bewforde, late Duke of
Somersett, and the castelle of Anwyke with the Lorde Hungerforde. And Bamborowe and Dunsterborowe were yoldyn be Syr
Raffe Percy and Syr Harry Benford, late Duke of Somersett, to the
Kyngys wylle, whythe the condyscyons that the sayde Raffe Percy
schulde have the kepynge of the ij castellys, Bamborowe and
Dunstarborowe. The sayde Syr Raffe Percy and Syr Harry Beuforde,
late Duke of Somersett, were sworne to be trewe and faythefulle as
trewe lege men unto owre kynge and soverayne lorde Edwarde the
iiij[the]. And they com to Derham, and there they were sworne
byfore owre kynge. And the kynge gaffe hem hys levery and
grete rewardys.

Ande thenn the for sayde Raffe Percys retornyde a-gayne in to
Northehumberlond, and hadde the kepynge of the sayde ij castellys
accordynge unto the poyntment. And the sayde Syr Harry
Beuforde a-bode stylle whithe the kynge, and roode with hym to
Lundon. And the Kynge made fulle moche of hym; in soo moche
that he loggyd whythe the kynge in hys owne bedde many
nyghtys, and sum tyme rode a huntynge be hynde the kynge, the
kynge havynge a boute hym not passynge vj hors at the moste, and
yet iij were of the Dukys men of Somersett. The kyng lovyd hym
welle, but the duke thought treson undyr fayre chere and wordys,
as hyt apperyd. And for a grete love the kyng made a grete justys
at Westemyster, that he shuld se sum maner sporte of chevalry
aftyr hys grete labur and hevynys. And with grete instans the
kynge made hym to take barnys uppon hym, and rode in the place,
but he wolde nevyr cope whithe no man and no man myght not cope
whythe hym, tylle the kynge prayd hym to be mery and sende hym
a tokyn, and thenn he ranne fulle justely and merely, and hys helme
was a sory hatte of strawe. And thenn every man markyd hym welle.

Edw. IV.
A.D. 1463.

But within schorte tyme aftyr the sayde Syr Raffe Percy by fals colysyon and treson he lete the Fraynysche men take the castelle of Bamborowe fro hym *nolens volo.* As for the castelle of Anwyke alle the men of werre that were of worschip brake owte of the castelle by fors and warre and rescuyd Syr Perys de Brasylle[a] on xij day by [v][b] the morne, and they that were with yn the castelle gaffe hit uppe by a-poyntement, &c. And then Kyng Edwar made Syr John Ascheley, the knyght that fought so manly in Smethe-fylde with an alyon that calengyd, he was made captayne of the castelle, and Syr Raffe Gray constabylle of the sayde castelle of Anwycke. And withyn iij or iiij monythys aftyr that fals knyght and traytoure, Syr Raffe Graye, by fals treson toke the sayde Syr John Ascheley presoner, and delyveryd hym to Queue Margarete, and thenn delyveryde the castelle to the Lorde Hungerforde and unto the Fraynysche men accompanyd whythe hym; and by thys mene he put the kyng owre soverayne lorde owte of possessyon. And thenne aftyr that come Kyng Harry that was, and the Quene to the Kynge of Schottys, Syr Perys de Brasylle,[a] with iiij[xx] M[l] Schottys, and layde a sege unto the castelle of Norham, and lay there xviij dayes. And thenn my Lorde of Warwycke and hys brother the Lorde Montegewe put them in devyr to rescewe þe sayde castelle of Norham, and soo they dyd, and put bothe Kynge Harry and the Kyng of Schotys to flyghte. And Queue Margarete whythe alle hir consayle, and Syr Perys de Brasey whythe the Fraynysche men, fledde a-wey by water with iiij balynggarys; and they londyd at the Scluse in Flaundyrs, and lefte Kyng Harry that was be hynde hem, and alle hyr hors and hyr harneys, they were so hastyd by my Lorde of Warwycke, and hys brother the Lorde Mountegewe, and by hyr feleschippe with them accompanyde. And at the departynge of Syr Perys de Brasyl and hys feleschippe was on manly man that purposyd to mete with my Lorde of Warwycke, that was a taberette, for he stode a-pon an hylle with hys tabyr and hys pype, taberyng and pyping as merely as any man

---

[a] De Brézé.　　　　　　　　[b] This figure is struck out.

myght, stondyng by hym selfe, tylle my lorde come unto hym he wold not lesse hys grownd; and there he be-come my lordys man; ande yet he ys with hym fulle good and to hys lorde.

Thenn the Kynge Edwarde the iiij purposyd to make an arme into Schotlonde by londe and by water, that the grete rebellyous Harry ande the Queue Margarete sbulde not passe a way by water. And the kyng made the Erle of Worseter captayne by water. And thenn there was ordaynyd a grete navy and a grete armye bothe by watyr and by lond. And alle was loste and in vayne, and cam too noo purposse, neyther by water ne by londe.

Alle so the kynge sone aftyr dysposyd hym, and was purposyd to ryde into Yorke schyre and to the contray a boute, to see and understonde the dysposyscyon of the pepylle of the Northe. And toke with hym the Duke of Somersett, and ij c of hys men welle horsyd and welle i-harnaysyd. Ande the sayde Duke, Harry of Somersett, ande his men were made the Kyngys garde, for the Kyng badde that duke in moche favyr and trustyd hym welle. But þe garde of hym was as men sbulde put a lombe a monge wolvysse of malyscyus bestys; but Alle myghty God was the scheparde. And whenn the kynge departyd from London he toke hys way to Northe-hampton, and thedyr the kynge com a Syn Jamys day the Apostylle,[a] ande that fals duke with hym. And the comyns of the towne of Northehampton and of the schyre a-boute sawe that the fals duke and traytoure was so nyghe the Kyngys presens and was made hys garde. The comyns a rosse uppon that fals traytur thee Duke of Somersett, and wolde have slayne hym with yn the kyngys palys. And thenn the kynge with fayre speche and grete defeculte savyde hys lyffe for that tyme, and that was pytte, for the savynge of hys lyffe at that tyme causyd mony mannys dethys son aftyr, as ye shalle heyre. And then the Duke [b] sende that fals Duke of Somersett in to a castelle of hys owne fulle secretly, for save garde of hys the dukys lyffe, and the dukys men unto Newe Castelle, to kepe the

---

[a] July 25. But there are privy seals of this year dated at Northampton on the 18th and 19th July.

[b] So in MS., evidently an error for " King."

towne, and gave hem goode wages fulle treuly payde. And the Kyng fulle lovyngly gave the comyns of Northehampton a tonne of wyne that they shulde drynke and make mery. And þe wyne was drunkyn merely in the market place, for they hadde many fayre pecys of sylvyr. I darsay ther ys no taverne that hathe not so moche of stuffe as they occupyde in hys[a] hyr tavernys. For sum fette wyne in basynnys, and sum in caudryns, and sum in bollys, and sum in pannys and sum in dyschys. Loo, the grete tresoure that they scheuyd þat tyme.

Mathewe Phylyppe,   { Muschampe   } Anno iiij°.
Mayre of London   { Basset   }

Thys yere, a-bute Mydsomyr, a the ryalle feste of the Sargantys of the Coyfe, the Mayre of London was desyryde to be at that feste. And at denyr tyme he come to the feste with his offecers, a-greyng and a-cordyng unto hys degre. For with yn London he ys next unto the kyng in alle maner thynge. And in tyme of waschynge the Erle of Worseter was take be-fore the mayre and sette downe in the myddys of the hy tabylle. And the mayre seynge that hys place was occupyd hylde hym contente, and went home a gayne with owt mete or drynke or any thonke, but rewarde hym he dyd as hys dygnyte requyryd of the cytte. And toke with hym the substance of hys bretheryn the aldyrmen to his place, and were sette and servyd also sone as any man couthe devyse, bothe of sygnet and of othyr delycatys i-nowe, that alle the howse mervelyd howe welle alle tynge was done in soo schorte a tyme, and prayde alle men to be mery and gladde, hit shulde be a mendyd a nothyr tyme.

Thenn the offesers of the feste, fulle evylle a schamyd, informyd the maysters of the feste of thys mysse happe that ys be-falle. And they consyderynge the grete dygnyte and costys and charge that longgyd unto the cytte, and a-non sende unto the mayre a present of mete, brede, wyne, and many dyvers sotelteys. But whenn they that come with the presentys say[b] alle the gyftys, and the sarvyse that was at the borde, he was fulle sore a schamyd that shulde doo

[a] So in MS.   [b] saw.

þe massage, for the present was not better thenn the servyse of metys was by fore the mayre, and thoroughe owte the hyghe tabylle. But hys demenynge was soo that he hadde love and thonke for hys massage, and a grette rewarde with alle. And thys the worschippe of the cytte was kepte, and not loste for hym. And I truste that nevyr hyt shalle, by the grace of God.

Ande thys same yere a-boute Crystysmas that fals Duke of Somersett, with owte any leve of the kyng, stale owte of Walys with a prevy mayny towarde the Newecastelle, for he and hys men were confeteryde for to have be-trayde the sayde Newecastelle. And in þe wey thedyrwarde he was aspyde, and lyke to have ben takyn be syde Dereham in hys bedde. Notwithstondynge he a schapyde a-way in hys schyrt and barefote, and ij of hys men were take. And they toke with hem that fals dukys caskette and hys harneys. And whenn that hys men knewe that he was aschapyd, and hys fals treson aspyde, hys men stale from the Newecastelle as very fals traytourys, and sum of hem were take and loste hyr heddys for hyr labur, &c.

Ande thenn the kynge, owre soverayne lorde Edwar the iiij, badde knowleche of hys fals dysposyscyon of thys fals Duke Harry of Somersett. The kynge sende a grete feleschippe of hys housolde men to kepe the towne of Newecastelle, and made the Lorde Scrope of Bolton captayne of the towne; and soo they kepte hyt surely alle that wyntyr. Ande a-boute Ester nexte aftyr the Schottys sewyd unto oure soverayne lorde the kynge for pes. And the kynge ordaynyde Commyssourys to mete whythe þe Schottys. The names of the Commyssyonourys be wretyn here aftyr folowyng :

The Chaunceler of Ingelond, And many othyr for the Eng-
The Erle of Warwycke, lysche partye, to brynge hyt
The Lorde Montegewe, to a conclusyon.

The poyntement was that they Schottys and þey shulde mete at Yorke. And thenn was my Lorde of Mountegewe assygnyd to fecche yn the Schottys pesseabylly, for he was Wardon of the Marchys. And then my Lorde of Mountegewe toke hys jornaye towarde the Newe castelle. And by the waye was fulle falsely i-purvyde that fals Duke Harry of Somersett and Percy, with hyr feleschyppe assocyat unto them, that there was layde by the waye, a lytylle from the Newecastel, in a woode, that fals traytoure Syr Umfray Nevyle, with iiij schore sperys, and the bowys there too. And they shulde have falle on the Lorde Mountegeue sodenly, and slayne hym sodenly, but, God be thonkyd, hyr fals treson was aspyde and knowe. And thenne the Lorde Montegewe toke a nothyr waye, and made to be gaderyd a grete feleschippe, and went to the Newecastelle, and soo toke hys jornaye unto Norham warde. Ande in the wey thedyrwarde there met with hym that fals Duke of Somersette, Syr Raffe Percy, the Lorde Hungerforde, and the Lorde Roos, whythe alle hyr company, to the nombyr of v M¹ men of armys. And thys metynge was a pon Synte Markys day;* and that same day was Syr Raffe Percy slayne. And whenn that he was dede alle þe party was schomfytyd and put to rebuke. Ande every man avoydyd and toke hys way with fulle sory hertys. And thenn my Lorde of Mountegeue toke hys hors and roode to Norham, and fecchyd yn the Schottys, and brought hem unto the Lordys Commyssyonourys. And there was concludyd a pes for xv yere with the Schottys. And the Schottys ben trewe hyt moste nedys contynu so longe, but hit ys harde for to tryste unto hem, for they byn evyr founde fulle of gyle and dyssayte.

Ande the xiiij daye of May nexte aftyr, my Lorde of Mountegeue toke hys jornaye toward Hexham from the Newecastelle. And there he toke þat fals Duke Harry Benford of Somersett, the Lord Roos, the Lorde Hungerforde, Syr Pylyppe Wenteworthe, Syr Thomas Fyndorne, whythe many oþyr; loo, soo manly a man ys thys good Erle Mountegewe, for he sparyd not hyr malysse, nor hyr falssenysse, nor gyle, nor treson, and toke meny of men and slowe many one in that jornaye.

The xv day of May folowynge thys good Lorde Mountegewe let to be smete of the heddys of thes men, the whyche that hyr namys here folowyn in wrytyng:

---

* April 25. This was the battle of Hedgley Moor.

Summa v. {
The Dukys bedde of Somersett,
Edmon Fysche, knyght,
Edmon Bradschawe,
Water Hunte,
Blacke Jakys.

At the Newecastelle, the xvij day of May, he let to be smete of the heddys, as the namys of hem done appere here aftyr in wrytynge:

Summa v. {
Fyrste, the bedde of the Lorde Hungerforde,
The Lorde Roos,
Syr Thomas Fyndorne,
Barnarde de la Mare,
Nycholas Massam.

Ande the xviij day of May he let to be smyte of* at Mydlam the hedys of thes men that hyr namys folowyn here in wrytynge:

Summa vij. {
Syr Phylippe Wentworthe, knyght,
Wyllam Penyngton,
Warde of Copclyffe,[b]
Olyver Wentworthe.
Wylliam Spyller,
John Senyer, of Yorke,
Thomas Hunte, foote man.

At Yorke, the xxvj day of May, he let to be smete of the heddys of thos men that hyr namys folowyn here in wrytynge:

Summa xiiij {
Syr Thomas Hoosy,
Thomas Gosse,
Robert Myrfyn,
John Butler,
Roberte Wattys, porter to Kyng Harry,
Thomas Fenwyke,
Robert Cockefelde,
Wylliam Bryce,
Wylliam Danson,

---

* *let to be smyte of.* he smot let to be smyte of, MS.
[b] *Copclyffe.* Should be Topcliff. See extract at end of Warkworth's Chronicle from Arundel MS. No. 5, f. 170, at the College of Arms.

John Chapman,
John Edyrbeke,
Rycharde Taverner,
John Russelle,
Robert Conqueror.

Ande be syde Newecastelle, the same monythe, þer was i-take Taylbosse[a] in a cole pyt, and he hadde moche mony with hym, bothe golde and sylvyr, that schulde have gon unto Kyng Harry: and yf [it][b] had come to Harry, lat Kynge of Ingelonde, hyt wolde have causyd moche sory sorowe, for he had ordaynyd harneys and ordenance i-nowe, but the men wolde not go one fote with hym tylle they had mony. And they waytyd dayly and howrely for mony that thys Taylebosse shulde have send unto hem or brought hyt; the summa was iij M^l marke. And the lordys mayny of Montegewe were sore hurte and seke, and many of hys men wer slayne by for in the grete jornays, but thys mony was departyd a-monge hem, and was a very holsum salfe for hem. And in the day folowyng Taylebosse loste hys hedde at Newecastelle.

Nowe take hede what love may doo, for love wylle not nor may not caste no faute nor perelle in noo thyng.

That same yere, the fyrste day of May be fore sayde or wrete, oure soverayne lorde the Kynge, Edwarde the iiij, was weddyd to the Lorde Ryvers doughter; hyr name ys Dame Elyzabethe, that was wyffe unto Syr John Grey, sone and heyre unto the Lady Ferys of Groby. And thys maryage was kepte fulle secretely longe and many a day, that no man kuewe hyt; but men mervelyd that oure soverayne lorde was so longe with owte any wyffe, and were evyr ferde that he had be not chaste of hys levynge. But on Alle Halowe day at Redyng there it was knowe, for there the kynge kepte hys comyn counselle, and the lordys mevyd hym and exortyd hym in Goddys name to ben weddyd and to lyffe undyr the lawe of God and Chyrche, and they wold sente in too sum stronge lond to

---

[a] Sir William Tallboys, of South Kyme, Lincolnshire, who had been already attainted with others of the Lancastrian party. See Rolls of Parl. v. 477, 480.

[b] Omitted in MS.

inquere a quenc good of byrthe, a-cordyng unto hys dygnyte. And thenn our soverayne myght not no longer hyde hys maryage, and tolde hem howe he badde done, and made that the maryage shuld be oppynde unto hys lordys.

Alle so the same somer my Lorde of Warwycke and hys brether the Lorde Mountegewe, that was made Erle of Northehumberlond by the kynge, they ij layde a sege unto the castelle of Anwyke a gate hyt by a-poyntement. And in the same wyse and forme they gate the castelle of Dunsterborowe by the same mene. And thenne they layd sege to the castelle of Bamborowe, and layde grete ordynans and gounys there too. And manly they gate hyt by fors, and toke there yn that fals traytur Syr Raffe Gray, and brought hym unto the kynge to the castelle of Pomfrete. And fro thens he was ladde to Dankester, and there hys hedde was smete of and sent to London, and hyt was sette a-pon Londyn Bryge.

| Raffe Gosselyn, | John Tate | |
| Mayre of Londyn | John Stone | Anno v°. |

And thys yere was hyt ordaynyd that the noubylle of vj s. viij d. shulde goo for viij s. iiij d. And a newe cune was made. Fyrste they made an Angylle and hit went for vj s. viij d., and halfe ande Angyl for xl d.; but they made non farthyngys * of that gold. And thenne they made a gretter cune and namyd hyt a ryalle, and that wentte for x s., and halfe the rvalle for v s., and the farthynge for ij s. vj d. And they made newe grotys not soo goode as the olde, but they were worthe iiij d. And then sylvyr rosse to a grytter pryce, for an unce of sylvyr was sette at iij s., and better of sum sylvyr. But at the be-gynnynge of thys mony men grogyd passynge sore, for they couthe not rekyn that gold not so quyckely as they dyd the olde golde. And men myght goo thoroughe owte a strete or thoroughe a hoole parysche or that he myght chonge hit. And sum men sayd that the newe golde was not soo good as the olde golde was, for it was alayyd.

Alle soo in thys yere in the monythe of May was Queue Elyzabet

---

* That is to say, no quarter angels.

crownyd at Westemyster. And many knyghtys were made of the Bathe, of the whyche the were v aldyrmen of the cytte of London i·made with hem. Thes v aldyrmen were made knyghtys of the Bathe:

Syr Hewe Wyche, mercer,
Thomas Coke, draper,
Raffe Gosselyn, draper,
Syr John Plomer,
Syr Harry Whafyr.

And no moo of the cytte but thes v, and hyt ys a grete worschyppe unto alle the cytte.

Alle soo that yere be·ganne a gre cyssym by twyne fryers and prystys, but the Fryer Charmys, that ys to saye the Whyte Freers, be·ganne hyt fryste at Poules Crosse. He that be·ganne thys matyr was borne in Flete Strete, a skyner ys sone, and hys name ys Syr Harry Parker; he blamyd men for there grete copy of hyr goodys, and in specyalle he blamy[d] benefysyd men that had grete benyficys and prestys that had temporalle lyffelod. For he sayd and affermyd that non of the xij Apostolys nor Cryste badde no thyng in propyr but alle in comyn, and sayd and affyrmyd by hys connyng, as strong as he cowthe, that Cryste was a begger and had nought but by way of almys. And that made men to groge and to muse passyng soore.

But the Sonday aftyr there was a docter of devynyte, Maystyr Wylliam Ive, the mayster of Whytyngdon ys College, sayde agayne the fryer, and prevyd that Cryste was poore and kepte noo grete tresoure, but as for beggyng he utterly denyde hyt, and by hooly scrypture prevyd hit soo that men undyrstode that the fryer erryd sore agayne Hooly Chyrche; ande thenne the fryers gan malyngne a gayne thys docter. Thenne in Advente they prevyde a docter of the Whyte Fryers, Mastyr Thomas Haldon,[a] and that he schulde preche agaynce þe Mayster Wylliam Ive before sayd, and there he talkyd moke of the beggyng of Cryste, and put the pepylle[b] that the

---

[a] Originally written "Waldon" and afterwards corrected.
[b] We should probably supply "in hope"·

same mater schulde ben determenyd in there scholys by twyne hym and a Grey Fryer at the White Fryers in Flete Strete the Wanysdaye vij nyght aftyr. And the Sonday folowyng, a docter of devynyte, Mayster Edwarde Story, person of Alle Halowys the More in London, and aftyr confessor unto the Quene, and aftyr that Byschoppe of Carlylle,[a] prechyd at Poulys Crosse, and as moche as he myght wolde have passefyde the mater, and sayde that hyt [was[b]] blasphemy soo to reherse and say by oure Lord Cryste. But that same Sonday the fryers set uppe byllys at every chyrche dore that the docter sayde nott trought, but the trought shulde be schewyd ande sayd by Docter Mayster John Mylverton, the pryor of the same place, and he was provyncyalle of the same ordyr. And that aftyr noone in hys sarmon he raylyd soore and grevysly to fortefy hys bretheryn ys sayyngys, that sum laye men were wrothe with the fryers and whythedrewe hyr almys from them; and sum men were not plesyd with hyr curettes, and sayde that they hadde noo ryght to have any offerynge but lyffe by almys as Cryste dyde; ande thys men were devydyd, sum welle and sum ylle.

But the Wanysday the docter, Mayster Halden, kepte the scholys with in the Fryers and dysputyd a gayne a Gray Fryer as he promysyd; and at that scholys were many grete docters and clerkys to geve hym audyens. And they thought he yode soo farre that Mayster Alcocke,[c] a docter of lawe and commyssary unto the Dene of Syut Martyns in the Graunte, assytyd the fryer that he shulde appere by fore the Arche Byschoppe of Cauntylbury at Lambeffe. And the fryer sayde he wold not obbey his cytacyon, for alle fryers ben exempte for alle the byschoppe ys power, but hit were for eresy; and the docter of lawe sytyd hym for eresy.

Thenne at the begynnyng of the terme aftyr Estyr the fryer apperyd by fore Mayster Docter Wynterborne, my lordys offycer and juge in suche causys and othyr as for spyrytualte. And þer were many worthy docters a gayne the fryer, but he lenyd evyr

---

[a] He was appointed Bishop of Carlisle in 1468, and was translated to Chichester in 1478.

[b] Omitted in MS.

[c] John Alcock, afterwards Bishop of Ely.

unto hys prevelege, but he schewyd non but a bylle unselyd.
Thenne the mater was put to my Lorde of London, by so moche
that alle thys trobylle was done in hys dyossy, and the Chaunceler
of Inglond, that was my Lorde of Warwycke ys brother,[a] toke
party a-gayne the fryers; and the day folowynge the provyncyalle
and Docter Haldon come to Poulys by fore my Lorde of London
and brought hyr prevelegys with hem, but þe prevelege wolde not
serve that tyme for noo cause of eresy.   And my lorde lawfully
a-sytyd them to appere by fore hym that same aftyr non, but they
come not, for the provyncyalle toke hys way a-non towarde Rome.
And Docter Haldon toke noo leve of the byschoppe.   And thenn
my Lord Chaunceler hyrde that they were gone, and send for the
yong fryer Harry Parker and commaundyd hym to preson.   And
he was take from preson and sende unto my Lorde of London.
And the Sonday aftyr the same fryer, Harry Parker, objuryd that
he sayd, and sayde as we saye, that Cryste ys lorde of ovyr alle
thynge, and he confessyd alle so that very nede causyd them to
saye that Cryste beggyd, by cause that men shulde take the ordyr of
fryers moste parfytyste of alle orders.

But one fryer couthe not be ware by a nother, for with a whyle
in the vacacyon tyme a Blake Fryer prechyd alle moste the same.
And he was exampnyd by fore my Lorde of London, and was
made to preche agayne and revokyd.   Thenne my Lord of London
cursyd thes ij docters, Mayster John Mylverton and Docter Thomas
Halden, at Poulys Crosse for there contymacy, and hyt happyd that
Docter Ive dyde the execucyon of the curse, and þat grevyd the
fryers soore, and sayde that he was sette alle in malys; but thys
Docter Ive myght not chese.

Ande be fore thys[b] tyme the fore sayde Docter Ive kepte
the scolys at Poulys[c] þat ys undyr the chapter house, and there he
radde many fulle nobylle lessonnys to preve that Cryste was lorde of
alle and noo begger, and he dyde hyt aftyr the forme of scholys, for

<hr>

[a] George Nevill, Archbishop of York.

[b] thys repeated in MS.

[c] The Cathedral School of St. Paul's, not the present St. Paul's School, which
was founded at a later date by Dean Colet and dedicated to the Child Jesus.

he hadde hys abyte and hys pelyon, and a vyrger with a sylvyr Edw. IV.
A.D. 1465.
rodde waytynge uppon hym. And the same fryer of Menors that
answeryd the Whyte Fryer answeryd hym onys, and many tymys
he dyspute and radde in that scholys; he kepte hyt more then ij
yere. Thenn the fryers straynyd curtesy whoo sholde answery
hym. And ssum fryers desyryd to answerye hym, but at the day
of hyr desyre þey apperyd not. And thenn men layde grete wagers
the Provyncyalle wolde come home and doo many thyngys, and
causyd that a fryer of Rome made a tretysse of the beggyng of
Cryste, that welle was hym that myght have a copy of hyt, and
they were to sylle at many placys in Rome, and sum were sende
home to the Whyte Freers, but yet hit happyd that they come to
thys Docter Ive, that he undyr stode the consayte welle i-nowe and
sayde fulle lytylle or nought.

Thenn the Pope* havyng woundyr of the complaynt of thys
fryer, and inqueryde of suche men as come late owte of Inglonde
of the mater; and whenne he undyrstode the mater, he wrote downe
to the Arche Byschoppe of Cauntyrbury and to the Byschoppe of
London, and thonkyd hem that they were so trewe to Cryste and
Hooly Chyrche, and desyryd to have alle the hoole mater and
proscesse i-sende unto hym by wrytynge. And so hyt was, every
thyng as ny as they couthe ymageny, puttyng alle favyr and parcyallyte and malysce a syde.

But the very trewe processe thys nobylle Docter Ive wrote unto
the Pope* the maner, sayyng, and prechyng in hyr^b sermonys,
bothe hys doyng and sayyng, as welle as the fryers, and the actys
of bothe scholys. And ix docters of devynyte and bachelers of
devynyte subscrybyd hyr namys with hyr owne hondys, and
testefyde that alle was trewe that thys sayde Docter Ive badde
wretyn, for hyt was exampnyd and radde by fore alle þe byschoppys
that tyme beyng at London, and by the same docters and clerkys
that subscrybyd. And that large and grete letter was sende with

---

* *Pope*. Altered into "busshope" in a later hand, both here and in several
instances after.

b *hyr* repeated in MS.

the byschoppys letters.   And yf that Docter Ivys letter badde ben
i-selyd with sum lordys sele spyrytualle, or an notarys syne there
on, the freer had ben brende in shorte tyme; hit hadde non othyr
sele but hys owne sygnett.

Ande the kynge toke a grete party on thys mater, for thes fryers
hadde causyd moche trobylle a monge hys pepylle, and therefore he
desyryd that holy fadyr the Pope[a] to chastysse suche trespasserrys
and brekers of the pesse, and send forthe a letter with the othyr
letters.

Thenne the Pope[a] ressayvyd thes letters, and undyrstode alle the
hoole processe, and made hys cardynallys to exampne the fryer, and
by hys answerynge they found ix moo poyntys that he erryd on,
and sone aftyr he was put into the castylle of Angylle in stronge
preson, and laye there yn alle moste iij yere.   And evyr hys frendys
and the fryers lokyd aftyr hys comyng home, but he may not, for
he hathe bund hym sylfe unto the Pope[a] by an yryn oblyacyn
faste i-selyd a-boute hys ij helys.   And Þen he lackyd mony and
frende schyppe, submyttyd hym to the Pope;[a] but whenn he shalle
cum hom I wotte not, but for sothe hys artyculys ben dampnyd,
whether he be or nought I wot ner; I truste ye shalle knowe aftyr
in tyme comyng by Goddys grace, hoo have us alle in hys blessyd
kepyng.   Amen for cheryte.

Raffe Vernay,   { Costantyne   } A° vj°.
Mayre of London   { Syr Harry Wafer }

That yere the mayr had a pesabylle yere and a plentefulle of alle
Goddys goode.   And he festyd the kyng, the quene, and the queue
ys modyr, the lady of Bedford, and many othyr lordys.   And
whenn they had done and dynyd the offesers [had][b] to there reward
the clothe of state that was ovyr the tabylle, honggyng ovyr hit.
And the substance of napery was gyffe with dyvers men of offyce.

Alle so that yere Kyng Harry that was come in to Lonkesschyre
owte of Schotlond; tylle he com in to Forneysse Fellys he was
nevyr i-knowe, but there he was knowe and take, and a pon Syn

_____

[a] "Bisshope" is written over in a later hand in all these instances.
[b] Omitted in MS.

Jamys eve he was brought to the Towre of London, and iij moo
with hym; ij were hys chapelaynys, Mayster Docter Bydon, Docter
of Devynyte, and Mayster Thomas Mannynge, Bacheler of Lawe,
and sum tyme Dene of Wyndesore and secretary unto the Quene.
But he was sone delyveryd owte of preson by cause þat he was
agyd and infecte with a whyte lepyr. But Docter Bydon was in
preson long tyme, and hys frendys laboryd for hym soore and payde
moche mony for hys delyverans. But he couthe not kepe hys
tounge, but in schorte tyme he was put yn a gayne, and was there
more thenne a quarter of a yere. and þen uppon hys othe he was
delyveryd and ys owte of donger, &c.

John Yonge,
Mayre of London; | John Brommer   } Anno vijº.
menne callyd hym | Harry Bryce
the good Mayre |

That yere the mayre beryd [his] * lady, and hys scheryffe and hys
swyrdeberer. And thenn Stocketon þe mercer was chose for Harry
Bryce, the scheryffe that was, and he was made scheryffe fro that
tyme tylle Mychellemasse, and no lenger.

Alle soo thys same yere there was an herryke i-brende at the
Towre Hylle, for he dyspysyd the sacrament of the auter; hys
name was Wylliam Balowe, and he dwellyd at Walden. And he
and hys wyffe were abjuryd longe tyme be-fore. And my Lorde of
London kepte hym in preson longe tyme, and he wolde not make
noo confessyon unto noo pryste, but oonly unto God, and sayde that
no pryste had noo more poner to hyre confessyon thenn Jacke
Hare. And he had no consyence to ete flesche aftyr Estyr, as
welle as thoo that were bothe schryffe and houselyd.

At the tyme of hys brennynge a Doeter, Mayster Hewe Damelet,
person of Syn Petrys in the Cornehylle, laboryd hym to be-leve in
the hooly sacrament of the auter. And thys was the herytyke ys
sayyng: "Bawe l bawe l bawe! What menythe thys pryste? Thys
I wotte welle, þat on Goode Fryday ye make many goddys to be
putte in the sepukyr, but at Ester day they can not a ryse them

* Omitted in MS.

selfe, but that ye moste lyfte them uppe and bere them forthe, or ellys they wylle ly stylle yn hyr gravys." Thys was that tyme of hys departyng from þat worschipfulle docter.

Alle soo that same yere there were many chyrchys robbyd in the cytte of London only of the boxys with the sacrament. And men had moche wondyr of thys, and sad men demyd that there had ben sum felyschippe of heretykys assocyat to gederys. But hyt was knowe aftyr that it was done of very nede that they robbyd, wenyng unto the thevys that the boxys hadde ben sylvyr ovyr gylt, but was but copyr. And by a copyr smythe hit was a spyde of hyr longe contynuans in hyr robbory. At a tyme, alle the hole feleschippe of thevys sat at sopyr to gedyr, and had be fore hem fulle goode metys. But that copyr smythe sayde, " I wolde have a more deynty mosselle of mete, for I am wery of capon, conynge, and chekyns, and suche smalle metes. And I mervyl I have ete ix goddys at my sopyr that were in the boxys." And that schamyd sum of them in hyr hertys. Ande a smythe of lokyers crafte, that made hyr instrumentes to opyn lockys, was þer that tyme, for hit was sayde at the sopyr in hys howse. And in the mornynge he went to chyrche to hyre a masse, and prayde God of marcy; but whenn the pryste was at the levacyon of the masse he myght not see that blessyd sacrament of the auter. Thenn he was sory, and a bode tylle a nothyr pryste wente to masse and helpyd the same pryste to masse, and say [a] howe the oste lay a-pon the auter and alle the tokyns and sygnys that the pryste made; but whenn the pryste hylde uppe that hooly sacrament at the tyme of levacyon he myght se no thynge of that blessyd body of Cryste at noo tyme of the masse, not somoche at *Agnus Dei;* and thenn he demyd that hit had ben for febyllenys of hys brayne. And he went unto the ale howse and dranke a ob.[b] of goode alle, and went to chyrche agayne, and he helpyd iij moo prystys to masse, and in no maner a wyse he ne myght se that blessyd sacrament; but þen bothe he and hys feleschyppe lackyd grace. And in schorte tyme aftyr iiij of hem were take, and the same lokyer was one of þe iiij, and they were

[a] Saw.   [b] *i. e.* a half-penny worth.

put in Newegate. And by processe they were dampnyd for that trespas and othyr to he hangyd and to be drawe fro Newegate to Tyborne, and soo they were. And the same daye that they shulde dy they were confessyd. And thes iiij docters were hyr confessourys, Mayster Thomas Eberalle, Maystyr Hewe Damylett, Mayster Wylliam Ive, and Mayster Wylliam Wryxham. Thenn Mayster Thomas Eberalle wente to masse, and that lokyer aftyr hys confessyon myght see that blessyd sacrament welle i-nowe, and thenne rejoysyd and was gladde, and made an opyn confessyon by fore the iiij sayde docters of devynyte. And I truste that hyr soulys ben savyd.

Lo, ye obstinat herytykys that holdythe a-gayn confessyon, here ys an exampylle grete i-nowe to converte you yf ye have any grace withyn you, for the boke saythe that *non est verior probacio quam oculorum demonstracio.* But ye ben soo i-blyndyd that thoughe ye hyre of suche men that have sene suche thyngys ye wylle not be leve but ye hit see, and thenn ye lese your demeryte; for scripture saythe, *Fides non habet meritum ubi humana racio habet experimentum.* God geve you to a mende. Amen.

Thys yere there come many inbasyters into Ingelond fro the Kynge of Fraunce for many dyvers thynges, but they desyryd a perpetualle pesse. And sum inbassyters com fro the Kyng of Spayne.[a] And a Patryarke come from the Emperoure,[b] and that Patryarke was of Antyoche. And from Schotlond come inbassyters. And sum com from the Duke of Burgon,[c] and sum from Bratayne. Also there com inbassyters from the Kynge of Napyllys.[d] And inbassytors com from the Conte de Perare.[e] And that same yere come a legatt from the Pope;[f] and he lay at Syn Bartholomewe the

---

[a] Probably Alfonso, who was proclaimed King of Castile on the deposition of his brother Henry the Impotent, in 1465.

[b] Frederic III.

[c] It is uncertain which Duke of Burgundy is here intended. Duke Philip died on the 15 June, 1467, and was succeeded by his son Charles the Bold.

[d] Ferdinand I.   [e] Borso Duke of Ferrara (not Count) is doubtless intended.

[f] "Bishop" in later hand written over.

Lasse in a grete place of a Lombardys, and he kepte a goode housholde, and hys men were fulle welle gydyd. That legat wolde nevyr come at noo festys nor dyners with no man, with kyng nor lorde, save with grete instance he rode to More with the Arche Byschoppe of Yorke, and dynyd there and com home to hys bedde. Where fore that he com to thys lond fulle fewe men can say, but he was the best Latyn man that com into Inglond many yerys, and fulle curtesse with alle. Men drede that in tyme comyng hit wylle be knowe that hys comyng hedyr was kept so prevely.

Alle so the same yere there was dede of armys done by fore Mydsomer in Smethefylde by twyne the Lorde Schalys, the Quenys brother, and the Bastarde of Burgoyn, bothe on horsse backe and in fote; but I wot not what I shalle say of hit, whethyr hit was fortune, crafte, or cunnynge, but thys ys a trought, that the Bastarde of Burgayn lay in the fylde bothe hors and man, and hys hors was so brusyd that he dyde with a whyle aftyr. Thenne the nexte tyme they fought on fote fulle welle. I reporte me unto hem that saye[a] thys : I doo aftyr hyryng. Or ax of em that felde the strokys, they can telle you best.

Alle so that sam tyme there was dede of armys done by twynne ij Gasconys of the kyngys house and other ij men of the Bastarde of Borgayn. And the ij men in the kyngys party ther namys were Thomas Dalalaund, and that othyr Lewys de Brytellys; and that orthyr ij men in the Bastard ys syde there namys were Syr John de Cassy, knyght, and that othyr Botton, squyer. But the kynges men were better thenn they, bothe an hors backe and on foote. And thes dedys of armys was for lyffe and dethe. And soo hyt was by twyne the Lorde Schalys and the Bastarde of Burgayne.

Thomas Olgrave, | Umfray Hayforde |
Mayre of London | Thomas Stalbroke | Anno viij°.

That yere were meny men a pechyd of treson, bothe of the cytte and of othyr townys. Of the cytte Thomas Coke, knyght and aldyrman, and John Plummer, knyght and aldyrman, but the kyng

[a] Saw.

gave hem bothe pardon. And a man of the Lorde Wenlockys, John Haukyns was hys name, was hangyd at Tyburne and be heddyd for treson.

And Umfray Hayforde, the Scheryffe of London, was a pechyd and loste hys cloke for the same mater; and many moo of the cytte loste moche goode for suche maters.

Ande that same yere the Kyngys suster, my Lady Margerete, was weddyd unto the Duke of Burgon; and she was brught thedyr with many worschypfulle lordys, knyghtys, and squyers. And the Byschoppe of Salysbury* resayvyd hyr, for he hadde ben in that londe many dayes before. And sum gentylly men that brought hyr there bare hem soo evylle in hyr gydynge, that they loste hyr heddys at London sone after that they come home. One Rychard Skyrys, squyer, Pounyngys, and Alphey, the iij were by heddyd at the Towre Hylle.

Alle so that yere the Lorde Herberd of Walys gate the castelle of Hardelowe in Walys; that castylle ys so stronge that men sayde that hyt was inpossybylle unto any man to gete hyt, but poyntment hit was gotyn.[b] And sum of the pety captaynys were be-heddyd at Towre Hylle at London, for that castelle was fortefyd and vytaylyd by suche at lovyd Kyng Harry; one of the men was callyd John Treublode.

Alle soo that yere, a lytylle be-fore the sege of that castelle, the olde Lorde Jesper and sum tyme Erle of Pembroke was in Walys; and he roode ovyr the contraye and helde many cessyons and cysys in Kyng Harrys name. But men wene that he was not owte of Walys whenn that the Lord Herberde come with hys oste; but favyr at sum tyme dothe grete ese, as hit ys prevyd by the hydynge of that lorde sum tyme Erle of Penbroke.

Alle so that same yere the men that come home from Brougayne[c] at hadde ben at the maryage of my Lady Margarete were purposyd to have myschevyd alle the Flemmyngys in Sowtheworke. And they wolde have take hyr conselle at a crosse be syde Redclyffe;

* Ric. Beauchamp.　　　　　[b] So in MS.　　　　　[c] Burgundy.

and alsosone as they myght have hadde any botys þey wolde have londyd at Horsey Downe and take the Flemmyngys owte of hyr beddys and slayne them; and many bot men were consentyng unto hem, but they were a spyde and lette of hyr purposse. And tho þat were the causers of thys mater were set in preson.

Alle so hit was reportyd by the moste party of thoo men that com from the maryage, that aftyr the dayes that were assygnyd that every man shuld wayte a pon hys owne lord, lady, or mayster, and com noo more at the dukys corte, that the Burgoners shewyd no more favyr unto Englysche men thenn they wolde doo unto a Jewe. For mete and drynke was dyre i-nowe as thoughe hit hadde ben in the londe of warre, for a schuldyr of motyn was solde for xij d. And as for beddyng, Lyard my hors had more ese thenn had sum good yeman, for my hors stode in the howse and the yeman sum tyme lay with owte in the strete, for las and[a] iiij d a man shulde not have a bedde a nyght. Lo howe sone they couthe play the nygardys!

Alle so that yere the Pope[b] sende a bulle for the Cordyners, and cursyd thoo that made any longe pykys passynge ij yenchys[c] of lengthe, and that no Cordyner shuld not sylle no schone a pone the Sonday, ne put no schoo a pon no man ys fote, ne goo to noo fayrys a pon the Sonday uppon payne of cursynge. And the kynge grauntyd in a conselle and in the Parlement that hyt shulde be put in excecussyon, and thys was proclaymyd at Poulys Crosse. And sum men sayd that they wolde were longe pykys whethyr Pope wylle or nylle, for they sayde the Popys curse wolde not kylle a flye. God amend thys. And with in schorte tyme aftyr sum of the Cordyners gate prevy selys and proteccyons to make longe pykys, and causyd tho same men of hyr crafte that laboryd to the Pope for the dystruccyon of longe pykys to be trobelyd and in grete donger.

---

[a] *and*, so in MS.   [b] "Bisshope" as before.

[c] *yenchys*. The initial y is dotted both above and below, perhaps to indicate that it should be struck out.

| Maystyr Tayler,
Mayre of London | Synkyn Smythe | Anno ix°. |

That same yere in the Lentyn, whyle men were at sarmonys the Sonday aftyr noon, a yong man that was watyng a pon a man of the kyngys house was soore vexyd and bound with the devylle. And that man aftyr tyme that he was unbound by mannys hondys lay specelys long tyme aftyr. And as sone as he myght speke men of worschippe com to hym, and sum grete statys alle so com to hym and desyryd hym to telle hem of hys syghtys that he had sene in hys ferfulle vexacyon. And he tolde them many thyngys that he say,[a] as ye shalle hyre here aftyr by wrytyng and by confessyon of hym selfe unto the Pryer of Chartyr Howse, and to many dyvers docters. For the Pryer of Chartyrhouse made a grete dyner to the docters,———[b]

[a] Saw.

[b] Here the MS. breaks off abruptly at the bottom of the page; but some leaves are certainly lost.

APPENDIX.

MAYORS AND SHERIFFS.

(See page 57, note.)

As there are some inaccuracies in the list of Mayors and Sheriffs contained in Gregory's Chronicle, it was my intention at first to have corrected them in footnotes on comparing them with other lists; but I found that the errors were in some cases very complicated, and that there is no such thing as a complete and accurate list existing. Very often, both in this and other Chronicles, the city officers for one year are assigned to another; sometimes the years are transposed; and sometimes the lists for a whole sequence of years are put one year too early or too late. Further, there are very great variations in the names themselves, many of which are obviously due to transcribers' errors, while many others are genuine *aliases*, owing to the frequent use in early times of different surnames for the same person. But as it is not in all cases certain to which particular cause each variation is due, and which authority is to be preferred, I subjoin a list, compiled from various sources, of the Mayors and Sheriffs from the beginning of King John's reign to the ninth year of Edward IV., showing all the variations and discrepancies to the end of Edward I.'s reign.

For the Sheriffs the most certain authority is the official list of Sheriffs compiled from the records of the Exchequer, which is printed in Report XXXI. of the Deputy Keeper of the Public Records, page 308. This is referred to by the letter O. There is, however, no similar list of Mayors. The other authorities referred to are as follows :—

Fabyan's Chronicle, referred to by the letter
Liber de Antiquis Legibus   „   „
Short Chronicle in Appendix to the preceding
MS. Harl. 565, referred to by the letter
MS. Cott., Jul. B. I.   „   „
MS. Cott., Vitell. A xvi. „   „

Year.	Mayors.	Sheriffs.
1 John, 1199 (1198, A., Ap.)	... ...	
2 John, 1200 (1199, A., Ap.)	... ...	
3 John, 1201 (1200, A., Ap.)	... ...	
4 John, 1202 (1201, A., Ap.)	... ...	
5 John, 1203 (1202, A., Ap.)	... ...	
6 John, 1204 (1203, A., Ap.)	... ...	
7 John, 1205 (1204, A., Ap.)	... ...	

Year.	Mayors.	Sheriffs.
8 John, 1206 (1205, A., Ap.)	... .	.,
9 John, 1207 (1206, A., Ap.) (9 John, 1208-9, F.)ª	... ...	.,
10 John, 1208 (1207, A., Ap.) (9 John, 1207-8, H.) ª	... ...	.,
11 John, 1209 (1208, A., Ap.)	Henricus filius Al-wynne; fiz Alwyn, F. ; or filius Eyl-wyni, A.ᵇ (The first mayor.)	
12 John, 1210 (1209, A., Ap.)	The same	
13 John, 1211 (1210, A., Ap.)	The same	;

ª Fabyan inaccurately places the sheriffs (or bailiffs) of this ninth year before those of the eighth; but calls both years "Anno ix." H. and J. give the names of the sheriffs for the tenth year as those of the ninth, and so misdate by a year the officers during the rest of the reign.

ᵇ According to the Liber de Antiquis Legibus his mayoralty began in 1188, the first year of Richard I.

Year.	Mayors.	Sheriffs.
14 John, 1212 (1211, A., Ap. 13 John, G.) *	Henricus filius Al-wynne	Joseus filius Pers; Josue fitz Pet, F.; Joceus filius Petri, A., O.; Goce fiz Peres, Ap.
		John Gerlande or Garlonde, G., A., Ap., O.
15 John, 1213 (1212, A., Ap. 14 John, G.)	The same	Rafe Holylonde; Helyland, A.; Ey-lande, F.; Rudulfus Elyland, Ap.
		Constantinus Joswe; Constantyne le Josne, F.; Constantinus Junior, A.; Costentin Juvenis, Ap.
16 John, 1214 (1213, A., Ap. 15 John, G.)	Rogerus fiz Aleyne	Martyn fiz Alesye ; Fiz Alis, F. ; filius Alicie, A., O.; fil Aliz, Ap.
		Petrus Batte, G., F., Ap.; Bath, A.
17 John, 1215 (1214, A., Ap. 16 John, G.)	Serle, mercer	Salman *Rasynge*, G.; Salomon Ba-synge or de Basinges, A., O., F., Ap.
		Hugo Basynge or de Basinges
18 John, 1216 (1215, A., Ap. 17 John, G.)	Willelmus Ardelle ; Hardell, F., A.	John Travers, G., F., A., Ap.
		Androwe Newland, G., F.; Nevelun, A.; Vevelun, Ap.
1 Hen. III. 1216-7	Jas. Alderman; after-wards Solomon Ba-sing	Benedictus Campanarius, A; or Benoit le Seynter, Ap.
		Willelmus Blundus, A., Ap.
	[Fabyan repeats the names of the mayors and sheriffs of 17 John under this year, and the official list of sheriffs is blank for this year; while Gregory gives as sheriffs Ricardus Sumpturer and Wyllelmus Blome Travers, and V. Richard Sumpte and William Blonte.]	
2 „ 1217-8	Robert Serle, mercer	Thos. Bukrelle
		Ralph Gylonde or Helylaunde; Eli-nant, O.; Eylond, V.
ɔ „ 1218-9	The same	John Vyele
		John Spycer, G.; Spencer, V.; Goce le Peseur, Ap.; Joceus Ponderator, A., O.
	[Fabyan gives as sheriffs Benet le Ceytur (? Ceyntur) and Will. Blounde, who appear to have been sheriffs in the first year; after which he places all the mayors and sheriffs a year later than they ought to be till the ninth year.]	

* Our Chronicle leaves the date of the thirteenth year blank, and dates every succeeding year of John's reign one year too early.

Year.			Mayors.	Sheriffs.
4 Hen. III.		1219-20	Robert Serle, mercer	
o	„	1220-1	The same	
o	„	1221-2	The same	
?	„	1222-3	Ric. Ronger; or Reynger	
o	„	1223-4	The same	
?	„	1224-5	The same	
10	„	1225-6	The same	
11	„	1226-7	The same	
12	„	1227-8	Roger Duke. F. dates Roger Duke's mayoralty in the eleventh year	
13	„	1228-9	The same	
14	„	1229-30	The same	
15	„	1230-1	The same	
16	„	1231-2	Andrew Bokerelle. F. continues Roger Duke this year, but old ed. has A. Bokerell	

APPENDIX.

Year.			Mayors.	Sheriffs.
17 Hen. III.		1232-3	Andrew Bokerelle.	
18	„	1233-4	The same	
19	„	1234-5	The same	
20	„	1235-6	The same	
21	„	1236-7	The same	
22	„	1237-8	Richard Renger; Ric. Roger, G.	
23	„	1238-9	William Joyner	
24	„	1239-40	Gerard Batte	
25	„	1240-1	Reginald de Bungey; Remon de Bengley, F.	.,
26	„	1241-2	The same	
27	„	1242-3	... ...	
28	„	1243-4	... ...	
29	„	1244-5	Michael Tovy; Tony, G., F.	
30	„	1245-6	John de Gisors	

Year.		Mayors.	Sheriffs.
31 Hen. III.	1246-7	Piers fitz Aleyn	Simon Fitz Mary
32 „	1247-8	Michael Tovy again; Tony, G., F.	
33 „	1248-9	Roger Fitz Roger, G., F.,H.,J. But according to A. Michael Tovy again, and Fitz Roger and the two next mayors each held office one year later than is here stated.	
34 „	1249-50	John Norman, G., F., H., J.	Ralph Hardel John de Tolesane
35 „	1250-1	Adam Basyng	Humphrey Basse ; Humfridus le Fevre, A., O.; Humfridus dictus Faber, Ap. William Fitz Richard
36 „	1251-2	F. and G. give in this year the mayor who held office in the thirty-seventh year, and so make the two following mayors also hold office a year earlier.	Nicholas Bat Laurence de Frowyk (He is inaccurately named in G. as a second mayor instead of a second sheriff.)
37 „	1252-3	John de Tolesano	William of Durham Thomas de Wimborne
38 „	1253-4	Nicholas Batte	Richard Picard; *Nicholas*, G. John de Northampton
39 „	1254-5	Richard Hardel ; *Radulfus* Hardel, A.	Ralph Ashwy, G., F.; Willelmus Eswy or Aswy, A., Ap. Robertus de Lintona, A., Ap.; Rob. Belyngton, F.; Bylton, G. *These sheriffs were removed, and their places supplied by—* Stephen de Oystergate; Stephen Doo, G. Henry Walemonde

Year.			Mayors.	Sheriffs.

[The removed sheriffs of this year are placed by G., V., and F. in the thirty-eighth year, and those who filled their places in the thirty-ninth; after which the sheriffs are assigned to their right years by these chroniclers, by F. till the forty-eighth year, and by G. to the end of the reign.]

40 Hen. III.		1255-6	Richard Hardel	Matthew Bokerell; *Michael*, G.
				John le Mynur; Lymnour, G.
41	„	1256-7	The same	Richard Ewell
				William Ashwy or Eswy, draper
42	„	1257-8	The same	Thomas fitz Thomas; fitz Richard, G., F.
				Robert Catylleyne; Catelyon or Cateleiger, F.
				The last-named sheriff died, and Matthew Bukerel was put in his place, but afterwards removed and William Grapefige was made sheriff.
43	„	1258.9	John de Gisors, pepperer	John Adrian
				Robert de Cornhill
44	„	1259-60	William Fitz Richard	Adam Browning
				Henry de Coventry; *Richard*, F.
45	„	1260-1	The same	John of Northampton
				Richard Picard
46	„	1261-2	Thomas Fitz Thomas	Philip le Tayllur (or Cissor); *Robert*, G.; *Richard*, F.
				Richard de Walbrook; *Philip*, F.
47	„	1262-3	The same	Osbert de Suffolk; *Robert*, F.; Obertus de Sowtheworke, G.
				Robert de Munpelers
48	„	1263-4	The same	Thomas de la Forde; Forthe, G.
				Gregory Rokisle

[Fabyan gives as sheriffs for this year Osbert Wynter and Philip Taylour, the edition of 1559 giving also Robert Munpilers in the margin as a correction.]

49	„	1264-5	The same	Edward Blunt
				Petrus de Aungers; Armiger, G.; filius Angeri, A.

[F. gives as sheriffs of this year those of the year preceding, calling the first Thomas de la Fourdeous.]

Year.		Mayors.	Sheriffs.
50 Hen. III.	1265-6	William Fitz Richard (Not mayor as in G. but custos)	John de la Lynde John Walerand, Waleraven, or Walrent
51	,, 1266-7	Alan Souche, custos of the City	John Adrian Luke de Batencourt
52	,, 1267-8	The same; but during the year he was replaced as custos by Thomas de Eppegrave or Ippegrave, and he by Stephen de Eddeworthe.	Walter Hervy; W. Henry, F. William de Durham; W. Duryseyne, G. (F. places these sheriffs in the fifty-third year.)
53	,, 1268-9	Hugh Fitz Otho, custos (Henry Fitz Thomas, G., which is certainly inaccurate, as also F., who calls him Thomas, and H. and J., which call him Hugh Fitz Thomas.)	The same sheriffs at first; afterwards Robert de Cornhill Thomas de Basinge (F. places these sheriffs in the fifty-second year.)
54	,, 1269-70	John Adrian, draper (F. calls him vintner.)	Philip le Tailur; *John*, G., F. Walter le Poter; W. Plotte, G.; W. Porter, F.
		[The mayor and sheriffs for this and the remaining years of the reign are placed a year later by Fabyan, who for this fifty-fourth year gives Thomas fitz Thomas as mayor, and William Haddistok and Anketyll de Alverne (de Auverne) as sheriffs.]	
55	,, 1270-1	The same	Gregory de Rokesle Henry le Waleys
56	,, 1271-2	Sir Walter Hervy, knight	John de Bodele; Bedell, G.; Bedyll, F. Richard de Paris
57 1 Edw. I.	,, and 1272-3 }	The same	John Horne Walter le Poter
2	,, 1273-4	Henry Waleys	Nicholas, son of Geoffrey of Winchester Henry de Coventry
3	,, 1274-5	Gregory Rokesley	Luke Batencurt; Patencourt, F.; Ratyncourt, G. Henry Frowyke
4	,, 1275-6	The same	John Horne Ralph Blount

Year.			Mayors.
5	Edw. I.	1276-7	The same
6	„	1277-8	The same
7	„	1278-9	The same
8	„	1279-80	The same
9	„	1280-1	The same
10	„	1281-2	Henry Waleys
11	„	1282-3	The same
12	„	1283-4	The same
13	„	1284-5	Gregory Rokesley, and afterwards Sir John Bryton
14	„	1285-6	Ralph Sandwich
15	„	1286-7 *	The same (Sir John Bryton, F.)
16	„	1287-8 *	The same
17	„	1288-9	The same
18	„	1289-90	The same
19	„	1290-1	The same
20	„	1291-2	Ralph Sandwich
21	„	1292-3	The same

* The sheriffs for the fifteenth and sixteenth years are transposed in our chronicle.

Year.			Mayors.	Sheriffs.
22 Edw.	I.	1293-4	The same; John Brytton, G.	Robert Rokesley Martin Aumbre or Aumbresbury
23	„	1294-5	Sir John Brytton	Henry Box Ric. Gloucester
24	„	1295-6	The same	John Dunstable Adam Halyngbery
25	„	1296-7	The same	Thomas de Suffolk Adam de Fullam
26	„	1297-8	The same	John de Storteford Will. de Storteford
27	„	1298-9	Henry Waleys	Richard de Refham; Ric. *Bosham*, G.; Riser le Mercer, Ap. Thomas Sely; Geli, Ap.; Tely, G.
28	„	1299-1300	Elys Russell	John Armenters, draper Henry Pyngrey, fishmonger
29	„	1300-1	The same	Luke Haveryng Ric. Champeis or de Campes
30	„	1301-2	John Blount	Robert Caller Peter de Bosham or Bosenho
31	„	1302-3	The same	Simon de Paris, mercer Hugh Pourte, fishmonger
32	„	1303-4	The same	Will.Combmartyn(orCombermartyn) John Burford
33	„	1304-5	The same	John Lincoln, vintner Roger Paris, mercer
34 *	„	1305-6	The same	Will. Cosyn Reynold Thundrylle; Doderell, F.; Sounderle, Ap.
35 *	„	and	The same	Geoffrey atte Conduit
1 Edw. II.		1306-7		Simon Bolete

[After this date I shall merely give names that seem pretty well authenticated, omitting most of the variations. Where a corrupt form seems to occur in G., I shall print it in Italics within parentheses.]

1	„	1307-8	John Blount	Nich. Pygotte (Pycok) and Nigel Drury
2	„	1308-9	Nicholas Faryngdon	William Basyng and John Butler

---

* The sheriffs for the thirty-fourth and thirty-fifth years are transposed by our chronicler.

Year.		Mayors.	Sheriffs.
3 Edw. II.	1309-10	Thomas Romayne	Roger Palmer and James of St. Edmunde
4 „	1310-11	Richard Roffham (*Bosham*)	Simon Croppe and Piers Blackeney
5 „	1311-12	John Gysors	Simon Merwoode and Ric. Wylforde
6 „	1312-13	The same (*Kysors*)	John Lambin and Ric. Lutekyn
7 „	1313-14	Nich. Faryngdon	Adam Burton and Hugh Gayton
8 „	1314-15	John Gysors	Stephen Habingdon and Hamond Chikwell
9 „	1315-16	Steph. Habingdon	Hamond Goodchepe and Will. Redyng (So in G. and F.; but F. gives in margin Bedington, which is also the surname given in J., while H. gives Golith.)
10 „	1316-17	John Wyngrave	Will. Caston (or Causton) and Ralph Palmer, Bulmer, or Balaunser
11 „	1317-18	The same	John Pryoure and Will. Furneux
12 „	1318-19	The same	John Pulteney and John Dallyng
		[G. gives the officers of the fourteenth year for the twelfth, and repeats them in their proper place.]	
13 „	1319-20	Hamond Chikwell	Simon Abingdon and John Preston
14 „	1320-1	Nich. Faringdon	Will. Proudeham and Reynold at the Conduit
15 „	1321-2	Hamond Chikwell	Ric. Constantyne and Ric. Hakeney (Habeney, G.)
16 „	1322-3	The same	John Grantham and Roger (or Richard ?) of Ely
17 „	1323-4	Nich. Faringdon (Simon Fraunces, F.)	Adam Salisbury and John of Oxenford
18 „	1324-5	Hamond Chikwell	Benet of Fulham and John Cawston
19 „	1325-6	Ric. Betayne	Gilbert Morden and John of Cotton
20 „ and 1 Edw. III.	1326-7	} The same	Ric. Roting (Rotinger, G.) and Roger Chaunceler
2 „	1327-8	Hamond Chyckewell	Harry Darcy and John Hawteyn (Hadden, G.)
3 „	1328-9	John Grantham	Simon Francis and Harry Combmartyn (Thonbyrmartyn, G.)
4 „	1329-30	Simon Swanne or Swaynlond	Ric. Lacer and Henry (Ric., G.) Gysors

Year.			Mayors.	Sheriffs.
5 Edw. III.	1330-1	John Pountney	Rob. Ely and Thos. Harewold or Harrewode
6	„	1331-2	The same	
7	„	1332-3	John Preston	
8	„	1333-4	John Pountney	
9	„	1334-5	Reynold at the Conduit (Ralph Cotymger, G.)	
10	„	1335-6	The same	Walter Morden and Ric. Upton
11	„	1336-7	John Pountney	Will. Brykelsworth and John Northall
12	„	1337-8	Harry Darcy	Walter Nele and Nich. Crane or Grave (Grene, G.)
13	„	1338-9	The same	Will. of Pountfreyt and Hugh Marberer
14	„	1339-40	Andrew Awbrey	Will. Thorney and Roger Forsham
15	„	1340-1	The same	Adam Lucas and Barth Mareys
16	„	1341-2	John Oxynford; afterwards Simon Fraunces	Ric. Berkyng and John Rokyslee
17	„	1342-3	Simon Fraunces	
18	„	1343-4	John Hamonde	
19	„	1344-5	The same	
20	„	1345-6	Ric. Lacer	
21	„	1346-7	Geoffrey Wichyngham	
22	„	1347-8	Thos. Legge	
23	„	1348-9	John Lovekin	
24	„	1349-50	Walter (or William ?) Turke	
25	„	1350-1	Will. Killingbury	John Notte and Will. Worcester
26	„	1351-2	Andrew Awbrey	John Wroth and Gilbert Steyndrop
27	„	1352-3	Adam Fraunceys	John Peche and John Stodey
28	„	1353-4	The same	John (or William?) Welde and John Lytell
29	„	1354-5	Thos. Legge	Will. Totenham and Ric. Smerte

Year.			Mayors.	Sheriffs.
30 Edw. III.		1355-6	Simon Fraunceys	
31	„	1356-7	Harry Picard	
32	„	1357-8	John Stodey	
33	„	1358-9	John Lovekyn	
34	„	1359-60	Simon Dolsell (Donfeld or Doffelde)	
35	„	1360-1	John Wroth	
36	„	1361-2	John Pecche	
37	„	1362-3	Steph. Caundish	
38	„	1363-4	John Notte	
39	„	1364-5	Adam of Bury	
40	„	1365-6	The same till 28 Jan.; afterwards John Lovekyn	
41	„	1366-7	John Lovekyn	
42	„	1367-8	Jas. Andrew	
43	„	1368-9	Simon Mordon	
44	„	1369-70	John Chichester	
45	„	1370-1	John Bernes	
46	„	1371-2	The same	
47	„	1372-3	John Pyell	
48	„	1373-4	Adam of Bury	
49	„	1374-5	Will. Walworth	
50	„	1375-6	John Warde	
51	„	1376-7	Adam Staple till 21 March; afterwards Nich. Brembre	

* F., J., and G. give the same Christian name to both the sheriffs of this year; but II. gives their names as Thos. Forster and Walter Brandon; Arnold as Walter Forster and Thos. Brandon.

Year.		Mayors.	Sheriffs.
[52 Edw. III.*		*Nich. Brembre* *	*Andrew Pykeman* * *and Nich. Twy-ford* *]
1 Ric. II.	1377-8	Nich. Brembre	Andrew Pykeman and Nich. Twy-ford
2 ,,	1378-9	John Philpot	John Boseham and Thos. Cornwaleys
3 ,,	1379-80	John Hadley	John Heylysdone and Will. Baret
4 ,,	1380-1	Will. Walworth	Walter Doget and Will. Knyght-cote
5 ,,	1381-2	John Northampton	
6 ,,	1382-3	The same	
7 ,,	1383-4	Nich. Brembre	
8 ,,	1384-5	The same	
9 ,,	1385-6	The same	
10 ,,	1386-7	Nich. Exton	
11 ,,	1387-8	The same	
12 ,,	1388-9	Nich. Twyford	
13 ,,	1389-90	Will. Venour	
14 ,,	1390-1	Adam Bamme	
15 ,,	1391-2	John Hynde or Hende	
16 ,,	1392-3	Will. Stawnden	
17 ,,	1393-4	John Hadley	
18 ,,	1394-5	John Frosh or Frensh	
19 ,,	1395-6	Will. More	
20 ,,	1396-7	Adam Bamme	
21 ,,	1397-8	Ric. Whittington	
22 ,,	1398-9	Drewe Barentyne	
1 Hen. IV.	1399-1400	Thos. Knolles	

* It is very strange that not only G., but F., J., and H. all give a fifty-second year to Edward III., though he died in the fifty-first year of his reign. The confusion doubtless arose from the election of a new mayor in the middle of the fifty-first year; and, as the mayor so elected was re-appointed in the first year of Richard I., the sheriffs of that year are named along with him.

Year.			Mayors.	Sheriffs.
2 Hen. IV.	1400-1	John Fraunceys	
3	„	1401-2	John Schadworth	
4	„	1402-3	John Walcote	
5	„	1403-4	Will. Askam	
6	„	1404-5	John Hynde	
7	„	1405-6	John Woodcock	
8	„	1406-7	Ric. Whittington	
9	„	1407-8	Will. Staundon	
10	„	1408-9	Drewe Barentyne	
11	„	1409-10	Ric. Marlowe	
12	„	1410-11	Thos. Knolles	
13	„	1411-12	Rob. Chicheley	
14 „ and 1 Hen. V.	1412-13	} Will. Waldern	
2	„	1413-14	Will. Crowmer	
3	„	1414-15	Thos. Fauconer	
4	„	1415-16	Nich. Wotton	
5	„	1416-17	Henry Barton	
6	„	1417-18	Ric. Merlowe	
7	„	1418-19	Will. Sevenoke	
8	„	1419-20	Ric. Whittington	
9	„	1420-1	Will. Cambridge	
10	„	1421-2	Rob. Chicheley	
1 Hen. VI.	1422-3	Will. Waldern	
2	„	1423-4	Will. Crowmer	
3	„	1424-5	John Mychell	
4	„	1425-6	John Coventry	

---

* Eboto in J., which agrees with F.; Enote in H. and V., which Nicholas has misread Cnote; Emot in Arnold.

Year.			Mayors.	Sheriffs.
5 Hen. VI.		1426-7	John (or Will.)[a] Rayn-well	Rob.[b] Arnold and John Higham
6	,,	1427-8	John Gedney	Henry Frowyk and Rob. Otley
7	,,	1428-9	Harry Barton	Thos. Dufhous and John Abbot
8	,,	1429-30	Will. Estfeld	Will. Russe and Ralph Holand
9	,,	1430-1	Nich. Wotton	Walter Chertsey and Rob. Large
10	,,	1431-2	John Welles	John Adyrley and Steph. Browne
11	,,	1432-3	John Parneys (or Parveys?)	John Olney and John Padysley
12	,,	1433-4	John Brokley	
13	,,	1434-5	Rob. Otley	
14	,,	1435-6	Harry Frowyke	
15	,	1436-7	John Mychell	
16	,,	1437-8	Will. Estfeld	
17	,,	1438-9	Steph. Browne	
18	,,	1439-40	Robert Large	
19	,,	1440-1	John Paddisley	
20	,,	1441-2	Rob. Clopton	
21	,,	1442-3	John Hatherley	
22	,,	1443-4	Thos. Catworth	
23	,,	1444-5	Harry Frowyk	
24	,,	1445-6	Simon Eyre	
25	,,	1446-7	John Olney	
26	,,	1447-8	John Gedney	
27	,,	1448-9	Steph. Browne	
28	,,	1449-50	Thos. Chalton	
29	,,	1450-1	Nich. Wyfold	
30	,,	1451-2	Will. Gregory	
31	,,	1452-3	Geoffrey (or Godfrey) Feldyng	
32	,,	1453-4	John Norman	
33	,,	1454-5	Stephen Forster	

[a] William in J. and in Arnold; but John in F., G., and H.

[b] Stowe and Orridge both give his Christian name as John, but the other authorities all call him Robert.

Year.		Mayors.	Sheriffs.
34 Hen. VI.	1455-6	Will. Marowe	
35 ,,	1456-7	Thos. Canynge	
36 ,,	1457-8	Geoffrey Boleyn	
37 ,,	1458-9	Thomas Scott	
38 ,,	1459-60	Will. Hewlyn	
39 ,,	1460-1	Ric. Lee	
1 Edw. IV.	1461-2	Hugh Wiche	
2 ,,	1462-3	Thos. Coke	
3 ,,	1463-4	Matt. Philip	
4 ,,	1464-5	Ralph Josselyn	
5 ,,	1465-6	Ralph Verney	
6 ,,	1466-7	John Yong	
' ,,	1467-8	Thos. Holgrave (or Owlegrave)	
ᵃ ,,	1468-9	Will. Taylour	
,,	1469-70	Ric. Lee	

SURRENDER OF FALAISE CASTLE.

(See page 121, note ᵈ.)

[These articles are not printed by Nicolas in the Chronicle of London, and as already stated only the two first are printed in Rymer in the original French. I therefore give the whole text of the treaty as given in the English Chronicle, MS. Cott. Jul. B. I. f. 43. After the words "first day of Feverer" in this MS., it is added]:—

Which day the capitayne and al they of the forseid castel desirid to trete with our sovereigne lord the Kyng, which committid the trete and appointment to be made with the worthie prynce the Duke of Clarence; which trete and appointment was made in maner and forme as foloweth:—

Here folowith the trete and appointment of the accorde made the first day of Feverer, the yere of our Lord m¹ iiij° xvij, by me Oliver de Mauny, knyght, capitayne of the castel and dongeon of Faloys, in my propre

ᵃ G. makes his christian name John, and Arnold makes it Robert; but it is Richard in F. and J.

persone grauntyng and bihotyng for me, and al tho of my compeigny and
garison to the ful worthy prince the Duke of Clarence to yelden the xvj
day of this present moneth the castel and the dongeon of Faloys into
the handis of the right excellent Kyng of England, or into the handes
of [other on] ᵃ his by half therto committid that to receyve if it so ne be
or sone come that thaboveseid castel and dongeon of Faloys be nought
rescowed the forseid day withynne the houre of mydday ᵇ by bataile of
the doutful lord, persone or persones of the right excellent Kyng of
Fraunce or of the right doutful lord the Dolphyn his eldist sone, or by
therle of Armonak, Constable of Fraunce, and upon [that] ᶜ the full
excellent Kyng of England to put or do put in the seid castel and
dongeon such kepyng that hym shal like.

Also it is tretid, accordid, and by hight by me thaboveseid Olyver de
Mauny that at the day of yeldyng of the seid castel and dongeon of
Faloys, I and al tho of my compeigny and garison, we shul yeld us
presoners to thaboveseid right excellent Kyng of England, out take
Geffrey of Chasteulx which shal abide and dwelle of al pointes, his body,
his lif, and al his goodes, to the grace and mercy of thaboveseid excellent
Kyng of England, he of his benigne grace to command upon the forseid
Geoffrey his good likyng.

Also it is set, tretid, and accordid and by hight by me aboveseid
Olyver de Mauney, that at the day of yeldyng up of the seid castel and
dongeon of Faloys, I and tho of my compeigny and garison shuld leven
in the forseid castel of Faloys all our horses, armures, staves, artilries,
without eny therof in any maner to bere away or to distroie atwix this
tyme and the yeldyng of the seid castel and dongeon of Faloys, and pᵗ
we shal take hede to put al the forseid armures, staves, and artilries sool
in an house of the forseid castel without eny thing therof to sparen.

Also it is tretid, accordid, and bihight by me aboveseid Oliver de
Mauney, in caas that rescowe as it is aboveseid be not done, that I and
al tho of my compeigny and garison at oure owne cost and expenses
shal do make ageyne and strengthe ageyne and reparaile the walles and
the diches of the castel and dongeon of Faloys, as wel without as withynne,

ᵃ Omitted in MS.   The original has " d'autre de par luy a ce commys."
ᵇ Orig. " de deux heure de mydye."
ᶜ Omitted in MS.   Orig " sur ce."

and forto put the dongeon and castel in such state, or as good, as it was bifore that thaboveseid Kyng of England there leide his worshipful sege.

Also it is tretid, accordid, and bihight by me above Olyver de Mauney and al hem of my compeigny or garison, that at the day of the yeldyng up of the seid castel and dongeon of Faloys we shul yelden, take, and delyver to the handes of such as it shall like to thaboveseid right excellent Kyng of England to committe, al the presoners, Englisshe subjectes obeisauntz, and other holding the partie of England, þᵗ for the tyme be presoned in the castel and dongeon of Faloys, without that any empechment be put to the forseid presoners by any of her maisters at this tyme or in tyme to come, be it by sommonyng, requyryng, or askyng in any maner what it be, but fynally al tho of the seid garison that seien or mowe seien hem han any right upon any of the condicion aboveseid, be it by fait of preson or of plegge, the forseid folke of the garison she[a] renouncen al the trouthes, feithes, bihestes, or othes that aboveseid presoners mowe have done bicause of takyng or in any other condicion or maner what so it be, without fraude or malengyne.

Also it is tretid, accordid, and grauntid by me aboveseid Olyver de Mauney that at the yeldyng up of the castel and dongeon of Faloys[b] into the handes of hem committid by the right excellent Kyng of England all thEnglissh born, Walshe, Irisshe, and Gascoigne that bifore this tyme han holden the partie of England, and nowe for this present tyme ben withynne the seid castel and dongeon, if eny be there.

Also it is tretid, accordid, and promittid by me Olyver de Mauney, and hem of my compeigny and garison, that al the vitaile and artilries, that is to sey, arblastes, bowes, arowes, quarelles,[c] poudres, gonnes, stanes, and all other abilementes for the werre and defence of the seid castel and dongeon of Faloys, be they alweies present in the forseid castel and dongeon fro the first day of thentreting of this present trete and appointment, and fro the date of this present trete shal dwel and abide in the forseid castel and dongeon of Falois without distruccion or wast in any

---

[a] shall.

[b] There is here an omission in the MS. corresponding to these words in the original: "jo delivrero et haider (*baillerai*) hors de dit chastell et dongou de Faluizo."

[c] *quarolles.* The word is "virtons" in the original French.

maner, sauf onely of vitaile, wherof reasonably we shal use and take our suffisaunce as we were wont to done bifore this present composicion.

Also it is tretid and accordid and grauntid by me aboveseid Olyver de Mauney, and al hem of my compeigny and garison, that in like wise of artilries aboveseid we shul not make ne suffre to be made eny broilyng, brekyng, beryng awey, ne none other distruccion in eny wise.

Also it is tretid, accordid, and bihight by me aboveseid Olyver de Mauney, capitayne of the castel and dongeon of Falois, aswele for me as for hem of my compeigny and garison, that unto tyme the forseid castel and dongeon of Falois be ageyne strengthid and reparailid and ageyn pat in thastate as it is aboveseid and declared, aswele without as withynne, we ne non of us shal not enarmen us ageyne thaboveseid excellent Kyng of England, ne ageyne his partie that* no maner maundementz that to us moowe be made ne for non other occasion what so it be. And that bihete we knyghtes and squiers of the seid castel and dongeon upon our feithes and honours, and al other of the garison bihoten it upon the Holy Evaungelies.

Also it is tretid, accordid, and bihight unto thaboveseid ful high and right myghtie prince Duke of Clarence by me aboveseid Olyvere de Mauney, knyght and capitayne of the castel and dongeon of Faloys, that upon this present trete and appointment I shal take and delyver viij gentilmen, knyghtes, and squiers notables, which shuld welle and abide to the commandment of thabove right excellent Kyng of England as for hostages, to that ende that the promyses aboveseid be the better togider holde for our partie.

Also it is tretid, accordid, and bihight by the ful high myghty prince the Duke of Clarence, in the name and by commaundment of aboveseid right excellent Kyng of England, his sovereigne lord, that whan the forseid castel and dongeon of Faloys, as wele withynne as without, be made ageyne, refortifieid, and repareilid, and put ageyn in the point and astate as it is above declarid, that I thaboveseid Olyver de Mauney, knyght and capitayne of the seid castel and dongeon of Faloys, with al tho of my compeigny and garison, shalbe dischargid and quiet of our prison ayenst aboveseid excellent Kyng of England, and that hath the Kyng accordid to us of his benigne grace.

* *that.* Should be "for." The original French has "pour."

Also it is to understand that the pleasunce of thaboveseid right excellent Kyng ne is nought that Geoffrey de Chastiaulx shal use ne have benefice of the grace of tharticle precedent.

Also it is tretid, accordid, and bihight by the ful high and myghty prince the Duke of Clarence, in the name and by the commaundment of thabove seid right excellent ˉKyng of England, and of his grace grauntid to me Olyvere de Mauney aboveseid, as wel as to hem of my compeigny and garison, al our goodes whatsoever thei ben, beyng nowe withyn the seid castel and dongeon of Faloys, out take our horses and armures and other goodes above expressid and declarid.

Also it is tretid, accordid, and grauntid by me Olyver de Mawney, knyght aforseid, capitayne of the castel and dongeon of Faloys, that by me, ne by hem of my compeigny and garison, ne other that ben withdrawen hem into the seid castel, shalbe askid, required, borne, ne[a] moevid out of the forseid castel and dongeon, under colour of this present appointment, none other goodes in no maner but onely oure propre goodes.

Also it is tretid, accordid, and grauntid, aswele on that oo partie as on that other, that hangyng the seid trete and appointment no maner of werre shalbe made bitwene hem and thoste of thexcellent Kyng of England and hem of the garison of the castel and dongeon of Faloys.

And for this present trete wel and truely to holde togidre have I, above seid Olyvere de Mawney, knyght, capitayne of the castel and dongeon of Faloys, for my partie to this present cedule of appointment set the seale of my propre armes and ensealid it with my signet of myn hand for the gretter approbacion of verite and trouthe bifore the seid castel of Faloys, the second day of the moneth and yere aboveseid.

And this present appointment entierly to holde and fulfill on our partie we Thomas, sone and brother of Kynges of England and of Fraunce, Duke of Clarence, Erle of Aumarle, High Steward of England, Chief Capitayne of the Vawarde, and Constable of thoste of my lord the Kyng, have done set to this cedule the seale of our armes, bifore the forseid castel of Faloys the second day of the moneth and yere above seid.

[a] *no.* me, MS.

NOTES.

Line 17.—"And the Monday was the terment of the Lorde Moumbrey at the Whytte Freerys in þᵉ cytte of London ys subbarbys."

Stowe also says in his account of Whitefriars : "There lay buried also, in the middle of the new Choir, Sir John Mowbray, Earl of Nottingham, 1398." But according to all our Peerage Historians Thomas Lord Mowbray, who was created Earl of Nottingham in 1383, did not die in 1398, but was created Duke of Norfolk in 1397.

Line 8.—"And the same yere, the xxx day of October, the Erle of Saulysbury was hurte." The chronicle in Vitell. A. xvi., which is here derived from the same source as Gregory's, gives "the xxxj daye of Octobre" as the date. As the second of November is given as the date of his death, this is in harmony with the statement in Grafton, that he died two days after his wound. But Monstrelet, who is followed by Hall, states that he languished eight days ; and the inquisitions *post mortem*, as cited by Dugdale, find that he died on the *third* of November. This date, it may be added, is given in no fewer than twenty-three different documents.

Line 14.—"And the secunde daye of Advente there were ij heretyks objuryd." For "daye," of course, we should read "Sonday," which is the reading in the Vitellius MS.

Lines 19, 20.—"And the xij evyn aftyr was i-broughte unto London, and hadde hys masse at Poulys, and hys bonys buryde at Birsham."

Owing to an omission in the MS. this sentence reads as if it referred to Wycliffe, which is absurd. In the similar chronicle, Vitell. A. xvi. (at f. 87) the passage stands as follows :

" And on the xij[th] even after the bonys of the Erle of Salisbury were brought to London, and had his masse atte Powles ; and than caried unto the priory of Birsham, and there y-buried with his auncestours the which were fownders therof."

Even here, however, there is a strange inconsistency, for in the preceding paragraph it is said that he was interred at St. Paul's on the first Sunday in Advent.

INDEX.

ERRATA.

Page 178. Marginal date should be " 1435-6."

Page 210, l. 12. *Dele* comma after " þe."

Page 211, l. 18. For " all eway " read " alleway."

Westminster : Printed by J. B. Nichols and Sons, 25, Parliament Street.

REPORT OF THE COUNCIL

OF

THE CAMDEN SOCIETY,

READ AT THE GENERAL MEETING

ON THE 2ND MAY, 1876.

THE Council of the Camden Society elected on the 3rd May, 1875, deeply regret the loss of one of their number,

WILLIAM DURRANT COOPER, Esq., F.S.A.

Mr. Cooper was not only the Editor of some of the Society's publications, in which character he is doubtless best known to most of the Members, but he was a constant attendant at the meetings of the Council, always ready to contribute valuable advice and criticism; his learning and his practical acquaintance with business will be often missed by those with whom he so heartily co-operated in the interests of the Society.

Another Member of the Society who has been removed from us during the past year and who deserves especial mention is

JOHN FORSTER, Esq.

Though ill health of late years precluded his attendance at the Council meetings, he always took a deep interest in the progress of the Society.

Mr. Forster's historical and biographical works are too well known to require any mention here. It is deeply to be regretted that the " Life of Swift," on which he was engaged at the time of his death, should have remained uncompleted.

The Council are sorry to add the following List of Members who have died during the past year :

JAMES BLADON, Esq.

J. W. THRUPP, Esq.

JAMES COBB, Esq.
WILLIAM BLANDY, Esq.
CHARLES BLANDY, Esq.
COSMO INNES, Esq.
The Very Reverend The Dean of CHICHESTER.
ROBERT DAVIES, Esq.
HENRY GREGORY, Esq.
The Right Hon. T. H. SOTHERON ESTCOURT.
The Rev. Dr. PARKINSON.

During the same interval the following new Members have been elected:

LORD DELAMERE.
The Honourable HENRY F. COWPER, M.P.
JAMES RAE, Esq.
EDWARD WALMISLEY, Esq.
Major FRANC SADLEIR STONEY, R.A.
J. ANDERSON ROSE, Esq.
The UNIVERSITY OF PRAGUE.
WENTWORTH HUYSHE, Esq.
NOTTINGHAM FREE PUBLIC LIBRARIES.
WALTER MONEY, Esq.
J. W. HALES, Esq.

The following books for the past year are now in the hands of Members:

I. The Camden Miscellany, Vol. VII. Containing, 1. The Boy Bishop. Edited by the late J. G. NICHOLS, F.S.A. and DR. RIMBAULT. 2. The Speech of the Attorney-General Heath in the Star Chamber against Alexander Leighton. Edited by the late JOHN BRUCE, F.S.A. and S. R. GARDINER. 3. The Judgment of Sir G Croke in the Case of Ship Money. Edited by S. R. GARDINER. 4. Accounts of the Building of Bodmin Church. Edited by the Rev. J. J. WILKINSON, M.A. 5. The Mission of Sir T Roe to Gustavus Adolphus. Edited by S. R. GARDINER.

II. Letters of Humphrey Prideaux to John Ellis. 1674-1722. Edited by E. M. THOMPSON.

III. The Autobiography of Anne Lady Halkett. Edited by the late JOHN GOUGH NICHOLS, F.S.A.

The books for the year 1876-7 will probably be—

I. Milton's Common Place Book. Edited by A. J. HORWOOD. (Ready.)

II. The Siege of Rouen, and other papers relating to the Reign of Henry VI. Edited by JAMES GAIRDNER. (In the Press.)

III. Papers illustrative of the Life of William Prynne. With a Biographical Fragment by the late JOHN BRUCE, F.S.A. To be edited by S. R. GARDINER.

The following books have been added to the list of suggested publications : --

Letters treating of the Domestic Affairs of the Priory of Christ Church, Canterbury in the fourteenth and fifteenth centuries. To be edited by J. B. SHEPPARD.

The Economy of the Fleet, throwing light on the condition of the Fleet Prison in the Reign of James I. To be edited by Dr. A. JESSOPP.

The Council are glad to think that the publications of late years, issued by the Society, fully maintain the character and value of those issued in its long series of historical works. They see no reason to think that there will in the future be any lack of materials, especially considering that the researches into ancient libraries by the Historical Manuscripts Commission yearly bring to light fresh treasures of knowledge. No effort will be wanting on their part to ensure to the Members a succession of works which shall maintain the character of the Society.

The Council has resolved to offer such of the copies as remain on hand of the volumes belonging to the First Series (only) at reduced prices, as there are no longer any perfect sets. Copies of the present list of prices are to be obtained at Messrs. Nichols, 25, Parliament Street.

By order of the Council,

SAMUEL RAWSON GARDINER, *Director.*
ALFRED KINGSTON, *Hon. Secretary.*

REPORT OF THE AUDITORS.

I, being one of the Auditors appointed to audit the Accounts of the Society, report to the Society, that the Treasurer has exhibited to me an A the Receipts and Expenditure from the 1st of April 1875 to the 31st of Ma and that I have examined the said accounts, with the vouchers relating the find the same to be correct and satisfactory.

And I further report that the following is an Abstract of the Receipts an diture during the period I have mentioned :—

RECEIPTS.	£	s.	d.	EXPENDITURE.
To Balance of last year's account..	582	11	6	Paid for printing 500 copies Quarrel between Man
Received on account of Members whose Subscriptions were in arrear at last Audit	23	0	0	chester and Cromwell. No. 12......................... Paid for printing 500 copies Autobiography of Lady Anne Halkett. No. 13 ....
The like on account of Subscriptions due on the 1st of May, 1875......	251	0	3	Paid for printing 500 copies Camden Miscellany Vol. VII. No. 14 ....
The like on account of Subscriptions due on the 1st of May, 1876......	16	0	0	Paid for printing 500 Copies Letters of Humphrey
To Repayment for Transcript	50	0	0	Prideaux. No. 15 .... Paid for Miscellaneous Printing...........................
One year's dividend on £466 3 1 3 per Cent. Consols, standing in the names of the Trustees of the Society, deducting Income Tax..	13	17	6	Paid for delivery and transmission of Books, with paper for wrappers, warehousing expenses (including Insurance) .... Paid for 500 Copies of three Fac-similes of Milton'
To Sale of Publications of past years.....................................	46	19	7	Common-place Book .... Paid for binding ....
To Sale of Promptorium Parvulorum (3 vols. in 1)	9	17	3	Paid for making various Transcripts...................... Paid for postages, collecting, country expenses, &c. ..
				By Balance
	£993		6	

And I further state, that the Treasurer has reported to me, that over a the present balance of £564 7s. 3d. there are outstanding various subscr Foreign Members, and of Members resident at a distance from London, v Treasurer sees no reason to doubt will shortly be received.

GEORGE F. SMIT